Humanizing Evil

Psychoanalysis traditionally has had difficulty accounting for the existence of evil. Freud saw it as a direct expression of unconscious forces, whereas more recent theorists have examined the links between early traumatic experiences and later "evil" behavior. *Humanizing Evil: Psychoanalytic, Philosophical and Clinical Perspectives* explores the controversies surrounding definitions of evil and examines its various forms, from the destructive forces contained within the normal mind to the most horrific expressions observed in contemporary life.

Ronald C. Naso and Jon Mills bring together an international group of experts to explore how more subtle factors can play a part, such as conformity pressures or the morally destabilizing effects of anonymity and show how analysts can understand and work with such factors in clinical practice. Each chapter is unified by the view that evil is intrinsically linked to human freedom, regardless of the gap experienced by perpetrators between their intentions and consequences. While some forms of evil follow seamlessly from psychopathology, others call this relationship into question. Rape, murder, serial killing and psychopathy show very clear links to psychopathology and character whereas the horrors of war, religious fundamentalism and political extremism resist such reductionism.

Humanizing Evil is unique in the diversity of perspectives it brings to bear on the problem of evil. It will be essential reading for psychoanalysts, psychotherapists, philosophers and Jungians. Because it is an integrative depth-psychological effort, it will interest general readers as well as scholars from a variety of disciplines including the humanities, philosophy, religion, mental health, criminal justice, political science, sociology and interdisciplinary studies.

Ronald C. Naso, Ph.D., ABPP, is a psychoanalyst and clinical psychologist in independent practice in Stamford, CT. The author of numerous papers on psychoanalytic topics, he is an associate editor of *Contemporary Psychoanalytic Studies* and contributing editor of *Division/Review* and the *Journal of Psychology and Clinical Psychiatry*. His book, *Hypocrisy Unmasked: Dissociation, Shame, and the Ethics of Inauthenticity*, was published by Aronson in 2010.

Jon Mills, Psy.D., Ph.D., ABPP, is a philosopher, psychoanalyst and clinical psychologist. He is Professor of Psychology & Psychoanalysis at the Adler Graduate Professional School, Toronto. A 2006, 2011 and 2013 Gradiva Award winner, he is editor of three book series in psychoanalysis, on the editorial board for *Psychoanalytic Psychology*, and the author and/or editor of 13 books including his most recent works, *Underworlds: Philosophies of the Unconscious from Psychoanalysis to Metaphysics* and *Conundrums: A Critique of Contemporary Psychoanalysis*, which won the Goethe Award for best book in 2013.

Philosophy & Psychoanalysis Book Series

Series Editor: Jon Mills

Philosophy & Psychoanalysis is dedicated to current developments and cutting edge research in the philosophical sciences, phenomenology, hermeneutics, existentialism, logic, semiotics, cultural studies, social criticism and the humanities that engage and enrich psychoanalytic thought through philosophical rigor. With the philosophical turn in psychoanalysis comes a new era of theoretical research that revisits past paradigms while invigorating new approaches to theoretical, historical, contemporary and applied psychoanalysis. No subject or discipline is immune from psychoanalytic reflection within a philosophical context including psychology, sociology, anthropology, politics, the arts, religion, science, culture, physics and the nature of morality. Philosophical approaches to psychoanalysis may stimulate new areas of knowledge that have conceptual and applied value beyond the consulting room reflective of greater society at large. In the spirit of pluralism, *Philosophy & Psychoanalysis* is open to any theoretical school in philosophy and psychoanalysis that offers novel, scholarly, and important insights in the way we come to understand our world.

Humanizing Evil
Psychoanalytic, Philosophical and Clinical Perspectives
Edited by Ronald C. Naso and Jon Mills

Humanizing Evil

Psychoanalytic, Philosophical and Clinical Perspectives

Edited by
Ronald C. Naso and Jon Mills

Routledge
Taylor & Francis Group
LONDON AND NEW YORK

First published 2016
by Routledge
4 Park Square, Milton Park, Abingdon, Oxon OX14 4RN

And by Routledge
605 Third Avenue, New York, NY 10017

Routledge is an imprint of the Taylor & Francis Group, an Informa business

British Library Cataloguing in Publication Data
A catalogue record for this book is available from the British Library

Library of Congress Cataloging in Publication Data
A catalog record for this book has been requested

ISBN: 978-1-138-82853-7 (hbk)
ISBN: 978-1-138-82854-4 (pbk)
ISBN: 978-1-315-71541-4 (ebk)

Typeset in Sabon
by codeMantra

Contents

Introduction and Overview

Ronald C. Naso

With a relatively modest initial investment, Bernard Madoff built a financial empire that prospered for more than 40 years. By age 70, he was successful beyond all imagination, actively sought out for his financial wisdom and hefty returns. This perception changed dramatically on December 11, 2008. Madoff was arrested in his multi-million dollar Manhattan apartment and charged with crimes related to the single largest financial fraud in Wall Street history, one spanning 20 years and involving billions of dollars.

Concerns about Madoff dated back to 1999, when a complaint was filed with the Securities and Exchange Commission by a financial analyst who had grown suspicious of Madoff's inflated claims. His returns were highly improbable given the market conditions at that time. Similar complaints in 2005 and 2007 also were ignored. The SEC's unresponsiveness and the complicity of other institutions would make a fascinating study in its own right—investment bankers and knowledgeable financial professionals standing on the sidelines while individuals and other institutions were ruined. It was a bystander effect of epic proportions. Madoff's misdeeds were the dirty little secret of greedy investors who profited from his crimes while remaining hidden behind a veil of deniability. But for the economic downturn of 2007 that made it impossible to attract new money, Madoff's scheme might have continued undetected.

There is no shortage of examples of man's inhumanity to man. Corporate malfeasance, genocide, terrorism, and state-sponsored torture are part of our everyday experience. In 1994, almost one million Tutsi were murdered in Rwanda. This was not a military action in the strict sense; nor were its horrors perpetrated on the battlefield. Rather, incited by local officials and the Hutu government, citizens committed unspeakable acts of bloodlust against their fellow Rwandans. Families were slaughtered, mothers and daughters raped and mutilated in a killing spree spanning approximately 100 days, forcing almost 2 million terrified Tutsi to seek asylum in neighboring countries.

The specter of evil reared its head in yet another form on September 11, 2001, when commercial airplanes were used to take down the World Trade

Center and severely damage the Pentagon. These bombings confronted citizens of the United States with evil in its most contemporary and horrific form—its victims chosen precisely because they had committed no crime; the al-Qaeda operatives who perpetrated this atrocity confident that their actions were justified and served a higher good. Driven by ideological commitments foreign to Western thinking, they acted with depraved and astonishing indifference to human life.

Principled relativism and respect for other points of view are difficult to maintain when they threaten one's well-being and way of life. This is one of the unfortunate realities of global terrorism. In the last century alone, more than 260 million people have been killed by their fellow countrymen in conflicts worldwide (Baum, 2008). No longer is evil a matter of tribal discord unfolding in distant lands. No longer is its devastation local and easily contained. For this reason, evil urgently calls for a response and for practical solutions. In the case of the 9/11 attacks, the U.S. answered this call. And it did so in a way that was anything but neutral. Unfortunately for many citizens of Afghanistan and Iraq, this response engendered evils of its own: war, the killing of innocent noncombatants and, later, abuse and torture of "detainees."

In the end, trauma begets only greater and more pervasive trauma. Innocents suffer alongside the guilty. And, more troubling, "collateral damage" is exposed for what it really is: a consequence never truly unintended or regretted, except when its horrors come to light. When one's strategy involves bombing villages thought to be harboring terrorists, claiming that one's killing of noncombatants was unintended is implausible. In what sense are the proximate results of military action unforeseen?

Each of the chapters in this book seeks to stabilize the meaning of evil and formulate a deeper understanding of its causes and dynamics. Each offers a unique perspective on the problem and, in so doing, bears witness to evil's diversity and the utility of applying different frames of reference to more fully appreciate its complexity. Despite the differences in perspectives presented in *Humanizing Evil*, its message returns us again and again to the centrality of narcissism, aggression, and the troubling human capacity for moral disengagement. All must be taken into account in any attempt to come to terms with the phenomenon of evil. I shall offer some preliminary thoughts about these concepts and the challenges they pose in order to orient the reader to the more comprehensive examinations that follow. Following this, I shall briefly sketch two forms of evil that occupy the attention of virtually every author in this volume.

On Narcissism

The concept of narcissism is robust and especially relevant for understanding those motivated by ambition and greed. At the clinical level, it unifies the key characteristics of psychopathy—the character type most closely associated with perpetration. Narcissism illuminates one central motive of individuals like Madoff who crave attention and are "contemptuous of those ... manipulate[d] into providing it" (Lasch, 1979, p. 38). Not only does pathological narcissism diminish shame, insecurity and envy, it enables one to act opportunistically and without compunction, exposing self-aggrandizing passions in individuals incapable of mourning.

Less clear is how narcissism's meaning, dynamics and implications operate in group behavior. Conceptually, narcissism throws into relief the entitled, self-interested motives of those who deceivingly present their immoral actions as altruistic and good—the unscrupulous investment banker whose charitable contributions build schools; the sadistic police officer who routinely abuses citizen's civil rights; the corrupt politician who profits from turning a blind eye to the harm caused by his policies; or the terrorist who beheads innocent victims to propel his personal (or group) agenda onto the global stage. It explains equally well the behavior of those individuals consumed by the need for power and complete control. By definition, narcissism seems to exclude empathy and feelings of genuine concern for the well-being of others, particularly when their interests are not aligned with one's own.

However, dislodged from its clinical context, narcissism's meaning is more difficult to stabilize. For example, how does one evaluate the claim that the torching of a Vietnamese village or the rape and murder of innocent Rwandans is narcissistic? At one level, the claim is self-evident: How else is one to understand actions that inflict unnecessary and horrific suffering on others when there are other means available to achieve one's strategic purpose? Upon closer inspection, it seems that individual and group behavior necessarily serves self-interest. One can always say, "they enjoyed (or profited from) what they did" or, perhaps, at bottom, "they did it because they could." If human behavior did not serve self-interests or provide pleasure, there would be no motive to act at all.

Whatever other motives it may serve, terrorism aims increasingly at garnering global attention. At the time of this writing, we are confronted by the very public executions of innocent journalists and relief workers by a newly formed terrorist group, the Islamic State of Iraq and Levant (ISIL), that claims religious authority over Muslims worldwide. Lest their claims be ignored, they post these executions on YouTube.

If one includes the pleasure derived from fulfilling one's duties and obligations as a motive for behavior, it will be recognized immediately just how difficult it is to *exclude* narcissism as an explanation. Therefore, for the term to have nontrivial explanatory force, it must do more than notice the satisfaction that follows from achieving virtually any goal. It must articulate reasons in the absence of which egregious actions would not occur.

This much is clear: When investigators describe group behavior as narcissistic, they do not deploy the term uniformly or in its strict clinical sense. Sometimes they use the term in a general way; at others, in a manner that references particular character traits. Rarely do they advance the claim, for example, that all, let alone most, of the individuals within these groups evidence pathologies of the self, of relationships with others, and of the superego—which is to say that each individual group member manifests the three anchoring symptoms of narcissistic personality disorder (Kernberg, 2007). While some group members meet these criteria, there is no evidence to support the claim that all do. Moreover, recent research on the personality characteristics of perpetrators of genocide suggests a wide array of motives and patterns of behavior that are neither fixed nor predictable (Clark, 2009). From the standpoint of motivation and personality structure, instigators of violence are often very different from perpetrators as well as from those whose actions serve to maintain the level of violence either directly or indirectly through inaction (Mandel, 2002). As a result, investigators who utilize the term narcissism to explain behavior often conflate its descriptive and diagnostic meanings. They exploit its resonances to explain the most horrific and unimaginable atrocities in the absence of any evidence of pathological or malignant narcissism. Such usage, I submit, is evocative but ultimately misleading. It provides little more than the illusion of explanation.

It is worth returning to the events of September 11, 2001 to highlight yet another danger posed by uncritically importing narcissism's syndromal features into explanations of group behavior. The events of 9/11 traumatized the nation and left its citizenry feeling powerless and confused. Having witnessed the World Trade Center's twin towers collapse in flames, people wanted to respond, to be active rather than passive. Does it therefore follow that the choice to support a military response aimed at punishing those responsible for the attack was nothing more than an expression of wounded narcissism? Is it narcissistic to confront, aggressively if necessary, significant threats to one's life? The fact that George W. Bush and his inner circle may have been machiavellian in their motivations has little bearing on what prompted others to support his policies or sacrifice their lives in service to the nation.

Individual and group behavior always expresses a variety of motives—not the least of which, in the case of the U.S. response to the 9/11 attacks, involved actions carried out in good faith and on the basis of incomplete or inaccurate information. The result: a tragedy of epic proportion—innocent U.S., Iraqi and Afghani lives lost in a search for nonexistent weapons of mass destruction; a violent and protracted military action aimed at nation-building that will fuel anti-American sentiment for generations. How else can these actions be described but as evil? Minimally, they highlight the complexity of the issues and multiplicity of motives and circumstances regarded as evil.

Taken as a whole, the following chapters underscore the notion that evil's incomprehensibility rests in part on its irreducibility to a single motive, cause, or perspective. While undeniably serving self-interests, evil exposes wide disparities among these interests, their consequences, and the frameworks most relied upon to conceptualize and respond to them. Given that its motives often are gratuitously instrumental, but ineradicably human, any answer that aspires to comprehensiveness must grapple with the question of why some people willingly violate the rights of others. This question leads some to conceptualize evil as a dimension of the Manichean struggle between the forces of light and darkness, as a metaphysical principle standing always in opposition to the good. For these theorists, whether referring to individual or group behavior, evil represents a transindividual force operating through human action. Others regard evil as distinctly human and always a product of choice. Yet, even here, there is disagreement as to whether some property might be identified that unifies its various instantiations. Is it an aberration or ontological structure that defines the human condition? The phenomenon of evil cries out for a new perspective, one that provides both greater understanding and a way to respond to a malignancy that has metastasized to virtually all people, countries and cultures. These are but a few of the issues addressed in this volume.

Aggression

Within psychoanalysis, aggression is conceptualized as one of two primary motives. Its relationship to destructiveness, in turn, is regarded as direct and self-evident. Like libido, Freud believed it structured personal identity as well as one's relationships with others, sometimes in ways fully accessible to awareness; at others, hidden in the deepest recesses of the mind. Unlike his romantic predecessors, however, he had no illusions about man's goodness, nor did he regard evil as a product of the corruption of man's essential purity or virtue. For Freud (1975/1930), man's viciousness expressed his nature as much as his sexuality. He famously stated, "man is a wolf to man" (p. 111). Rather than

> gentle creatures who want to be loved, and who at the most can defend themselves if they are attacked[, men] are ... creatures among whose instinctual endowments is to be reckoned a powerful share of aggressiveness. As a result, their neighbor is for them not only a potential helper or sexual object, but also someone who tempts them to satisfy their aggressiveness on him, to exploit his capacity for work without compensation, to use him sexually with his consent, to seize his possessions, to humiliate him, to cause him pain, to torture and to kill him. (p. 111)

Given the opportunity, man is a "savage beast to whom consideration towards his own kind is something alien" (p. 112).

Psychoanalysis has struggled with Freud's view of human aggression and has preferred to locate it largely within fantasy or unconscious mental life.

Strictly speaking, this claim does not misread Freud so much as it fails to take account of ideas promulgated in his later works. For example, Freud championed the view that the viability of civilization depended on redirecting inclinations to aggressiveness toward the self. One thesis specifically advanced by Freud was that morality represented precisely this reversal and internalization of aggression. Whereas detection by others can be avoided, one cannot evade the scrutiny of one's own conscience. Yet, the larger point about man's predatory nature remained central to Freud's thinking. The juxtaposition of aggression and sexuality made conflict real and foundational rather than illusory and incidental to the human condition. Conflict between these powerful inclinations was intrinsic; it conditioned all thought, feeling and behavior. Left to his own devices, Freud believed man would exploit and destroy indiscriminately and without compunction, his aggressiveness constrained only by the fear of retribution or the threat of loss. Even those theorists who regarded aggression as reactive to frustration without reference to drives generally did not question its role in transgression and violence.

In positing a death drive, Freud memorialized the tendency to destruction and dissolution. Freed from the civilizing effects of repression or under the sway of identification with corrupt and aggressive authority figures, especially in group settings, evil was an ever-present possibility. Whereas libido bound one to others, the death drive undermined unity, preservation and attachment; it opposed, negated and destroyed.

Although generating interest among interdisciplinary scholars, Freud's views on aggression remain unsystematized within psychoanalysis both clinically and theoretically. Skepticism among practitioners dedicated to helping others has created confusion about the complex relationship between aggression and evil. For example, while it is true that aggression is discerned in evil actions, it is simply false to claim that evil is reducible to this single motive or drive. Perhaps better put, the truth of this claim can be established only at the expense of a clear understanding of aggression as a complex phenomenon. Why? Because aggression is neither exclusively nor inherently murderous, destructive or undermining of attachment. The soundness of this claim is buttressed by data from ethological studies in which aggression is found repeatedly to serve important evolutionary aims (Boehm, 2002; Midgley, 1984). In its broadest sense, aggression offers a means of dispute resolution in many animal species, including subhuman primates. Rather than necessarily destructive, it strengthens community bonds and organization. It also is effective in driving off threats to one's survival, rivals for resources and sexual reproduction. Aggressive behavior accomplishes these ends without killing, causing significant harm or "seriously interrupt[ing] social life" (Midgley, 1984, p. 87). Evil and aggression therefore are distinguishable both conceptually and practically. Evil depends on aggression joining with other attitudes, beliefs, inclinations and goals into a superordinate, complex and highly destructive motivational system.

Perversion and Moral Flexibility

At the clinical level, Freud discerned indicants of the death drive in acts of overt destructiveness as well as in unconscious enactments revealed in phenomena like the repetition compulsion, perversions, negative therapeutic reactions and group behavior. Freud understood sadism, for example, as a twisting of the sexual drive such that one experienced pleasure through the infliction of pain. However, one of the most important discoveries made possible by the study of perversion, one particularly relevant to the understanding of evil, is the identification of the unique forms of mentation it engenders. Especially in fetishes, perception and cognition are narrowed, bringing about alterations in reality testing.

Importantly, the breeches of reality testing observed in perversions rarely betoken psychosis; rather, they represent refusals to test fantasies against norms and rules as well as against potential consequences (Grossman, 1996). Closely linked to denial and rationalization, these failures of "reality" or "value" testing heighten the potential for transgression. They do so by forestalling the activation of moral emotions typically responsible for restraining misconduct. Different from repression, the "perverse attitude toward reality" (p. 9) narrows perception to a degree that effectively sequesters from awareness information key to the activation of moral restraint. One lives in the moment, in an altered state of consciousness or a dream-like state; one inhabits a world in which the rules no longer apply. Such mental states are not as unusual as one might initially suspect—they emerge in various ways when one must confront uncomfortable realities. Isn't it commonplace to greet disappointments, loss and trauma initially with disbelief and incredulity? Isn't it natural to hope that what one sees or hears is not *really* real? Problematically in fetishes and, as I am claiming, in mental states productive of some forms of evil, these lapses tend to be chronic. They are self-reinforcing and intensely pleasurable.

The perverse attitude toward reality encompasses an array of evils that transpire insidiously as well as in single, dramatic acts. What is important is that this concept offers a means of understanding enactments under conditions that diffuse the agent's experience of moral responsibility. For example, the white-collar criminal lines his coffers simply by manipulating numbers on a spreadsheet; the pharmaceutical executive by releasing tainted products, both with devastating effects on unsuspecting victims. Neither necessarily acts out of enmity, at least in any obvious way; neither experiences himself as destroying a hated adversary. There may be little recognition in the perpetrator's mind of the connection between his actions and the disproportionate human harm they cause. This disconnection is believed more easily when his actions are carried out from a location far from those likely to be victimized. Anonymity increases the likelihood of evil.

While evil depends on one's intentionally doing wrong, knowing one could have done otherwise, it does not require one's intentions to be fully formulated or clear. One can act in a machiavellian way, exploiting opportunities that present themselves spontaneously rather than by design. One might act sadistically toward those perceived as threatening, while simultaneously evincing capacities for loyalty and compassion for others in one's life. In this way, evil is easily rationalized, its dissonance diminished.

Dissociation facilitates the engagement with evil because it promotes detachment and moral disengagement. Simply put, it narrows the range of considerations deemed relevant to one's deliberations. Not only does it bias perception and information processing, but it engenders moral tunnel vision, allowing one to think and act in ways sequestered from identity and the values one otherwise holds. Could psychoanalytic thinking about dissociation and the perverse attitude toward reality offer a way of understanding what transpires intrapsychically in the phenomena described by social psychologists like Milgram (1974) and Zimbardo (2007)? Does it illuminate the dynamics of obedience to authority, bystander effects and the readiness of some individuals to engage in abuse and torture? Can these concepts be deployed to bridge the vast divide between the so-called "situational" and "character" explanations of evil? The reader should keep these questions in mind in thinking through the arguments advanced in each chapter.

Perversion is important to the problem of evil because it offers an understanding of transgression that does not rest on ignorance or psychopathy. Nor does it depend on a personality in which aggression plays a prominent role. Instead, evil sometimes is facilitated by failures to activate values of restraint or to integrate them with identity. In this view, perpetration does not rest on the absolute absence of inner morality so much as it reflects a choice, whether conscious or unconscious, to remain a bystander. It is a failure to honor the call of conscience. Without such integration, the other's humanity is easily diminished, making moral intervention unnecessary. Sometimes, this lack of integration transforms the other into an impersonal object to be manipulated as one wishes. Put another way, dissociation may be conceptualized as encompassing an array of cognitive processes like psychological distancing or moral disengagement; it may well facilitate euphemistic redescriptions of wrongdoing that, in turn, reinforce intergroup prejudice and justify perpetration (Bandura, 1999). In the end, perhaps evil depends on the intersection of contextual variables, like the anonymity described by Zimbardo and the pleasures, both conscious and unconscious, that accompany the fulfillment of forbidden wishes (Rangell, 1980).

Evil as a Distinctly Human Problem

We expect our lives to make sense, to fit within an intelligible framework. Evil challenges this cherished belief, confronting us with a world that is truly indifferent to our needs and wishes. In a world stripped of any higher authority whose benevolence somehow insulates us from the harsh realities of life, our suffering no longer serves any obvious purpose. Our pain is incoherent and arbitrary.

Neiman (2000) regards the refusal to relinquish our illusions as the greatest obstacle to coming to terms with evil. Evil is more than a concept or interpretation of experience: It presents us with real and practical problems that call for a response. While it resists facile definition, we recognize evil when we see it, despite the fact that its forms continue to evolve and transform. Bernstein (2002) goes so far as to claim that "there is a plurality of types of evil, with no common essence" (p. 226). He agrees with Neiman that there is no unifying theme or origin that makes evil intelligible, no essence that stabilizes it conceptually or makes it less horrifying.

Camus (1948) was well aware of the potential for evil and its inevitable unfolding. *The Plague* is a cautionary tale about the unreliability of memory and our readiness to forget collective trauma, despite the constant reminders of our own destructive capabilities. At any given moment, evil seems to be everywhere: armed fighting in the Middle East, Africa and Ukraine; terrorism threatening virtually all countries around the globe; and the murder, rape and torture of innocents. Shock and horror at these events slowly and inevitably gives way to amnesia; only for those most directly affected does mourning painfully endure. For the latter, there is no closure, no return to who they were before evil infected their lives. However much they move forward and find meaning and value in their lives, it is *in spite of* what evil has wrought.

The proliferation of technologies that permit instantaneous global communication makes our amnesia all the more striking. How can we forget when we have constant and instantaneous reminders of man's inhumanity to man? How else can it be explained but as denial, a refusal to see? In forgetting—or perhaps in a process more aptly described as suppression—a false innocence is restored at the expense of any ability to face the problem of evil courageously. The residue is incomprehension and astonishment. Is not this naïveté compelling evidence of our collective guilt?

Pure Evil

There is a second, self-protective dynamic operative in the workings of evil. Not only do we deny our knowledge and collective culpability, but we distance ourselves from evil-doing by demonizing those who perpetrate it. Demonizing should not be confused with moral condemnation. The latter expresses outrage; it communicates our disapproval of an action in the strongest possible terms. Demonizing does this as well, but also something more—it erects an insuperable barrier between perpetrators and others, between them and us. To be sure, there are real and absolute differences between evil and normative acts. What is at issue, however, is whether we gain any deeper understanding of the motives for evil by regarding those who perpetrate it as other-than-human. Rather than driven by recognizably human forces—like wrath, avarice, sloth, pride, lust, envy, and gluttony—evil agents become monsters whose actions uniquely express a principled commitment or dedication to evil. For the monster, evil is transformed into the good and undertaken sincerely and authentically. In this view, whatever pleasure accrues to evil-doing, whatever instrumental purpose it may serve, duty and obligation are its primary motives. While pure evil of this kind is a conceptual possibility, it is at best rare and fails to explain the vast majority of human wickedness.

Equally important is how conceptualizing evil as an essence, supernatural force or monstrous and other-worldly distracts us from its central challenge: the impact and consequences of evil. Evil is horrific and worthy of condemnation because of what it accomplishes—unimaginable pain and suffering, whether in a single, unanticipated action or repetitively over time. The tension between treating evil as an essence and as a practical and moral problem is one that will be maintained throughout this book. To gloss over this tension is to offer false reassurance about our fundamental humanity, to achieve a degree of comfort at the expense of understanding evil as an ever-present human possibility. Limiting the possibility of evil only to the deranged, disturbed, diabolical—to the "not me," preserves the assumption of our humanity. It allows us to experience astonishment at its manifestations and consequences.

Structures of Evil

There are two additional forms of evil that will be discussed from a number of different perspectives in the chapters that follow. The first, often referred to as *instrumental evil*, describes actions aimed at satisfying a wide variety of needs—in fact, virtually any need, whether pressing or trivial. Importantly, these needs do not necessary include the infliction of suffering in any intrinsic way; in other words, their primary purpose need not be to do harm. Rather, the *evil* of instrumental evil resides in the agent's willingness to knowingly and intentionally do harm in order to fulfill one or more of these needs. He chooses one course of action rather than another, with consequences that are foreseeable to any rational agent. His inner experience of intentionality and choice notwithstanding, it is a requirement of instrumental evil that the agent is free to act otherwise.

Formulated in this way, instrumental evil does not challenge understanding in the same way that contemporary forms of evil do. It is at once comprehendible and confirms our worst suspicions about how readily moral restraint is deactivated. We condemn such actions but do not struggle to grasp, perhaps identify with, their goals and motives. We rightly condemn the actions of a Bernard Madoff for his greed. We condemn him especially for the devastation he caused in so many lives, for so many organizations and charitable causes. But, truth be told, who among us has not felt the allure of this and other motives? Who has not wished for money, power or status at one point or another in their lives?

Given their ubiquity, it is unlikely that these motives define or explain evil. Rather, they engender thoughts, feelings and beliefs that influence our choices. Better put, they pose dilemmas that require moral deliberation. Under the sway of shame, anger, deprivation or want, some individuals willingly harm others to delete inner conflict and discomforting emotions. These actions sometimes rise to the level of depraved indifference. The instrumentally evil agent recognizes the wrongness of his actions; he recognizes his failure to respect the dignity of others, using them as objects to achieve a selfish end.

Second and lastly, we collectively face the threat of *ideological evil*. While not entirely new, it has evolved in such a way that its devastation strains comprehension and poses a threat of truly global proportions. By ideological evil, I refer to the indiscriminate torture and murder of innocent people, sometimes carried out on a massive scale, on the basis of ideological commitments. Importantly, these commitments make it possible to commit acts of unthinkable violence while regarding them as justified, moral, even good. From the perpetrator's perspective, the ends truly justify the means.

Strenger (2011) views ideological evil as nurtured in the cradle of "closed worldviews" (p. 171), perspectives that are rigid, inflexible and dogmatic, reflecting the essence of what is regarded as fanaticism. Whereas advances in communication and social media underscore the degree to which we all are members of a global community, with many intersecting interests, closed worldviews rest on paranoia and a tribal mentality that imagines its values and way of life always under attack. Individuals in these systems feel certain that they possess the "ultimate truth and final solution to all human problems" (p. 171). Their certainty short-circuits critical reflection and moral deliberation and creates conditions in which evil is not only possible but desirable and reinterpreted as moral.

Overview

This book offers a contemporary psychoanalytic perspective on the problem of evil, written by investigators internationally recognized for their scholarship. It is inspired by Freud's insight that one of the greatest sources of human suffering results from the vicissitudes of our relationships, whether with other individuals or among groups and nations. Whereas "natural" evil betokens suffering that bears no mark of human intentionality, moral evil—which, in essence, comprises the subject matter of this book—concerns itself with harms intrinsically linked to human freedom. Rather than an impersonal force of nature, moral evil depends on choice and agency and, for this reason, implicates obligations and responsibilities however much they may go unrecognized by any particular agent.

Humanizing Evil is divided into three parts. The first, entitled "Formulating Evil," examines evil from a broadly psychoanalytic-philosophical perspective. In chapter one, Dr. Mills surveys and evaluates various claims about the nature of evil in order to identify its essential features. Once stabilized, he interrogates the coherence of this concept as a purely human phenomenon, one that stands dialectically in relationship to the good. He argues that evil is an ineradicable human possibility, separated from the good only by the agent's effortful control over the ever-present lure of enactment. His conclusion is controversial: we are all evil.

In Chapter 2, Dr. McGrath revisits the perspective of Freud and Jung on the problem of evil through the lens of Böhmean theogony. In contrast to Freud's superego, which turns on what is publicly forbidden, and Jung's view of evil as part of a cosmic whole that must be acknowledged and owned without moral condemnation, evil for Böhme is real and grounded in divine law. Put another way, it is not reducible to that which opposes self-flourishing or group cohesion, but rather is intrinsically linked to the good. More than this, McGrath sees psychoanalytic practice as rooted in a theory of self in which good can be formulated only by virtue of its relationship to the ever-present possibility of aggression and destructiveness. For McGrath, the unconscious is theological and Böhme's work brings it about that both good and evil may be understood to issue from the very same source.

Dr. Beebe's develops Jung's concept of evil as a form of destructiveness that can be organized in accordance with an eight-function, eight-archetype model of the psyche. Following Jung, he understands the archetypes teleologically as shaping the expression and instantiation of evil thoughts, feelings and actions. Utilizing clinical examples and literary sources, Beebe completes the third chapter by reminding the reader of the vital connection between the capacities for reflective self-assessment and self-regulation and their impact on what he calls "demonic consciousness."

In Chapter 4, in the second section of *Humanizing Evil*, "The Psychology of Perpetration," Dr. Naso develops the concept of "breaking bad" in order to explain engagements with evil aimed at undoing dramatic reversals of fortune. He is led to this formulation on the basis of his psychoanalytic treatment of a 30-year-old man who turned to criminality when his hopes for success by legitimate means were dashed. Critical to Naso's thinking is the fact that this man was not psychopathic, nor was he incapable of establishing and maintaining deep relationships with others. For most of his life, he had been committed to "playing by the rules." These findings lead Naso to conclude that breaking bad represents a unique and coordinated expression of personality and situational factors, including chance.

In Chapter 5, Dr. Prince develops the idea of *predatory identity* as a source of evil. As he understands it, predatory identity cannot tolerate dissonance and reacts with disproportionate destructiveness to anything and anyone who threatens it. Although conceptualizing identity broadly as encompassing gender, ethnicity and group belonging, Prince focuses on the impact of belief systems in this chapter. He concludes that predatory identity poses a risk in virtually any arena where belief systems are rigid and inflexible.

Dr. Stone offers a detailed taxonomy of evil, focusing in Chapter 6 on the psychological forces that prompt the commission of evil acts. Pathological narcissism is seen as playing a central role. However, Stone also pays careful attention to the role of trauma and other unfavorable circumstances in the lives of perpetrators as well as to evidence that supports the claim that genetic predisposition also plays a key role—especially those whose personalities fulfill criteria for psychopathy. Stone concludes with the hypothesis that changes in post-1960 culture, along the lines outlined originally in part by Christopher Lasch (1979), illuminate the heinousness of contemporary forms of evil. The decline of religion, the proliferation of mind-altering drugs, and the increasing and exclusive focus on the self are some of the key variables he sees as transforming perpetration.

Part III of the book, "Clinical Applications," examines the concept of evil as it manifests itself in a number of different clinical settings. In Chapter 7, Dr. Gozlan turns his psychoanalytic gaze from the patient to the witness's response to exposure to evil; he explores this theme through the case of Dr. John Bradford, a forensic psychiatrist who did not believe in the diagnostic criteria of PTSD until experiencing the symptoms himself following exposure to videos made by Russell Williams, a colonel in the Canadian Army convicted in the murders of two women and the slaying and sexual torture of two others. His paper explores the traumatic effect of witnessing acts of murder, dismemberment and rape and poses the question of whether it is ever possible to enter evil without being affected by it.

In the eighth and final chapter of this book, Dr. Covington returns the reader to the Lithuanian city of Kovno in 1941 where a man beat to death 50 Jewish men between the ages of 30 and 50. This event marked the beginning of the Nazi pogroms in Lithuania known as Operation Barbarossa. By engaging the question of: "Who could stand by and let such cruelty happen?" psychoanalytically, she illuminates the complex psychodynamics of those who witness evil and fail to intervene. Specifically, she argues that identification with the aggressor powerfully undergirds witnessing, providing the subject with a sense of mastery over trauma at the same time that it destroys core beliefs and threatens relationships with internal objects.

Taken together, all of the papers included in *Humanizing Evil* bring to bear on the problem of evil the full array of conceptual tools available within contemporary psychoanalytic thinking. In so doing, they offer an affirmative response to the current impasse surrounding this topic, one that seems to accept human evil as fundamentally mysterious and incomprehensible. Rather than rejecting the ideas of investigators from other moral, religious, social-psychological or philosophical traditions, each chapter critically evaluates and integrates these ideas within a psychological perspective.

The result is one that respects these traditions but refuses to lapse into a stance that demonizing others or engages in self-blame. Evil is formulated as a plurality rather than an essence, as an inescapable human potential coextensive with the possibility of good. At bottom, *Humanizing Evil* is an integrative effort that portrays evil as a multifaceted phenomenon expressive of psychological, situational and historical factors, broadly conceived.

No project of this magnitude is completed without the ongoing support and guidance of others. Dr. Mills and I both wish to express our gratitude to Kate Hawes, Senior Editor of Routledge, and Sue Wickenden, also of Routledge, for making this project a reality. I also want to acknowledge and thank my mother and father who have supported me in everything I do. I feel blessed to have them in my life as well as in the lives of my wife and children.

References

Bandura, A. (1999). Moral disengagement in the perpetration of inhumanities. *Personality and Social Psychology Review, 3*, 193–209.

Baum, S.K. (2008). *The Psychology of Genocide: Perpetrators, Bystanders, and Rescuers*. New York, NY: Cambridge University Press.

Bernstein, R. (2002). *Radical Evil: A Philosophical Interrogation*. Cambridge, UK: Polity Press.

Boehm, C. (2002). Conflict and the evolution of social control. In L. D. Katz (Ed.), *Evolutionary Origins of Morality: Cross-Disciplinary Perspectives*, 79–102. Bowling Green, OH: Imprint Academic Press.

Camus, A. (1948), *The Plague*. Translated by: Stuart Gilbert. New York, NY: Knopf.

Clark, J.N. (2009). Genocide, war crimes and the conflict in Bosnia: Understanding the perpetrators. *Journal of Genocide Research, 11*, 421–445.

Freud, S. (1975). Civilization and its discontents. *The Standard Edition of the Complete Psychological Works of Sigmund Freud, 21*, 59–148. London, UK: Hogarth Press. (Original work published 1930).

Grossman, L. (1993). The perverse attitude toward reality. *Psychoanalytic Quarterly*, 62, 422–436.

Kernberg, O. (2007). The almost untreatable narcissistic patient. *Journal of the American Psychoanalytic Association, 55*, 503–539.

Lasch C. (1979). *The Culture of Narcissism*. New York, NY: W.W. Norton.

Mandel, D.R. (2002). Instigators of genocide: Examining Hitler from a social psychological perspective. In L.S. Newman and R. Erber (Eds.), *Understanding Genocide: The Social Psychology of the Holocaust*, 259–284. New York, NY: Oxford University Press.

Milgram, S. (1974). *Obedience to Authority*. New York, NY: Harper & Row.

Midgley, M. (1984). *Wickedness. A Philosophical Essay*. London, UK & New York, NY: Routledge.

Neiman, S. (2000). *Evil in Modern Thought*. Princeton, NJ: Princeton University Press.

Rangell, L. (1980). *The Mind of Watergate. An Exploration of the Compromise of Integrity.* NewYork, NY: W.W. Norton.
Strenger, C. (2011). *The Fear of Insignificance: Searching for Meaning in the Twenty-first Century.* New York, NY: Palgrave MacMillan.
Zimbardo, P. (2007). *The Lucifer Effect: Understanding How Good People Turn Evil.* New York, NY: Random House.

Part I

Formulating Evil

Chapter 1

The Essence of Evil

Jon Mills

Does evil exist, or is it a social invention? Is evil an action, a disposition, a property, a consequence, and/or a characteristic that necessarily makes it what it is, essentially? Does it hinge on creating pain for others—from relatively benign modes of discomfort to harm and gratuitous suffering? Does malicious intent have to be involved or simply just intent, even if not malicious? Surely, pain can result without intent, so what is the relationship between harm and human motivation? What if an event that brings about harm and suffering was not due to a direct action but rather a failure to act, such as in a weakness of will, the bystander effect or a miscarriage of moral courage? Here we may describe evil as the abnegation of responsibility, the failure to choose, the denial of freedom. But what happens if these failures are unconsciously informed, even chosen, the product of an unconscious will toward evil? Or are these queries contingent upon value judgments we ascribe to events and their causal attributions?

The question and nature of evil have been a human preoccupation since the rise of civilization, yet we can find no consensus on what constitutes its essence. The instantiation of evil unequivocally contributes to the necessary social manufacturing of law and order, religion, morality, justice and systemic mechanisms of restraint, as well as punishment, that govern individual and collective relations within all societies. Psychoanalysis generally has tended to focus upon the pathological dynamics that motivate evil actions, from primary, malignant, and traumatic narcissism to primitive defensive enactments, superego lacunae, failure in internalization and empathy, sociopathy, selfobject deficits, developmental trauma and attachment pathology, rather than on the question of evil itself. For example, is evil a human phenomenon, or does it have a metaphysical structure? What makes evil (by necessity) what it is? Is it merely a relative enterprise fashioned by our subjectivities? Any determination of evil stands in relation to the meaning of value and the value of meaning, for what differentiates a natural act (such as animals killing prey, extreme weather phenomenon resulting in environmental disasters with loss of life, and so forth) from a human act is the construction of meaning and value inquiry within ethical agency. Furthermore, are actions in themselves sufficient to determine the essence of evil, or does psychological intent become a necessary ingredient? What if such intent was unconsciously harbored yet unacknowledged by the conscious subject, let alone enacted, the evil within? And what about the consequences of both action and intention as a touchstone by which to adjudicate evil? These questions tend to situate the problematic of evil within a moral realm. But what if the question and nature of evil have nothing to do with morality whatsoever?

In this chapter, I wish to explore the essence and ethics of evil. What I will conclude is both controversial and counter-intuitive. But, before we get there, I will need to prepare our discussion. After laying out various philosophical problematics, our analysis will center around the domain and structure of violence as: (a) natural phenomena, (b) subjective interiority, (c) objective instantiation, (d) systemic perpetuation, and (e) ontic universality. The degree to which our natural constitution derived from evolutionary pressures predisposes the human animal toward evil will be contrasted with developmental currents that are cultivated as a result of social interaction and the interiority of suffering. What marks the qualification of evil is the degree of ethical agency within an individual and society determined by the objective attainment of self-consciousness and voluntary choice. The evil that inhabits man in thought, intention, and deed is beyond psychological dynamics, I suggest, for violence is a metaphysical principle that saturates the natural world as a *mysterium tremendum*, at once a frightening necessity governing life yet one that signals the non-violent domain of ideality we attribute to moral idealism, paradoxically, itself a violent imposition as ethical demand.

What is Evil?

Let us first begin with basics. In classical Greek, κᾰκός historically signifies that which is intrinsically "bad," whereby the term "evil" is a transliteration. Etymologically the origin of the word is unknown, but many philologists believe it is derived from the proto-Indo-European root *kakka*, taken from κακκάω—to defecate. In other words, evil is shitty. The term is taken up in numerous contexts in classical antiquity and has generally informed our modern conception of all valuative discourses today. κᾰκός refers to: (a) persons and their character: *bad*, *lowly*, *wretched* (see Herodas, 1922, 3.42); (b) of appearance: *ugly*; (c) of birth: *ill-born*, *mean*; (d) of courage: *craven*, *cowardly*; (e) of kind: *worthless*, *sorry*, *unskilled*; (f) of things: *pernicious* (see Homer, *Odyssey*, 10.64); (g) of omens: *unlucky*; (h) of words: *abusive*, *foul*; (i) of actions: *to do harm or ill to another* (*Illiad*, 2.195); and (j) in the moral sense: *base*, *evil*. Interestingly, κᾰκός is a cognate of καλός, its opposite, namely, the good, the beautiful.[1] Here we may see how good and evil are dialectically related and mutually implicative. In other words, we cannot have any discussion of either concept without invoking the other.

This makes evil, by definition, contingent on a notion of good, which is itself equally presupposed, debatable and problematic.

There is a natural simplicity to splitting based upon a perfunctory economy. This is an elementary aspect to mental functioning and observed endlessly as a normative process, whether in society or in the clinic. This natural (hence normal, inborn, instinctual or organic) tendency to think in terms of binaries—same/different, good/bad—is a rudimentary mechanism of thinking that is superimposed on all experience. It is only with cognitive development and the acquisition of self-consciousness or a reflective function (often referred to as mentalization) that the binary proclivity is breached through attempts at entertaining complexity, holism, integration of opposite perspectives, and synthetic attempts at unification or reconciliation of opposition and difference. But this synthetic function, I argue, is a developmental or ideological ideal that is never fully achieved as a hierarchical reality when it comes to certain matters, especially those involving the human emotions, including the notions of right and wrong. In fact, an ideology of right can intensify this bifurcation and fortify a rigid antithesis that blinds us to the opposing perspective, which further introduces a danger of imposing an absolutism on phenomena, phenomena that by definition are open, transient, fluid and pluralistic, thus radically resisting unification. Here there is no transvaluation of values, no *Aufhebung*, no discernible space beyond good and evil; rather we have an impasse, a gap, lacunae, or parallax where there is no synthesis between the two polarities. We cannot make each opposition—the fork between good and evil—a unified position based on fanciful logic alone. It defies all social realities. It betrays what we know about the human psyche as an unconsciously desirous and conflicted animal. There will always be a firm obstacle, limit or check between these opposing forces in the mind. Yet it all depends upon what perspective you take.

Evil is typically construed on the negative pole of the dialectic, a construct defined in relation to absolute difference. Evil as contrast to its opposite highlights its one-sided polarity, one based on pure negation, yet this duality forms an ontological unit. Since antiquity, evil has been signified by its privative function and formally instantiated as innate badness, viz., that which deracinates and generates social disharmony by lacerating all semblances of moral order. It is none other than the introduction of radical negativity, to the degree that existential preoccupations with its recalcitrant presence has generated the psychological need for elaborate systems of theodicy to explain its occurrence. Here reconciling the appearance of evil with the good and with the question and meaning of God has elevated the notion of evil to a metaphysical factor. Historically, God has been extricated from evil, and it is attributed instead to fallen angels or man, yet this fantasy is hardly intellectually worthy of support. In today's secular world, the reification of evil to a supernatural hypostatization (i.e., the Devil) is an untenable explanation for the atrocities committed by human beings. In the absence of divine presence or intervention, evil is exclusively a human phenomenon.

What would a secular theory of evil look like? First we must explore whether we can pinpoint its essence, namely, that which necessarily circumscribes and defines what it is, without which it would not and could not exist. Here I am chasing after the question of universality: Can evil be shown to have an essence, and if so, does it apply universally across modes of human phenomena that are adjudicated to be or deemed as evil? This would imply, all things being equal, that any universal attribution of evil would carry epistemological and hermeneutic agreement to warrant such generalizations, even if only confined to theory. But is this possible? This would mean, hypothetically, that no one instance or particularity would elude the label of evil if it was deemed a universal attribution. This surely would challenge the notion of context, contingency, accident and chance. Perhaps we should not assume that universality and context are mutually exclusive, especially when they ontically inform each other. Perhaps evil may be viewed as a certain positionality as fixation on one side of its dialectical polarity, what may also be said of the good, whereby both positions form a tension arc between their oppositions. Here we may posit that both good and evil involve a radical splitting of the other, one that is obstreperous to mediation or synthesis.

Because evil is historically by definition the absence or privation of good, opposition is required for it to have structure and meaning. Here evil is value laden, hence it stands in relation to the question and nature of morality. This presupposes that evil cannot be amoral as it signifies a judgment about value and agency. But what if evil is in itself a relative construct and there are no absolutes? What if it has no value? This would imply that there is neither good nor evil, for valuation itself is either held in abeyance, neutralized, suspended, non-existent or devolves into a meaningless construct. But how can a material act or embodied event lack valuation, how can it escape human judgment? Perhaps we may conclude there are no absolutes due to the relativity of conferring value judgments while still observing appearances of evil that are universal. Conversely, can the notion of pure negativity carry with it a metaphysical value even if it lies outside of human valuation? In other words, can evil exist without agency? These are difficult questions to sustain.

Evil is often defined as an act of transgressing, which in many cultures corresponds to something that is wrong, yet we immediately encounter the thorny issues of determining what constitutes wrongness, the non-good, and what it means to transgress, as these determinations stand in relation to a contextual and collective attribution of meaning as valuation. Here evil is not merely an intellectual concept or the religionization of human desire and action, for it stands in relation to an absolute value that has been contravened, devalued or occluded. Because value judgments are determinative and transpire within a given material culture and linguistic social structure replete with local customs and prejudices of meaning, the question of absolute value may succumb to relativity. Regardless of the questionable antipodes and extremity of either absolutism or relativism, the essence of evil is found in its contextual valuation whether absolute, universal or relative in its instantiation and scope. This necessarily places valuation at the heart of any determination of evil, and since valuation stands in juxtaposition to greater collective-meaning structures within any given society, evil becomes a social artifact.

The term "evil" is burdened by its history. In the Judeo-Christian tradition that has dominated Western thought, evil is considered to be that which violates God's will. We may already see an ideology at play by presupposing a Supreme Being to begin with, one that dominates world discourse and preys on the fears, emotional vulnerability, ignorance and religious prejudices of contemporary cultures. Promulgating such a way of thinking further reinforces the unconscious social fantasy that such a reified Ideal exists by which all humans will be compared to and judged by divine authority. In ancient times, the God posit served many pragmatic and psychological purposes, but it hardly serves as a touchstone let alone justification for an operational definition of evil. I see no valid rational argument for perpetuating this psychomythology that evil is deviation from God's way, when God is merely a social construction born of a fantasy principle and instituted as a cultural symbolic (Freud, 1927; Mills, 2016).

But we must take seriously the notion that evil is the privation or absence of good. This was set out by Aquinas in his *Summa Theologiae* (see Part I: Treatise on The Distinction of Good And Evil [Q 48–49]), which was earlier echoed by Augustine (*Confessions*, Bk 3, vii [12]), what Plotinus believed was a psychic or subjective event, hence belonging to the soul (*Enneads*, I, 2.1–3; 8.8), not a godhead, yet at the same time an ontological condition based upon the fact that we are embodied. But the privation (*steresis*) theory of evil (*kakon*), although debatable, may be said to have its genesis in Aristotle who discussed the notion of lack, such as when something is deprived of an attribute belonging to its nature, for "a thing comes to be from [it's] privation" (see *Physics*, bk 1: 191b15). With stipulations, this may be (loosely) interpreted to mean that which is evil comes into being from what it is lacking. Perhaps this is merely an inverse tautology: evil is the lack of goodness. Of course this sentiment is inherited from Plato: evil is the destroyer and corrupter of all things (*Republic*, 10.608e), which can never be done away with (*Theaetetus*, 176a). That which is deemed objectively beneficial is good, and that which is deemed evil is not. As for the nature of evil, it is derived from the natural "desire of food of drink of sex," but not for the momentary pleasure it produces, but rather from its "consequences" (*Protagoras*, 353c-e). Here we may see a kernel of Neo-Platonism influencing the Christian perversion of pathologizing human nature as sinful. Despite the fact that discourse on the nature of evil was inspired by the pre-Socratics and can be historically found in virtually all records of early civilization, good and evil have become the positive and negative exemplifications of moral absolutes.

Radical Evil

Kant's treatise on evil does not attribute evil to original sin or to a turning away from God, nor does it conform to the Augustinian denial of evil since it is nothing but the privation of good (*privatio boni*). It does not even conform to human want or desire, but rather is due to free choice (*Willkür*). Evil is the product of our determinate powers of choice because, for Kant, we are radically free to determine the grounds for the sake of which to behave. This places the onus of responsibility squarely on the existential agent making such choices and not on natural inclination, impulse or desire, for as Kant (1793) tells us, "the source of evil ... can lie only in a rule made by the will for the use of its freedom, that is, in a maxim" (p. 17). So even though we are born with innate needs, desires, leanings, dispositions, and impulses, man is the author of his nature due to acts of freewill as choice that either conform to or neglect the moral realm. This so-called freedom of the moral will that generates maxims upon which all human beings supposedly construct for themselves, is a purely determining, autonomous spontaneity of choice and is therefore influenced by many "incentives." And for Kant, "the moral law, in the judgment of reason, is on itself an incentive, and whoever makes it his maxim is *morally* good" (pp. 19–20), whereas deviation from the moral injunction makes one an "evil man."

Kant believes that such a disposition toward choosing good or evil is a matter of free choice, and as such, natural a priori predeterminations are contradictory to the principles of choice as one cannot freely choose what is given or thrown. But are dispositions always freely chosen? Are not urges, impulses, inclinations and wants also mediated by forces outside of one's immediate agentic will, awareness and intent? Propensities, he argues, are acquired, and therefore not necessarily innate, although they are naturally predisposed by virtue of the fact that we crave and have penchants and susceptibilities; but how can he justify the claim that we are predisposed to be inclined to freely choose any course of action unless we are subjected to particularized experiences? Moreover, if we are predisposed to be free agents, are we not necessarily conditioned on naturalized tendencies? Our corporeality is a necessary condition for actualizing free choice, although it is far from a sufficient one.

If we are naturally predisposed to freely choose, then are we not naturally predisposed to choose evil, necessarily so? Left to our own natural devises, would we not likely choose what feels good in the moment regardless of any moral maxims, much like a child in the candy store? Moral laws are not naturally given, for they are acquired: Morality is the education and imposition of culture.

We can no more presuppose the moral law as a transcendental good than we can as evil, for every human activity is based in naturalized psychology. Kant behaves as though the so-called moral imperative is a metaphysical given in the universe much like the physical laws governing our world and the cosmos, when it may be forcefully argued that morality is a human phenomenon. When Kant repeats his ethical mantra that "there is no propensity to moral evil, for such a propensity must spring from freedom ... in the moral capacity of the will" (p. 26), he is presupposing a moral capacity adapted as a rational decision to live one's life according to moral maxims. On the one hand Kant wants to champion a radical freedom by virtue of our capacity to choose evil, while on the other denying an *inherent necessity* to such a choice that is by nature a "natural predisposition" (p. 27). In the end, for Kant, all choices derive from maxims of the will.

What is "radical" for Kant is the deliberate act of choosing evil in light of our conscious awareness of the moral law, which is tantamount to the free choice of violating our moral duty, hence a corruption of the will in selecting evil maxims; although we are naturally inclined to do so, we are nonetheless responsible and accountable for it, which is brought on by ourselves (p. 28). Evil is radical in the sense that it "corrupts the ground of all maxims" (p. 32), which is subjectively chosen through perversity of the heart, human frailty, impurity and vulnerability to wickedness and vice (see p. 24), for it ultimately "puts out of tune the moral capacity to judge" (p. 34). Yet, for Kant, the moral law is transcendentally given, hence presupposed, as is the notion that human beings freely choose their actions through rational means. Here Kant's theory of radical evil suffers from a theoretical prejudice to begin with, namely, the belief in sober rationalism, as though people conduct their lives in deliberate fashions that embrace ethical principles and rules of behavior conforming to logical axioms in choice and action. This could not be farther from the truth of our primordial natures, for moral deliberation is a developmental triumph of the will mediated by many psychological dynamics that ultimately inform any rational comprehension of choice.

Kant ultimately makes evil a rational enterprise of choosing to follow a maxim in discord with duty and allegiance to the moral law, or what duty demands, as if morality is a purely rational decision. Furthermore, ethical attunement is either aligned or misaligned with some realm of moral metaphysical realism, once again freely chosen or ignored, rather than attributed to a moral idealism invented by humanity. Kant fails to reconcile the tension arc between the faculty of desire and free will and begs the question of ethical duty by presupposing a transcendental moral law, as though it is preordained; not to mention that we choose maxims to follow in rational ways rather than as emotionally expedient, mediated events under the press of a whole host of extraneous factors and cultural environs. For example, when he says that "the predisposition to *personality* is the capacity for respect for the moral law as *in itself a sufficient incentive of the will*" (pp. 22–23), he fails to understand human nature as driven by other competing dynamic processes and conflicts that condition this will, especially those imposed by unconscious currents and environmental determinants. Here evil impositions can come from a multitude of directions having very little to do with free will. Evil begets evil whether chosen or not.

Is not the moral law an achievement of culture, at once an invention and imposition of civilization? Kant's view of good and evil as rational choice succumbs to the prejudices of his day concerned with upholding a Christian explanation of man's aberrant behavior while salvaging a theodicy that insulates God from allowing evil. In the end, it is hardly a satisfactory account of the irrational, emotional, libidinal and aggressive predilections that fester within our human natures clamoring for release in various forms, under various guises and valences, and in various circumstances that stimulate their appearance. Contra Kant, moral law is not the provenance of "*divine command*" (p. 37), but rather a human calling.

The Relativity of Evil

I have a country home on a modest fishing lake surrounded by many acres of forest and bush in the lush Canadian wilderness. My closest friend was visiting from the States when my wife, while taking a walk with our daughter on the property, called me on her cell phone alerting me to her discovery. There were several large fish pooling together in a shallow area of the lake near a water drain that connects to a stream. She had no clue what kind of fish they were, but she found the discovery of concern. I immediately feared they were Asian carp attempting to migrate upstream to spawn in the spring. Asian carp are an invasive species that kills practically everything in its ecosystem and have received much attention from anglers and ecologists in Ontario, hence stimulating governmental campaigns designed to combat their contamination of indigenous waters. The invasion of Asian carp have been so damaging in the United States that it is estimated that approximately 90 percent of the ecosystem in the Mississippi River has been decimated. I am a catch-n'-release bass fisherman, forester and conservationist, and the last thing I want is my precious fishing paradise destroyed by unwelcome intruders. Upon this news, I immediately grabbed a large fishing net and walked briskly with my friend to the scene of the crime.

As I feared, these were not largemouth bass but one-to-two-foot carp waiting for the right moment to swim upstream. I instinctively started to scoop them out one by one with my net in a frenzied manner and threw them onto the shore to die. Only a few escaped back into the lake. When the deed was done, I looked at my friend's face and could immediately see his visible discomfort with my murderous act. Was this evil? From my perspective, I was protecting my lake. From his, this was morally reprehensible. Here, witnessing the killing of living creatures was disturbing, and I must admit I did not enjoy it one bit, but I felt compelled to safeguard my habitat. One could even say this basic instinct, as biologists will tell you, is evolutionarily programmed despite the elevation or sublimation of self-consciousness we typically confer onto reason and moral conscience. But herein lies a clash of values that provoke basic ethical questions. Despite the fact that we are hardwired toward predation, adaptation and survival, should human consciousness be obliged to rise above its naturalized tendencies? Should one kill another living thing? Is it evil to set a mousetrap or swat a fly? Moreover, is it innately base? Necessarily so? Or do we value some entities more than others to justify our acts of killing? World societies face these dilemmas every day. In other words, is killing intrinsically evil?

Of course we may differentiate the act of killing from murder, as the world masses must eat and have no malicious intent when harvesting grain, plants and vegetables, or slaughtering animals to put food on the table in order to be healthy and thrive. The cold brute fact of nature is that we must necessarily kill in order to live. Despite the well-intentioned, ethically conscientious objector who demands that we as humanity transcend our primitive natures as desirous, self-enhancing agents, most of the world pays very little attention to this moral question when a hungry stomach cries out to be fed. Here we value our own sustenance over an axiological category or lower form of life that we determine is secondary to human need. But here I had no intention of eating these fish. They were an atrocious enemy that needed to be eradicated in order to preserve what I have and value. This basic splitting in my consciousness at the time may be compared to a simple economy that justifies hurting others, including murder and warfare, based on the notion of relativized experiential value.

On Universality

On January 10, 2015, Nigeria's militant Jihadist group Boko Haram (which literally means "Western education is forbidden"), after going on a mass killing spree in Baga on Lake Chad, strapped explosives to a 10-year-old little girl and sent her off into a market in Maiduguri as a human detonator (Nadeau, 2015). This atrocity comes after the April 14th, 2014, kidnapping of nearly 300 schoolgirls from the Chibok Government Secondary School by the terrorist group; the girl is believed to be one of the abductees. Although reported accounts vary, as many as 276 are still missing, all of which are believed to be used as sex objects and domestic servants.

On December 16, 2014, seven members of a Pakistani Taliban extremist group entered the back door of an army public school in the dustbowl border city of Peshawar and indiscriminately opened fire with machine guns and explosives strapped to their vests, killing 132 schoolchildren. The

Taliban proclaimed the attack was a vendetta for an army offensive in North Waziristan in June that beset militant insurgents. Pakistan's Taliban spokesman Mohammed Umar Khorasanin plainly stated their motive: "We targeted the school because the army targets our families ... We want them to feel our pain" (Inayat, Qazi & Bacon, 2014). Among the copious voices of world outcry, Canadian Prime Minster Stephen Harper said in a news conference:

> I think it's hard for any of us as rational and compassionate people to understand terrorism, to understand why people would want, in the name of some political cause, to simply terrorize, hurt, kill innocent people, whole sections of society, but I think it is just beyond, it is beyond our comprehension why somebody would target children. (Canadian Press, 2014)

These words read alone do not convey the felt emotionality of his speech. This psychological perplexity of disbelief nicely encapsulates the unfathomability of bearing witness to a universal horror. What is beyond comprehension is that innocent helpless children would be brutally murdered by deliberate, malicious and calculated actions of men. It is as if the response of the collective psyche were to say: "How could human beings do this? Only animals prey, for they are instinctual evolutionary organisms that have no self-reflective function or moral conscience by natural design. Humans are supposed to be different." But whether we accept the inherent animality to humanity or not, the line has been crossed.

It is only on the condition that slaughtering innocent children in cold blood would be permissible in any possible world that one would even question its moral significance. In other words, it would never occur to most civilized people to ask whether it is moral or immoral to kill innocent children who have done nothing to others, for the Kantian categorical imperative already speaks a universal language of prohibition. In such instances, where the masses identify with the purity and holiness of childhood, whether as a cultural symbolic or through the direct empathic identification with their own families and personal lives—namely, their own relatives and the child within, the immediate dissociation of understanding any rational means behind such atrocities is emotionally unfathomable for the simple fact that it disrupts our psychic need for a moral order in the universe. Such an imposed confrontation with universal horror forces us to question the presupposed universality of a moral universe to begin with, for it eclipses all value as we know it. Here our rational "unfathomability" that is "beyond comprehension" is none other than our own emotive dissociation to the realization (that must be disavowed) of the *dissociation of ethics*—hence the renunciation of "right"—perpetrated by the Other. In other words, we would have to suspend or abandon a universal concept of what is right and wrong, not to mention entertain a mentalized stance that others would not share our own sense of values. Here lies the pathological breach, an incipient a priori knowledge, that human nature is at base a primitive, feral process that fractures all illusory notions of a civilized, just, and loving world, for it only takes one act of barbarism to remind us that evil is no illusion.

On the Question of Essence

Let us begin to try to sketch out a more refined definition of evil. First of all, as stated earlier, I categorically reject the notion of the personification of evil as a supernatural force or being derived from theosophic perspectives, theodicy or onto-theology.[2] Having said this, there are certain metaphysical principles that are operative in any account of evil, such as the institution and/or experience of pure or radical negativity, disorder, disharmony or disintegration as a structural process endemic to the instantiation of destruction and decay, but these factors may also be viewed as a necessary complementarity to life, for without such events, there can be no change or growth, only stasis. I cannot conceive of the universe without process; therefore without privation, variation, difference, conflict and negation, there would be no motion, evolution or creativity; hence negativity in itself cannot be condemned as evil and in fact may be deemed a metaphysical good because it leads to variation, heterogeneity and plurality. But this discourse on metaphysical evil hardly satisfies our quest for an answer to essence.

Natural disasters and tragedies happen every moment, from the Lisbon earthquake that sparked the theodicy movement to overcome the aporia of how such systemic destruction could even be allowed by a benevolent godhead, especially now when the problem of evil and gratuitous suffering remains the most severe challenge to justified theology (Frances, 2013), to the banality of death, from the butcher's block to political warfare and military science; but we do not impart a malevolent intent to the impersonal hands of cosmic forces. They merely happen through the blind random mutation of organic nature, as well as influenced or expedited by human intervention, as we may readily observe as global populations slowly destroy our planet through climate change, global warming, pollution, exploitation of natural resources, desertification and the despoliation of our ecosystems. But when people burn coal to warm their homes or cook food, there is no malignant intent to cause harm, only to survive. Despite the fact that these continued practices, if allowed to go unrestrained or unchecked, may bring about the demise of our planet, to call them intrinsically evil would mean that we must abort our natural inclinations toward self-sustenance dependent upon a social infrastructure that promulgates and provides the necessities of life. This is not to say that societies should not improve upon such cultural institutions through collective education and social consciousness, but to call them inherently evil, I suggest, is misguided. After all, most people value their own immediate concrete lives over an abstract principle or a fish in the sea, even if such suspension of reason or ethical myopia leads to slow global suicide.

We must first attempt to isolate a key ingredient before formulating an answer to the question of the essence of evil. In paraphrasing Aristotle, for something to be, it must necessarily contain certain essential qualities, elements or forms that make it what it is, without which, it could not be or exist. In other words, if something does not possess certain features, it would not be fundamental to its nature, hence it would not be a vital aspect to its ontological structure. The essence of anything must be indispensable, critical, requisite or basic, hence the lifeblood of its being. Does evil have an essential form? Does it have essential properties? And what would they be?

If evil necessarily encompasses pure negativity, and negativity is an indispensable property to its constitution and appearance, then its instantiation must issue forth or bring about a modicum of violence. Violence may have many appearances, from the pulsating threat of passion or power to the intensity of fear, intimidation, felt aggression, overt hostility, brute force, abuse, ferocity, fury, viciousness, cruelty, savagery, death, and so on. Violence may also be lulled, implicit or expectant, an immanent looming presence that suffuses our world, even if conspicuously absent, an invisibility that is felt. In this regard, violence is hidden but is always there. We may say this is metaphysical violence, as origin, as *arkhē*, the violence of Being. Mind is an original form of violence, a violent coming into being, an awakening as internal rupture, as upheaval, as the self-violent manifestation of interruption.

Slavoj Žižek (2008) identifies *subjective* violence as the phenomenon of subjective experience, which is the most salient among the masses perpetrated by an identifiable agent or entity. By contrast, *objective* violence[3] is both symbolic, that which is constituted through language and semiotic orders of understanding, and the myriad forms it may sociologically take. In fact, language itself is violent: It places a proverbial demand on the other whether solicited or not through aggressive encroachments and superimposed universals of meaning; while *systemic* violence is instantiated through our economic and political institutions that are operating as concretely inscribed mechanisms within our cultural infrastructures and social ideologies. Here we must differentiate the ontological structural elements of evil from their subjective phenomenological-hermeneutical counterparts.

A defining characteristic that differentiates subjective from objective evil is that subjective experience or its qualitative, hermeneutic equivalent may elude a universal appraisal of its definition. This may be due to a lack of shared personal experience or history, linguistic meaning, social convention, consensus, or objective standards of measurement and their interpretation that separates the individual from the collective. We have already encountered this with the problem of relativity. Here empathy may play a key ingredient in sympathizing with how another may interpret a particular personal experience as evil or not, but the form of the experience and its adjudication is nevertheless a solipsistic enterprise. The question becomes whether or not it is universalizable. Here a potential objective dimension materializes, namely, does it resonate with other subjects and their subjectivities that can form some basis of consensus that is adopted as social convention? Whether this makes something objective is still another matter, for one can envision a community of others that hold onto propositional attitudes, false beliefs, emotional prejudices, distortions of truth and realty and socialized delusions based on intersubjective fantasies peculiar to a group, mass or culture. The God posit is a good example.

Let us propose a distinction between: (a) an evil *act* and (b) an evil *intention*. An act always leads to some form of a consequence, while an intention may be passive, active, conscious, unconscious and either linked to a motive or action, suspended, disavowed, or even held in check, hence non-enacted. For example, an act that brings about death may be accidental, such as a motor vehicle accident, but there was no intent to kill. The same applies to forces of nature, such as a tornado or tsunami: Weather has no personal intention to destroy; it is merely a series of random or teleonomic physical events. In these cases death and destruction result from acts without intent; despite being tragic, dreadful and disastrous, I would not classify these as examples of evil. Hence for something to be evil, it requires *agency*. This implies that a certain modicum of intentionality is at play in operationalizing evil. Here an intention always possesses an *aim*. And when it comes to the human psyche, this would necessarily require consciousness (even if consciousness lies on a continuum) that aims at a particular act as an intentional meant object. This means that an act that brings about a certain negative consequence we deem evil must stem from an intentional stance, hence it is deliberate although not necessarily deliberated, as acts may be spontaneously enacted and not particularly well thought-out; albeit it would have to stem from an intention all the same, for no action is devoid of a motive or purpose driving an act, even if it is unconscious.

This brings us to speculate that a certain state of mind must be operative in acts of evil, whether this be: (a) *dispositional* or (b) *intentional*, as well as bearing a particular (c) *qualia* or (d) *psychic form* (e.g., emotion) attached to the intentional act. Here is where we may consider a state of mind that is ontically or dispositionally aggressive, which is the manifestation of the purely negative split of the dialectic. Here violence becomes an ontological feature structurally infused in the very essence of evil. This commits us to accepting a universalizing principle to evil, for every form of evil must participate in a rudimentary violence. We may further say that in its pure (abstract) form, dispositional violence is the inscription of radical negativity, while evil is the manifestation (hence the appearance or enactment) of dispositional violence. Not only is this subjectively constituted in each person (viz., dispositional evil), it materializes in empirical reality when externalized in society. In other words, it takes on objective properties and consequences, is institutionally organized, signified and represented in the concrete universals that comprise our social, economic and political suprastructures and as Žižek points out is systemically politicized through reinforced ideologies operative within hegemonic, socio-symbolic and cultural unconscious processes. Not only is there a phenomenal appearance to evil, it is ontologically encrypted in the very fabric of worldhood itself.

From the side of phenomenology, the qualitative appearance of intentionality manifests as a certain mode of dispositional violence that takes on a malevolent form: namely, there is a certain malignancy, spitefulness and maliciousness directed toward an object of aggression. Therefore, there must be a certain desire to hurt or cause pain to another person or thing, even if this is a prereflective act. Here the *agent*, the *intent* and the *act* must display its dispositional violence, while the consequence may or may not bring about an evil outcome based upon the success or failure of the intentional act to achieve its goal. For example, the intent to inflict pain, suffering or death on another may be thwarted, but the intentional act itself is nevertheless evil. Here we may say it is predisposed. The corollary is that dispositional violence ontically informs intentionality and action, including the act of thinking itself. This means that people are evil and not merely their behavior. Here we may conclude that the disposition toward evil is structurally constituted, because human nature is predisposed toward violence in thought and deed. This means that the customary, hackneyed definition of evil as deliberate malicious intent falls short because it fails to account for its innate, deep structural psychic precursors. Evil exists without malicious intent; it merely becomes a question of disclosedness or concealment. Hence the ontology of evil may or may not be enacted based on impulse and restraint, therefore relegating the domain of evil to a bifurcation of desire, emotionality and thought on the one hand, and the behavioral instantiation of intentional action on the other. In other words, we are inherently evil (as that which is onto-structurally innate), but not all people engage in evil endeavors. Here a principle of restraint supersedes our base primitive constitutions, if not for the beacon of reason attuned to the reality principle, due to identification and empathy for others, the development of conscience, and the pursuit of the good or virtue as an ethical comportment. But this involves a process of socialization and domestication based on self-renunciation and a taming of the inner shrew, as Freud (1930) famously points out, the sublimation and foil to our primitive propensities.

Thus far we have deconstructed evil as having an ontological (hence a necessary and universal) edifice based upon our primordial psychic constitution that interpellates the individual and society by natural proclivity and desire, as well as through the objective institutionalization of social, semiotic and symbolic practices that condition our being in the world. Therefore, the psychic dimension of evil is *structural* as both: (a) innate disposition due to our organic embodiment fueled by drive and desire and (b) socially superimposed by concrete (hence environmental) materiality via our thrownness into culture. Here structuralization accounts for the universality of our corporeal and cultural embodiment as an objective fact suffused with metaphysical violence. But the *phenomenal* dimension of evil is concerned with lived subjectivity or *psychic qualia*. This may be radically relative or germane to personal experience under hermeneutic variants even if shared by a collective ethos.

We have already determined that a degree of intentionality must be operative (even if prereflexive) in conditioning the phenomenology of evil, but the qualitative forms of such appearances must emerge from dispositional violence that ingress in the intentional act. The subjective state of mind is pertinent, as there is an affective qualitative manifestation of maleficence that is mobilized in evil intentionality through a negative emotional intensity of the will. However, we cannot restrict our definition to conscious intentionality or recapitulate the narrow, pedestrian view that evil is born from malicious intent, or in the words of Heidegger (1978) that "the essence of evil is in the malice of fury, not in the mere baseness of human action" (p. 355). Evil is not merely about intention and action or destruction of the moral law or institution of the signifier, but rather is unconsciously structuralized as primordial, ontological violence in the very masonry of the human psyche itself, hence the humanization of evil; yet one we can't help but moralize.

The Normativity of Evil

If evil is structurally constituted in all human beings, then evil is normative. It exists in all cultures, conditions our social relations with others, and is carried out in a variety of ways by people just like you and me. No one is immune from its signature or affliction. This is part and parcel of our fermenting *pathos* (πάθος). It is the new psychopathology of everyday life. Psychoanalysis has cogently shown, like the Zimbardo and Milgram experiments, that human nature is oriented toward hurting others, including ourselves. All human beings have sadistic wishes and impulses and aggressive tendencies—from jealousy, envy, rivalry, hate, the diabolic, death wishes, punishment fantasies and the need to humiliate and destroy—this is part of our unconscious animal nature morphed by experiencing the world; while personal and social defenses keep us from consciously embracing our unconscious destructive principles vying for pleasure, greediness, decadence, excess and egoistic hedonism. These empirical facts speak toward our unconscious motivations that condition our waking conscious choices. Of course there are different instantiations of evil as qualitative classifications of the wrong offering gradations in concrete appearance, but my point is that evil is ontologically prepared as a primordial violence permeating Being itself. Asteroids collide, cosmic dust flickers and every astronomical event is a physical-energetic negotiation: there is no ontic difference in this basic proposition governing the universe *or* human relations, for each is merely a modification of the metaphysics of experience.

In most discourse on evil, no one talks about unconscious intentionality, the evil within. And it is only by accident, on the occasion and condition of a non-conscious choice through the proverbial slip or faulty achievement (*Fehlleistung*), that evil is allowed expression. The fact that we are dominated by reflective choice via the puissance of consciousness does not eradicate the force and reverberation of unconscious teleology. In psychoanalysis, which has discovered the fact that universally, we not only have the *capacity* to kill, we all have the *wish* to commit murder. In those who have developed sufficient superego defenses of conscience and moral values, this wish is bulwarked against a strong desire for denial, repression, renunciation and undoing—even reaction formation, such as those going into helping professions to reverse or annul this unconscious artifact by making reparation for our lingering guilt. The violentization of human proclivity is historically proven and biologically conditioned, the backbone of civilization, one that is far more civil today than in its *arkhē*. But the way we come to apprehend our "nature" is humanized, as mentioned earlier, by our freedom to choose certain paths of thought and action, even under the strain of a lack of mentalization or affect regulation that colors our penumbra of ethical choices.

In what Adam Morton (2004) refers to as the "barrier theory of evil," he emphasizes that "the essence of evil motivation is the failure to block actions that ought not even to have been considered" (pp. 55–56). Here, he insists, most people filter out harmful actions to others when considering the right course of action; however, this does not displace motivation itself. Furthermore, it does not consider the fact that many actions are motivated and executed by unconscious telic forces that scarcely recognize the foreseeable results or outcomes they may have on others, especially when such prereflective enactments are carried out unconsciously. This framework with which to adjudicate evil also presumes a Kantian bias that moral motivation and behavior are rationally contemplated with self-conscious foresight to consider the penalties of our actions. The notion of instituting barriers and refraining from the wrongful breach of barriers once put into place are important factors in understanding patterns of motivation, yet motivation and action are not always amenable to following a learned strategy or habitual procedure as rational deliberation of choice; rather people simply act and deal with the consequences later. Here we may observe that consciousness is often foreshadowed by overdetermined, psychodynamic events that affect the conscious motivation and action of the agent, even if under disinhibition or self-deceptive currents. This may explain, in part, why the great majority of evil acts are committed by normal or average people rather that criminals and violent sociopaths. The failure to construct barriers affecting our conscious choice of actions is only one such component of evil, regardless of whether it is unconsciously conceived or organized. Therefore, the barrier theory of evil conforms to a deeper structuralization process we may refer to as the "defense theory of evil," which is subject to the free reigns of imagination mediated by unconscious fantasy and compromise formation.

As a semiotic, the word "evil" has become too readily equated with moral outrage, which always stands in relation to a value judgment. And since value judgment is a human phenomenon, the criteria of determining a proper interpretation of a *concept* of evil remains our task. We have already determined that evil may be ensconced in the realm of thought and not merely action and that violence is interred in thought. Thoughts can do violence to those who think and harbor them, who suffer, let's say due to unremitting hate, and they manifest in the most normative of situations, such as through symptoms, somatization, affect dysregulation, sleep dysfunction, memory disturbance, and so forth. Here thought may be a form of self-evil, even if it is self-instituting and involuntary, hence the product of one's own self-victimization, even if such original victimization was due to the encroachment and internalization of the Other.

Evil as Appearance

Rather than focus on the myriad forms of evil that appear throughout humanity, and they are innumerable, let us address evil as appearance as such. It was Hegel (1830) who famously argued that "essence must *appear*" (§ 131), for appearance is the requisite for anything to be made actual. This simple yet sophisticated observation is logically prepared: the coming into being of any phenomenon is ontologically conditioned on its essential a priori fulcrum. Here we may summon the principle of sufficient reason: every mental event must stand in relation to its original form from which it is derived. In other words, there must be an original ground for every mental event that stands in relation to every mental object. For Hegel (1807), "appearance is essence" (§ 147), for nothing can exist unless it is real, hence has being or presence. Here evil appears as essence revealed through its marbled modes of manifestation.

Hegel's doctrine of essence is conditioned on the notion that whatever comes into being is always mediated by its previous appearances. Evil is mediated by prior shapes, the conduit that allows psychic reality to appear as concrete reality. This includes human history, as well as any contextualization of our thrownness, what I have referred to as "archaic primacy" (Mills, 2010). This further means that evil has a prehistory and a metaphysical structure: appearance emerges from a primordial ontic ground. In the *Phenomenology*, Hegel (1807) tells us:

> The inner world, or supersensible beyond, has, however, *come into being*: it *comes from* the world of appearance which has mediated it; in other words, appearance is its essence and, in fact, its filling. The supersensible is the sensuous and the perceived posited as it is *in truth*; but the *truth* of the sensuous and the perceived is to be *appearance*. The supersensible is therefore *appearance qua appearance*. (§ 147)

This "inner world" is none other than a psychic one, an unconscious presencing that has been made objectively real—the instantiation of the evil within. Essence appears and appearance fills *its* essence; more specifically, appearance fills *with* essence. The "truth" is "posited" in itself as a supersensible beyond, but it may never be beyond appearance, for truth is equated with appearance as such. In Hegel's (1830) words, "Essence therefore is not *behind* or *beyond* appearance, but since the essence is what exists, existence is appearance" (§ 131). In other words, by extrapolation, evil is "really actual," or it would not appear. This makes evil an ontological presence within humanity. But the ontology of evil is not a static or hypostasized thing; rather it is a process of emergence that is always transforming, leaving debris in its path. In fact, Hegel warns us that evil is not fixed or simply contained in an absolute unity with the good, but rather it "*wants* to be on its own account" as "semblance of inward negativity" (§ 35, *Zusatz*), one that is exteriorized. The negativity within must manifest; it must materialize in order for evil to be actual. Its reality is to be found in its appearances, but it lies deeply hidden within its interior, an interior that conditions all appearance, evil or otherwise.

Hegel (1830) argues that evil is to be equated with "cognition" itself due to a "schism," split or "universal separation" from the "immediate knowledge" or unity with the good, a cleavage introduced through the act of thinking and self-reflection, a turning away from the simple unity of "innocence in the moral sphere" (§ 24, *Zusatz* 3). Here he evokes the Mosaic myth of the Fall. Man is sinful by nature, and here we need no sophisticated theory to argue that humankind transgresses on itself and within itself, that it surpasses limit and restraint, and by definition, this is the same function ascribed to thinking itself. Thinking violates innocence; it breaches simplicity and breaks up unities through instituting negation, difference and self-reflection as internal relation. As Hegel puts it, "It is thinking that both inflicts the wound and heals it again" (§ 24, *Zusatz* 3). In the Garden lies the tree of life and the tree of knowledge, the cognition of good and evil; and herein stands our "entry into the antithesis," the forbidden, the realm of the *not*. Cognition wants to surpass itself, to explore new territory, to enact its desire, the desire to know, and to transgress its curtailment of knowledge. This is the saga of the human spirit (*Geist*) as mind discontent with its immediacy, the fate of desire enslaved as self-relation wanting to satiate the lack.

What Hegel concludes is nothing other than profound: mankind by nature is evil, not because we are born of original sin, but because we think. It is only on the condition that we are autonomous subjects that make us evil, for this is the price of freedom, one that "wills in his particularity without reference to the universal," that is, without considering others. This is why Hegel concludes that "evil" is individual "subjectivity." In other words, our subjective experiences and actions are the locus of ignobility, which stand in opposition to an objective corollary holding itself up to be a universal ideal, namely, humanity's symbolic godhead.

The Greeks defined truth through a privative expression—ἀ-λήθεια, through the *via negativa*, a negation or reversal of the closed, the unseen. Evil is disclosed through its openings, or more precisely, through its openness into the light of being. Evil as appearance is everywhere, even if hidden, concealed or non-manifest, dwelling below in the cellar of non-appearance, waiting to be born, unveiled, released. Evil's disclosedness or unconcealment reveals a particular truth about the inherent nature of our *pathos*, one that feels compelled to no longer remain hidden. This holding fuels a festering that cannot be contained, as it is destined to make itself known, to show itself, to shine. The shining of evil is the face of man, the image of a fallen ideal, the petty iteration of subjectivity, the human mirror of self-negativity.

The Ethics of Evil

We live in a sick society, one chosen yet unconsciously determined. Here evil is the natural consequence of the cost of freedom. We kill people for this cost, for the privilege, politics and principle of freedom, itself a lamentable and ethically dubious dilemma. Military intelligence has studied and strategized about the best way to kill people, to deracinate, to dismember their spirits, to rob them of soul, to crush entire peoples of their dignity to the degree that warfare and state murder have become both a technological and mechanized industry. A weapon is an instrument designed to kill—from the steel and bronze age to a drone. The atomic bomb was invented for one thing: human extermination.

The technology of evil is witnessed everyday on our television sets, from Wall Street to mass scale corporate corruption, to Internet fraud and cyber bullying, all abetted by advances in computer science. The use of global information exchange, digital communication, social media, robotics, nanotechnology and the engineering of terror has become its own science. From WikiLeaks and Edward Snowden to the Arab Spring and *Charlie Hebdo*, no nation is immune from its own homegrown transgressions. Sometimes the craft or art of *techne* enlists a certain psychological intelligence condoned through state torture, such as inducing learned helplessness through waterboarding and "rectal rehydration" at Guantanamo or rape warfare used in the ethnic cleansing campaigns perpetrated in Bosnia, Croatia, Kosovo and Rwanda.

The ethics of evil is the distortion of an inverse relation, namely, the justification of self-righteousness while perpetrating evil under the guise of moral superiority. When ethical arguments are employed to justify evil acts, we reason in a hegemonic circle of self-interest that betrays a philosophy of right, even if such actions are deemed necessary in order to combat an identifiable threat. Ethical rationale can be exercised by any individual, group or nation state to legitimate its activities and foreign policies affecting other lives regardless of the legitimacy of one's belief system, veracity of events or the flimsiness of moral reasoning employed. Under the rubric of national security and the crusade against terror, people simply "disappeared" into CIA custody, were detained against their wills without criminal charges laid, and systemically subjected to the use of "enhanced interrogation techniques," a euphemism for torture, in the hopes that reliable intelligence could be procured despite the legal and ethical prohibitions against torture instituted since the Geneva Conventions' forbiddance of it even during times of war. Not only is this a good example of moral hypocrisy under the justification of state ethics, as are drone attacks, military commissions and mass electronic surveillance by a superpower that bases its global political platform on democracy, freedom and human rights, it furthermore underscores the universality of national self-interest at the expense of democracy itself.

When nation is against nation, narcissistic national identity forms a firm antithesis against the other that becomes legalized within state foreign policy or totalitarian rule, even if duped or deluded. Under the Bush Administration following 9/11, the United States manufactured a war on terror because it needed to have enemies to pillory as revenge for its castrated ego. Here the Other becomes alien, a xenophobic object prone to hurt us. And after they found Saddam Hussein tucked away down a spider hole, there were no weapons of mass destruction to be found. But he served a utilitarian public purpose: he was the symbolic Bad Man who was put to death under state execution, itself a practice deemed evil despite enjoying a cathartic welcome by the West.

We may readily observe the paranoid position at work on a global scale: otherness is the enemy. This primal fear is even further spread within our own nations and communities, where private lives are under state surveillance, neighbors spy upon neighbors, race riots are on the rise, and home invasions are the norm. Under Big Brother, anyone could disappear. And with global economic unrest due to the fuel crisis, Russia's infringement on the Ukraine to seemingly attempt to recover its lost Soviet Union has generated a new paranoia where citizens can't speak freely due to fear of police arrest or public assassination. Paradoxically, after the country had lost almost half of its value and people couldn't afford a mortgage payment, the nation's approval ratings for Vladimir Putin skyrocketed. Whereas in the United States, the disgruntled public craves a swing of the pendulum toward any politician selling hope for a recovering economy, Russia can't get enough of its leader while blaming the greedy West for its own financial malaise.

When the class genocide in Rwanda occurred, initiated by rival ethnic tensions between the Hutus and Tutsis, where mass mayhem organized by Hutu paramilitary personnel and locals having much to gain from the systematic extermination of the Tutsis, the world remained curiously passive and silent. Even after reports of entire villages and individual family members killing their own kind with machetes and the crudest of utensils were known to be factual, the West looked on as a detached spectator unwilling to do anything until it was too late. Lethargic in its enthusiasm to intervene, after nearly a million dead, world superpowers finally felt motivated to lift a finger to stop the genocide at the U.N.'s beckoning. The Dark Continent, I suggest, held little value to democratic and developed countries who had little to gain and many economic costs to bear for intervening in a country that is (symbolically) associated with poverty, famine, AIDS, overpopulation and disease, hence the alien Other. But when SARS, Swine-Flu (H1N1) and Ebola can conjure up the paranoid position and threaten a global epidemic, the world has become more gracious and attuned to social realities that affect us all. The cold hard facts are that some peoples and countries are valued over others based upon their discernible worth, others on their discernible threat. Even humanitarian aid is never devoid of political self-interest, especially if it means thwarting global anxiety.

Is it evil not to think of other peoples, cultures and continents, to not consider their needs and social challenges? This would not only imply an admonition as failure to acquire self-consciousness and empathic attunement for the other, but incite an intransigent condemnation for not caring to do so in the first place. Yet Levinasian ethics barely occur to the masses engrossed in their everyday lives, let alone being handed down a moral sentence for not thinking about the plight of the disenfranchised abstract sufferer residing somewhere in an arbitrary land. It is too much for the individual psyche to bear; that's why it is turned over to the collective social psyche to contemplate and do something about. Even in the most well-intentioned and conscientious soul who envisions a better humanity and wishes to serve altruistic causes, in the end we do what we can, because that's all we can do. Is it evil that we don't do more, that we cease to try because we value our own needs over others? Or do we merely accept our humanism that we cannot live up to the demands of our own ideals we place on ourselves? Here I am reminded of Hegel's beautiful soul: when we become aware of our imperfections we bear an unhappy consciousness. Here the self is divided: we can posit the Ideal but simply can't actualize it. Here moral lassitude becomes another banality.

Institutionalization

When we think about the institutionalization of evil in recent times, from colonial imperialism, totalitarianism and fascism, we often think of large scale suprastructures that superimpose an oppressive bureaucratic machinery on its citizenry, but we may observe how these unconscious cultural fantasies operate as entrenched ideologies unquestioned by the masses. The caste system in India may be said to foster a form of institutional racism where social class is determined by blood, history, custom and skin color. The upper class or Brahmans hold wealth, power, status and education, while the Untouchables are held in contempt and allocated the most unpleasant and revulsive of all vocations in the most horrid conditions of sanitation, domestic servitude and back-breaking manual labor. Aryan descendants with lighter-skinned pigments are more aesthetically valued while the darker-skinned Indians are viewed as ugly, an attitudinal phenomenon we may also witness in Africa. There is an air of superiority by birth and provenance and an aura of disdain, condemnation and vilification of the underclass, even though the advantaged groups rely on the sweat and subservience of the underclass for their privileged lifestyles. Huge discrepancies between rich and poor determine the social infrastructure, where the elite govern the masses, political and social institutions are rife with corruption and abuse of power, and the citizenry have no tangible access to housing, education or work. The subcontinent is suffocating in pollution, and every major city is a conglomeration of slums. Poverty, death, disease, crime, infestation, filth, lack of sewage, vagrants, panhandlers, homelessness, frantic desperation and abject hopelessness abound; the majority of its billion people are illiterate, disenfranchised and penniless. In fact, India has the highest illiteracy rate in the world (United Nations, 2014), followed by China and Sub-Saharan Africa. Abandoned children, the deformed and handicapped and destitute mothers with emaciated babies in their arms roam the streets begging for food. An endless swarm of hovering hands pounce on tourists and locals alike hoping to get a rupee or American dollar for free.

Fairy tale romances are non-existent, for marriages are arranged by patriarchy based on caste, birth and class as a union of families, not love, where relationships are determined, not freely chosen, lest one betrays the family, established social order and the entrenched cultural tradition that sustains this institutional practice. It is no wonder that Buddhism branched off from Hinduism and Islam was successful in converting much of the underclass, each under the teachings that all men are equal regardless of race, caste or custom.

In other developing countries, such as in the Middle East, where despots, dictators and autocrats rule their totalitarian regimes, women and children are systematically oppressed, often under the edicts of Islam. Here we may observe a widespread institutional practice in most Arab countries that grant men both legislative and property rights over their wives and children, where strict observance of Muslim law is harshly imposed, including denying women access and rights to education, individual autonomy and independent finances in order to keep them enslaved, including controlling their dress, physical mobility and behavioral practices, and granting them virtually no criminal protection or civil liberty rights under the law. Women and children may be beaten or raped by men with practical immunity from prosecution, and transgressions by females may be punishable by death. Public stoning, immolations and honor killings (from Pakistan to Canada), where women turn on other accused women, including mothers and family members who are willing participants, are salient phenomena fueled by culturally engrained misogyny.

In vast parts of China and India, female (sex-selected) infanticide is ubiquitous due to the cultural devaluation of women. Concentrated in northeast Africa, Yemen, Iraqi Kurdistan, the Middle East and portions of Asia, female genital mutilation (circumcision) is legally imposed against their will (usually in childhood), often under horrendous unsanitary conditions that permanently disfigure and endanger the survival of its victims, and condoned under the dominion of male patriarchy. These primitive practices are designed to fortify a man's power and authority by turning women into functional objects of domestication, obedience and sexualization where only a man has the right to pleasure. Furthermore, in many of these countries, as throughout South and East Asia, children are sold into slavery by parents to pay for family debt or for profit, as are human organs offered on the black market to help pay for passage to another land. Human trafficking and the child sex trade industry have become an international pandemic, often abetted by institutional corruption and systemic pathology thriving on high profit margins with no signs of a conscience.

Israeli legislative policy is designed to promote and privilege an exclusive Jewish state. Israel actively recruits immigration from European Jewry, hence lending asylum and giving economic and material benefits (including housing, transportation and tax-shelters) to Jews over non-Jewish Israelis, imposes higher costs of living and excise taxes on domestic Palestinians and other Israeli Arabs who refuse to live and work in the West Bank, although entire generations had previously owned property and run family businesses throughout the country before the declaration of Israel. A democratic state that maintains class privilege and financially rewards one ethnic group over others who live and work in the same country, own property, and are equally part of the same society would be an unfathomable occurrence in North America.

Israel is concerned with occupying rather than compromising over disputed land, and retaliates with military bombardments that deliberately target civilian neighborhoods where innocent lives are lost. And with Palestinian resistance compelled to fight and galvanize subversive insurgencies and initiate clandestine missile fire, keeping hate and resentment alive, Israeli citizens break out the lawn chairs, crack a beer, and watch the military pick off houses in Gaza. Here each side points the finger while calling the other "terrorist." This is a good example of the paranoid-schizoid position at play where radical splitting and projective identification leads to reiterations of violence as proportional exchange, like a ping-pong ball traversing each side of the net until one opponent slams a victory. But this is followed by endless rounds of repetition in fixed perpetuation of retaliatory aggression to the point that systemic acrimony toward the Other justifies state institutional racism and military barrages. It is understandable that Israel suffers from dread due to centuries of European and Russian anti-Semitism while living in the shadow of the Holocaust, but with the messianic clash of religions and fundamentalist supporters of Islamic State (e.g., ISIS/ISIL) recently killing Jews in Paris and Copenhagen, the tinderbox could explode without warning, especially if Iran continues with its nuclear development program, a spark that could ignite a Third World War.

The Evil Within

When my daughter was not quite four years old, my wife gave birth to our second child. Upon bringing our daughter to see her mother and newborn baby sister for the first time in the hospital with roses in hand, we visited them both at bedside, our new baby swathed in a blanket. After receiving a flower to give to her mother, our older daughter took the stem and started poking her baby sister in the belly as if the rose were a knife. To my daughter, this wasn't her baby sister, but rather a *thing*, an intruding object that commanded special attention and displaced her importance in a fraction of a second. There was nothing playful about her action: she wanted to hurt or kill it, for she wanted it to die, or simply vanish. It came to steal away her mother. It had taken her place. We may joke about Oedpalization, sibling rivalry over parents' affections or the feelings of abandonment and hatred for the replacement object, but there was an air of innocence to this event, an evil normalcy, so to speak, conveyed in this automatic behavior.

Everyone is intrinsically evil: it is a structural invariant of the human psyche as normativity. Why is this so? Because everyone is predisposed to aggressivity and violence, to mistreating others, to intentionally inflicting verbal, emotional, relational and/or physical pain, even abuse of various forms and vicious maliciousness no matter how unsavory the thought, or how one vociferously objects to or disavows such characteristics, or how saintly a person may appear. Show me one person who has committed no evil! Who has not demonstrated some form of violence? In Derrida's (1978) words, "A Being without violence would be a Being which would occur outside of the existent: nothing; nonhistory; non-occurrence; nonphenomenality" (p. 147). To uphold the proposition that there are humans without evil would be a ludicrous denial of our humanity.

Psychoanalysis has illuminated this psychological fact to the point that it bears no further justification or empirical demonstration, for all one has to do is observe a child in daycare or turn on the evening news. Our world is a festering cesspool of pathology, but we cannot say the same about the good. Goodness or virtue is not structurally intrinsic like evil; rather it is a developmental achievement acquired through socialization and education, unless one prefers to define goodness as a purely biological-ethological category belonging to our animal bodies, such as nurturing and protecting one's young. But this also requires aggression to meet its aim. Animals kill in order to eat, nurture, protect and defend. Just as this innate inclination belongs to our natural constitutions, so does our dispositional urge toward violence. It is as natural as breathing to have aggressive fantasies and to kill—for food, self-preservation, out of fear, protection of others and so forth, hence falling under the rubric of natural law theory. The naïve notion that we are born good and become bad is as infantile as the most guileless fantasy that we have fallen from God's grace into sin by natural desire, corruption and choice. Not only is this illogical, for it would mean denying our embodied facticity, it also negates all empirical facts that we are libidinal and aggressive creatures by virtue of our evolutionary phylogenetic pressures. Many psychoanalysts today do not take seriously the notion of drive theory or phylogeny, when it is a biological fact that human psychology is conditioned on and derived from our naturalized material embodiment. It is beyond dispute. We are capable of anything, from killing to loving, to giving into instinct and impulse, to ethical sociality, to self-sacrifice for an ideal, to transcending our basic animality for the greater Other.

It seems superfluous to even have to argue for the obvious, but I shall briefly recapitulate why evil is structurally inherent as part of our unconscious ontology. Roughly, the argument goes, because we (the human race) are biologically conditioned toward aggression through dispositional violence, it is a natural predisposition that can be both activated and inhibited. Potentiality (< Lat. *potentia*) is enough to warrant the ontological label of dispositional evil, for if there were neither a potential for evil, its inhibition or its actualization, then we would not be human. The potentiality is inherent within everyone, and a variety of circumstances can kindle or defuse its possible occurrence. These sociological factors do not concern us here, but suffice it to say that drives are stimulated by external factors.

The inner a priori ontological preconditions toward evil, however, do not mean that all human beings will enact their evil tendencies. This is subject to many factors including inhibition, defense, compromise and transformation, as well as their failures, which always stand in relation to social systems, institutionalization and intersubjective relations. The point here is to emphasize that to be human is to always stand in relation to the evil within. In fact, our humanization requires us to confront our evilization. We would not be human without such a confrontation, for this demands that we examine our interior and social environs and analyze what is preferably good from what is characteristically bad. Although this conundrum is a contentious enterprise that is inscrutable and open to many estimations, it is also a social requirement that influences the parameters of institutional law and order. Without such dialogue, we would merely be slaves to self-interest and biological instinct at our own peril.

It is rather elementary to remind the reader of the primacy of the drives (*Triebe*); I do not find it necessary to regurgitate a dissertation of their defense (cf. Mills, 2010). The basis of Freudian theory from its inception allowed for the polymorphous perversity of the drives if not for the simple fact that desire has no bounds. Desire is free-floating and can attach to any object. While desire is unbounded in itself, only a drive can appear bound, whereby its aim is to achieve satisfaction. Although drives may be temporarily sated by infusing or incorporating an object in reality or fantasy (which is completely variable and arbitrary), desire is always an incessant craving that is never satiated. Because the fantasized object of a wish is always transient and never permanent, unconscious fantasy and its potential foci are fodder for the imagination ripe for the enactment of evil. This means that our libidinal investments will always entail aggressive complementarities in the strife and gratification of any wish fraught with controversy, competition, compromise formation, and defensive countermeasures that define psychic process. This structural tension produces antithetical dialectical relations that influence the internality and manifestation of our *pathos*.

Whether derived from instinct or simple learning theory, the pleasure-pain principle that is operative in all psychological motivation driving human action is an ontological given. The human organism is hardwired or preprogrammed to process mental events in concord with basic biological parameters that inform our disposition to think and act. But these parameters are nevertheless subject to modification, realignment, and redistribution of psychic energies that give shape and content to their contextual expressions. Our ontological thrownness presupposes the logic of the interior based on a simple economy of splitting objects of experience into counterparts, each with a positive and negative vector. This dialectical division must be instituted in thought, as Kant, Fichte and Hegel demonstrate at the most fundamental level, and hence a determination of difference through negation is unconsciously interjected into every mental act while mediating any experiential object. What follows is that early fantasy life is dominated by evil impulses, sadistic urges, primitive affects and paranoiac anxieties we project onto objects and re-introject or re-gather back into our internal constitutions. Here we may say that inborn aggression as instinct is a *primary evil*, for it is structurally constituted in nature as dispositional violence and not merely chosen. What is chosen is how it shall be autonomously processed by mind. That which is not equiprimordially given a priori is retroactively mediated by consciousness. Since the disposition-toward-violence is ontologically given phylogenetically, it is no surprise that we see it everywhere.

The human psyche has a peculiar tendency to use and abuse objects of functional immediacy, namely, for disposable means of gratification. This is often hidden and unacknowledged because it takes place behind the back of consciousness. The phylogenetic or tribal evolutionary origin of aggression as dispositional emotional violence is part of our thrownness into the human race. The theoretic speculation of an inherent death drive (*Todestrieb*), although controversial, does not preclude the reality of dispositional violence oriented toward human aggression, but rather accounts for it as a destructive ontological principle channeling negation and conflict within a psychobiological framework. The human psyche is born/e of negativity and radical splitting, which initiates a procreative or generative process that is simultaneously life enhancing yet paradoxically self-destructive. The logic of the interior that suffuses unconscious organization fuels this antithetical impulse as a will toward life and death, hence creating antinomies and impasses in their ability to meet resolve or find a synthetic node of unification. But as Freud (1920) reminds us, before the will toward murder as an externalized aggressive fantasy belying our true primitive natures, there is also a primal impulse of suicidal self-negation that may be equally enacted through volitional eruptions in psychic space. The analyzed mind cannot deny these human predilections, because they materialize every day in the clinic and the social world, which tells us something irrefutably profound about human nature. The human animal fights the evil within on a daily basis as an inherent self-renunciation we are obliged to accept on the one hand, and as the refusal to take ownership of our desire on the other, that which is part of our clashing dialectical symmetries, hence the formal dynamics underlying the structural tensions bolstering our unconscious *pathos*. Here self-repudiation is only possible on the condition that we secure a psychic space for the fulfillment of our pathologies, where we may unconsciously enjoy our evil fantasies mired in the kingdom of *jouissance*, that realm of excess so satisfying yet so repugnant that it *cuts*.

The dispositional wickedness of urge, affect, fantasy, behavioral impulse and thought is scarcely capable of being eradicated, only mitigated. What ultimately matters is control over its enactment. This is the functional introduction of an ethical social introject as a prohibitive law or ideal that facilitates human sublimation over brute instinct often initiated by empathic identification with others based in human attachment. But the fantasy life of world masses carries on in a sordid underworld where satisfaction is achieved through the contemplation of the nefarious as a fantasized internal drama that brings about both horror and relief, but only on the condition that it is consigned to fantasy with our self-reflective awareness of such. Those who are not able to maintain an internal reflective ego or mentalized stance of self-consciousness may beckon the dark call of the shadow, the demonic, or whatever term we may wish to employ to signify the destructive forces of evil. Thinking evil thoughts and wishing evil deeds or events is not the same as doing them. This defensive containment of self-restraint makes all the difference between a civilized human being and a criminal. And this frames our problematic: it is in the locus of decision, of concreteness, where we find evil. Despite the fact that we are all dispositionally evil, it may never come to light.

So here we have a crucial difference in the value parameters we assign to our definition of evil. Although we may be constitutionally predisposed toward evil, it does not always appear. That is, evil dispositions and intentions may be relegated to thought rather than actions, hence inhibited and transformed. What this means is that evil remains hidden in some while disclosed, unconcealed or enacted by others. This makes the qualia and empirical quantification of evil contingent upon evil's modes of manifestation, or how it appears. But our pithy unsavory conclusion is anything but trite: everyone by nature is evil; it's just a matter of degree.

Acknowledgements

I owe many thanks to philosopher Janusz Polanowski for hours of stimulating conversation on this topic.

Notes

1. Initiated in the 19th Century, and now in its 9th revised edition, Liddell and Scott's *Greek-English Lexicon* is generally considered among classicists to be the finest compilation to date of the classical works of antiquity where the etymological sources of ancient words derive and correspond to contemporary linguistics and modes of discourse. See pages 870 and 863 respectively of Volume 1 for καλός and κᾰκός (good and evil).
2. It is for this reason that I have deliberately omitted any discussion or critique of Boehme and Schelling, whose projects were to reconcile evil with human freedom and God.
3. Here Žižek annexes the notions of subjective and objective forms of violence from the Jains, where *ahimsa*, or the principle of non-violence, is central to Jainism as a religious valuation practice.

References

Aquinas, St. Thomas. (ca. 1256–1272). *Summa Theologiae*. (Trans.). The Fathers of the English Dominican Province [1947]. http://www.sacred-texts.com/chr/aquinas/summa/.

Aristotle. Physics. (1984). In J. Barnes (Ed.). *The Complete Works of Aristotle. 2 Vols*. (The revised Oxford trans.). Princeton, NJ: Princeton University Press, 1984, pp. 315–446.

Augustine. (2008). *Confessions*. Henry Chadwick (Trans.). Oxford, UK: Oxford University Press.

Canadian Press Video. (2014, Dec. 16). Stephen Harper calls Pakistan attack heart-breaking.*Globe and Mail*. http://www.theglobeandmail.com/news/news-video/video-stephen-harper-calls-pakistan-attack-heartbreaking/article22106356/. Retrieved December 28, 2014.

Derrida, Jacques. (1978). *Writing and Difference*. Alan Bass (Trans.). London, UK: Routledge & Kegan Paul.

Freud, S. (1920). *Beyond the pleasure principle*. In Freud 1966–95 [1886–1940]. *The Standard Edition of the Complete Psychological Works of Sigmund Freud*, Vol. 18, pp. 1–64.

Freud, S. (1927). *The future of an illusion*. In Freud 1966–95 [1886–1940]. *The Standard Edition of the Complete Psychological Works of Sigmund Freud*, Vol. 21, pp. 1–56.

Freud, S. (1930). *Civilization and its discontents*. In Freud 1966–95 [1886–1940]. *The Standard Edition of the Complete Psychological Works of Sigmund Freud*, Vol. 21, pp. 57–145.

Francis, Bryan. (2013). *Gratuitous Suffering and the Problem of Evil*. London, UK and New York, NY: Routledge.

Hegel, G.W.F. (1807). *Phenomenology of Spirit*. A.V. Miller (Trans.). Oxford, UK: Oxford University Press, 1977.

Hegel, G.W.F. (1830). *The Encyclopaedia Logic*. Vol. 1 of *Encyclopaedia of the Philosophical Sciences*. T.F. Geraets, W.A. Suchting, and H.S. Harris (Trans.). Indianapolis, IN: Hackett Publishing Company, Inc., 1817/1827/1830/1991.

Heidegger, Martin. (1978). *Wegmarken, 2nd Ed*. Frankfurt am Main: Klostermann.

Herodas. (1922). *Mimographus*. Walter Headlam (Ed.). Bristol, UK: Bristol Classical Press.

Homer. (800 BCE). *The Odyssey*. Samuel Butler (Trans.). http://classics.mit.edu/Homer/odyssey.html.

Homer. (800 BCE). *The Iliad*. Samuel Butler (Trans.). http://classics.mit.edu/Homer/iliad.html.

Inayat, Naila, Qazi, Shereena, & Bacon, John. (2014, Dec. 17). Death toll reaches 141 in massacre at Pakistan school. *USA Today*. http://www.usatoday.com/story/news/world/2014/12/16/taliban-storms-military-school/20469711/.Retrieved December 28, 2014.

Kant, Immanuel. (1793/94). *Religion Within the Limits of Reason Alone*. 2nd Ed. T.M. Greene & H.H. Hudson (Trans.). New York, NY: Harper Torchbooks, 1934.

Liddell, H.G. & Scott, R. (1843). *A Greek-English lexicon*. 2 Vols. Oxford, UK: Clarendon Press.

Mills, Jon. (2010). *Origins: On the genesis of psychic reality*. Montreal, Quebec: McGill-Queens University Press.

Mills, Jon. (2016). *God: The Invention of an Idea*. London, UK: Routledge.

Morton, Adam. (2004). *On Evil*. New York, NY: Routledge.

Nadeau, Barbie Latza. (2015). Nigeria is letting Boko Haram get away with murder. January 13, 2015. *The Daily Beast*. http://www.thedailybeast.com/articles/2015/01/13/nigeria-is-letting-boko-haram-get-away-with-murder.html. Retrieved January 13, 2015.

Plato. *Protagoras*. In *The Collected Dialogues of Plato*. E. Hamilton & H. Cairns (Eds.). Princeton, NJ: Princeton University Press, 1961, pp. 308–352.

Plato. *Republic.* In *The Collected Dialogues of Plato.* E. Hamilton & H. Cairns (Eds.). Princeton, NJ: Princeton University Press, 1961, pp. 575–844.
Plato. *Theaetetus.* In *The Collected Dialogues of Plato.* E. Hamilton & H. Cairns (Eds.). Princeton, NJ: Princeton University Press, 1961, pp. 845–891.
Plotinus. (1992). *The Enneads.* Stephen MacKenna (Trans.). Burdett, NY: Larson Publications.
United Nations. (2014). India tops in adult illiteracy: U.N. Report. January 29, 2014. *The Hindu.* http://www.thehindu.com/features/education/issues/india-tops-in-adult-illiteracy-un-report/article5629981.ece. Retrieved February 23, 2015.
Žižek, Slavoj. (2008). *Violence.* New York, NY: Picador.

Chapter 2

The Psychoanalytical Relevance of Jacob Böhme's Concept of Evil

Sean J. McGrath

Introduction

The theology of Jakob Böhme (1575–1624) is not merely an esoteric religious philosophy, a fusion of Protestant pietism, Rhineland mysticism and Renaissance Kabbalah; it also contains one of the most sophisticated doctrines of personality to emerge out of early modernity. As such, Böhmian theology had a decisive influence on the first philosophers to seriously consider the psychology of the unconscious (in particular Schelling and Hegel).[1] Böhme expands the orthodox Trinitarian paradigm of personhood (essential relationality) into a dynamic psychology: For Böhme personality is a being that is only related to others insofar as it has achieved a difficult relation to itself through a moral negotiation of conflicting unconscious drives. One drive directs *eros* within, toward the self; the other drive directs *eros* without, toward the other. But the second drive presupposes the subordination and support of the first. Relatedness to the other is not simply a negation of narcissism; to speak in the language of Freud, love is the *sublimation* of narcissism. When it fails, evil divides the soul against itself and plunges it into ignorance, shame and self-loathing.

Without official training as either a theologian or a philosopher, and inspired by peculiar religious experiences, Böhme blended the limited sources he had available to him (the Luther Bible, the alchemical writings of Paracelsus, the preaching of the German mystics) into a strikingly original vision of God's relation to creation. At the same time he constructed a new paradigm of personality, the functional soul as an *imago Dei*—the product of a resolution of conflicting unconscious drives.[2] The unconscious ground of personality extends as far as demonic evil and provides Böhme with an answer, however heterodox, to the question of the origin of evil. For Böhme, good and evil are mutually exclusive yet connected at the root. Christ's love is born of the same principle as the devil's hate. Böhme calls this common root the wrath (*Zorn*) of God, the narcissism of the father, which is forever balanced by his mercy. The notion of an original unity of divine wrath and mercy originates in the Kabbalah, which posits them as respectively the left and right hand of God.[3] United, divine wrath and divine mercy hold each other in check. Without mercy, wrath becomes the spite of the devil. Evil is ingrown personality, the self-assertive principle sundering itself from the other and willing to be infinite. The result of this break is a loss of interior balance and capacity to grasp reality. The others who ought to be occasions for love became hateful and sources of pain.

In his lectures on the philosophy of history Hegel goes to some lengths to prove the philosophical respectability of Böhme, whom he regards as the spiritual voice of modernity, the representative of "the protestant principle" (Hegel, 1965, vol. 19, p. 300) In Hegel's reading Böhme re-conceives all that which was previously considered to be "beyond" as immanent in human experience: God and the devil, heaven and hell—the whole cosmology and theology of the Middle Ages—is re-inscribed within the human soul. That this interiorization would produce the breakthrough to psychology characteristic of modern thought seems obvious. As Böhme puts it, "external Reason supposes that hell is far from us. But it is near us. Every one carries it in himself" (Böhme, 1623, p. 108). Plainly we are on the cusp of the cultural transformation whereby exorcism will become Mesmerism, that is, proto-psychoanalysis.[4] What was vilified in the former as an invasion of the soul by an external demon is pathologized in the latter as a health problem to which the soul is prone.

It is my hypothesis that Böhme's greatest influence on the contemporary age manifests itself through the dissemination of psychoanalytical notions of the self, which one way or another, and via a labyrinth of transformations, lead back to his speculative theology. And yet Böhme's influence on depth psychology and psychoanalysis has scarcely been explored. The Bömian thread shows that psychoanalysis is only on the surface a secular and agnostic practice; its roots are buried deep in Christian self-experience. Böhme is not the *only* theological root of psychoanalysis: we must also include the early Christian experience of interiority, medieval mysticism, the rite of exorcism, the medieval practices of confession and *Seelsorge*. Nevertheless Böhme is the most important root, for only in Böhme's theogony does psychoanalysis find the metaphysical terms necessary to accurately formulate the psychological structures that show themselves in psychoanalytical practice. Böhme's notion of unconscious drive (*Trieb*) as the root of consciousness, his principle of polarity, and his understanding of the necessity of a sublimation of otherwise self-destructive narcissism, are concretized and enacted in psychoanalytical experience.

Demonstrating a theological origin to psychoanalysis flies in the face of Freudian atheistic-biologism, Lacanian structuralism, and although it lends some credibility to Jung's turn to alchemical and mystical texts as prefigurations of psychoanalysis, it also throws into question the clinical foundations of Jungianism. Böhme's persistence shows us that Christianity, seemingly dead in mainstream Western intellectual culture, is in fact not finished with us: It continues to influence us in the form of floating theologoumenon. By this neologism I mean seemingly rootless secular concepts, such as "authenticity," "individuation" or "the unconscious," operative in Western societies that are fed by concealed theological roots. The hidden theological sources of these concepts, however unacknowledged they maybe, are largely the cause of their affective power and influence.

A solid historical argument is to be made concerning the influence of Böhme on the founders of psychoanalysis. Freud often spoke disdainfully of philosophy, but he read the major German philosophers and had a love of German literature. As early as *The Interpretation of Dreams* he cautioned his followers against drawing hasty connections between his theories and philosophical theories of the self: "What we call [unconscious] does not coincide with the unconscious of the philosophers" (Freud, 1994, p. 464). The disclaimer suggests that, indeed, some kind of relation exists between Freud and the unconscious of the post-Idealists. Among the philosophers whom Freud cites most frequently are Schopenhauer and van Hartmann, both of whom were deeply influenced by Böhme (Weeks, 1993, p. 230; von Hartmann, 1893, vol. 1, pp. 360–61).[5] Freud is also explicitly indebted to the nineteen-century natural scientist, Gustav Fechner, the first to coin "the pleasure principle" (*das Lustprinzip*), the basic unconscious energy of life inclines everything toward a resolution of the tension of desire. Fechner imbibed the spirit of Romantic philosophy of nature, particularly Schelling and Goethe, both of whom were informed by Böhme.[6] Jung references Böhme in many places, reading him alongside other alchemical and mystical writers as a source for psychological insight.[7] Some work has been done exposing Lacan's debt to Böhme, whom Lacan learned of from his friend and colleague, Alexandre Koyré, the author of arguably the most important study of Böhme in the Twentieth Century.[8]

However significant the historical argument, the systematic argument for Böhmian resonances in psychoanalysis is more vital to the point I wish to make. The structure of personality *performatively* defined in psychoanalytical *practice* enacts Böhme's concept of God. In what follows, I can only gesture here to some of the evidence for this claim.

Neither Freud nor Jung can follow Böhme in his explicitly moral assessment of the structure and dynamics of the personality. For Böhme evil is a real possibility for the self and only in the light of that possibility is pathology to be understood. For Freud, the distinction between good and evil tends to give way in the face of the relativity of the super-ego injunction: without a divine law, evil becomes simply that which is publicly forbidden. A pragmatic necessity still maintains the distinction between good and bad: to let the Id express itself unchecked is to imperil human civilization, and since the latter is the condition of the possibility of the survival and flourishing of the individual, a utilitarian imperative underwrites the normal super-ego.

With Jung the relativity of good and evil in the self, which is the union of opposites, is explicit.[9] The denial of the real distinction between good and evil cost Jung his friendship with the theologian Victor White (Lammers, 2007). While the degree to which Jung recommends the indulgence of evil inclinations as a method for integration is greatly exaggerated by Jung's detractors, in principle it becomes difficult to say that anything for Jung is evil, strictly speaking, that is, always to be avoided. Böhme on the other hand sees evil as finally and irreducibly distinct from good, and while the two are connected at the root, there is no doubt in Böhme's mind that at the end of time, God will cast evil back into the nothingness from whence it came.

Böhmian Elements in the Early Freudian Model of the Personality

Freud develops many theories of personality over the course of his long career, from the triad of unconsciousness, consciousness and censor in his earliest work (*The Interpretation of Dreams*, 1900) to the polarity of life-instinct and death-instinct in the mature work (*Beyond the Pleasure Principle,* 1920), to the final system of id, ego and superego (*The Ego and the Id*, 1923). In the following I will concentrate on the early work, noting in passing that at each stage of his development Freud articulates a basic polarity in the psyche, a tension between two opposing forces, one that says Yes (to unconsciousness, desire, pleasure, life), the other that says No, and gives rise, through the negation of the absolutistic claims of the first, to mature conscious life and human civilization.

When Freud turned from a physicalist account of psychic life toward talking-therapy (the transition from the 1895 *Project* to *The Interpretation of Dreams*) he inadvertently returned to the Böhmian narrative of the birth of God from the divine unconscious or *Ungrund*: the soul does not appear ready-made but is achieved over the course of time through a process of suffering, negation and sublimation of primitive desire. Freudian adaptation involves a struggle with two opposing tendencies in the human being, on the one hand, the drive toward self-assertion, the libidinal drive, the primary process, narcissim, or later, the Id (Böhme's first principle), on the other hand the opposite drive toward recognition of otherness and self-abnegation, the reality principle, the secondary process, or later, work and love (Böhme's second principle). It is only by overcoming the original tendency of the soul to resist development and relation to otherness and turn in on itself, feed on itself, pleasure itself, that consciousness emerges from the maternal night of the unconscious.

For Freud as much as for Böhme, where there is no other, there can be no consciousness. *The Interpretation of Dreams* describes a painful birth of consciousness out of a struggle between two opposing forces, one that unconsciously affirms only itself, and a second that negates the narcissism of the first and establishes functional relationships between self and other. Freud describes the dialectic as a tension between a "primary" and a "secondary processes": the primary process, the power of the psyche to satisfy itself by generating an image of its desire (a "cathexis" or *Besetzung*), can only say Yes; if it is allowed to rule unchecked, consciousness is stillborn. The secondary process blocks the cathexes of the primary process, establishing the distance from desire necessary to functional relationships to reality, the reality of the world and the reality of other people (Freud, 1994, pp. 453 ff.). Without the No in the primary process, consciousness would not develop out of the unconscious. In the development of the child, the No is enacted in the break with the mother and the identification with the father, which resolves the Oedipus complex.

Nothing could be further from Freud's intentions than a teleology of psychological life. Teleology implicates us in metaphysics. Teleology attempts to explain the lower in terms of the higher; in Freud's view it runs inexorably into the arms of religion. Freud therefore insists on stopping with an archeology of the psyche: the Freudian unconscious is a residue of the past, not a forerunner of the future: it does not unfold but reacts. The primal memory of the child's oceanic unity with the mother, the paradisiacal time when nascent needs were satisfied before they were felt, is necessarily forgotten or repressed as the child learns to live with the daily frustration of desires and becomes, at the same time, differentiated from the mother. Yet the memory of the lost object, the body of the mother, persists in the unconscious, only to reappear in dreams and neurotic symptoms. The work of psychoanalysis is primarily one of unearthing the frustrated desires of infancy, bringing them to language, naming them, so the massive energy they harbor ceases to obstruct interactions with the objective and inter-subjective worlds and can be put to the service of cultural and social activities. The sex drive exceeds the purposes of reproduction and the confines of civility. Its only sustainable option is repression or sublimation, redirection to non-sexual achievements, such as art and science. Psychoanalysis is damage control on the tragic, ultimately futile passions of the psyche. The memory of the Oedipal bliss is never fully excised from the soul but haunts us in our dreams (Freud, 1994, pp. 269–70).

Paul Ricoeur points out that Freud's desire to avoid teleology is thwarted at every turn by the teleology implicit in his theories and performatively exhibited in his therapeutic practice. "In order to have an *arche* a subject must have a *telos*" (Ricoeur, 1970, p. 459). The teleology manifests itself in the tendency of the Freudian unconscious toward language and inter-subjective relation. The experience of the hysteric healing herself by naming in analysis the traumas at the root of her symptoms shows that the unconscious wants to speak, and not only to itself, but to others; it wants to be revealed. "If Freudianism is an explicit and thematized archeology, it relates of itself, by the dialectical nature of its concepts, to an implicit and unthematized teleology" (Ricoeur, 1970, p. 461). Ricoeur asks why the unconscious content presses upward toward the light of language. What impels it to break with itself? It would seem that the psyche has an agenda; it is not enough to say that it madly and blindly wishes; it rather acts for the sake of an end—the psychoanalytical work itself: the maximum possible broadening of consciousness, self-consciousness that can only be achieved through relation to another. The end of suffering sought through analytical work could perhaps be characterized reductionistically as a sophisticated expression of the pleasure principle. The psyche finds itself at odds with reality because it cannot adjust inner expectations to outer fact; the analyst assists it in this regard, helping it to recognize the impossibility of its desires. But what is the psychological reductionist who denies psychic *telos* to make of the transference, the phenomenon in which the analyst finds he must encourage the analysand's emotional attachment to him for the sake of the cure? It would appear that the psyche not only wants pleasure, it wants another psyche to whom it can relate; it craves not only satisfaction, but above all recognition. "The entire analytic relation can be reinterpreted as a dialectic of consciousness, rising from life to self-consciousness, from the satisfaction of desire to the recognition of the other consciousness. As the decisive episode of the transference teaches us, insight or the process of becoming conscious not only entails another consciousness, the analyst's, but contains a phase of struggle reminiscent of the struggle for recognition" (Ricoeur, 1970, p. 474).

To summarize: Freud's early theory of the unconscious describes a dialectical struggle between an autistic, unconscious self-assertion of the psyche and an increasingly conscious negation of the self-assertion, with the implicit end of: (1) functionally relating the soul to others and (2) growing in self-consciousness. The energy of primal desire is not merely negated but rather redirected (sublimated) to cultural and social pursuits. We begin to discern, however faintly, and no doub, with need of more precise elaboration in the texts of Freud, the three features of Böhmian personality: personality emerges out of a dark and unconscious state of desire (*der Ungrund*); it is an achievement of balance of polar, opposed drives; it is ultimately a work of redirecting primitive self-will toward self-abnegation and relation. When the *telos* is refused and self put in the place of the other, evil ensues. In effect evil wishes to return to the non-being from whence all things have arisen.

Böhmian Elements in Jung

Freud erased as best he could the lines connecting his theories of personality to the history of early psychology and its admixture of occult philosophy. His prodigal son, Carl Gustav Jung, an amateur occultist since his doctoral dissertation on table-turning, re-opened this history, immersing himself in mesmerism, Romanticism, and the history of the occult, mythology and religion. These opposed attitudes to the pre-history of psychoanalysis largely account for the conflict between Freud and Jung. For Freud the psyche is if not material, still a product of material evolution; it is driven from behind by natural and biologically explicable conditions (appetite, desire), and its behavior can be in principle reduced to regular laws of nature. For Jung, the psyche is drawn toward the future; it not only cannot be reduced to material laws or mastered by empirical science; it opens out into a world that proves the limits of empirical science and the merely phenomenal nature of matter, a world that has been testified to by mystics, poets, philosophers, and theologians.

In the book that marked his break with Freud, *Symbols of Transformation*, Jung introduces his master concept of transformation of psychological energy, which includes but is not confined to the sex drive (Jung, 1977a). Jung's notion that libido is subject to transformations is not far from Freud's notion of sublimation (Jung, 1969, para. 60–69). However, Freud could not accept Jung's characterization of libido as an energy teleologically directed toward wholeness (an ideal harmony of inner and outer reality), nor could he see the point of an interiorization and regression that was at the service of health. He intuited early on in Jung's career that Jung's identification of libido with psychic energy displaced sexuality as merely a symptom rather than a cause of libidinal movement. By doing so, Jung overturned the biological and evolutionary determinism informing Freudian analysis.

Like the medieval alchemists, for whom the task of the scientist was to bring about the transformation of base into sublime substances (*transmutio*), Jung sees the goal of psychotherapy as one of unearthing the primitive, the archaic, the base, the inferior, for the sake of transforming it into something higher. The transformation is not an act of violence, not a coercion of raw materials into forms that are foreign to it, but an assistance and acceleration of processes that occur naturally. The *telos* of all psychological events, from dreams to psychotic hallucination, from "the mid-life crisis" to the nervous breakdown, is the expansion of the center of psychic life from the narrow confines of the conscious ego to the circumference of "the self," which embraces not only the conscious and unconscious aspects of the personal ego, but also the conscious and unconscious aspects of the collective psyche. The self for Jung is protean, mercurial or alchemical: subject to constant and progressive transformations, recurring oscillation between opposites, as it strives to take up more and more of the "alien" and "other" into its conscious life (Jung, 1966).

Jung realized that if he was to make any contribution in this regard he would need to limit the scope of his research into "the collective unconscious": the field threatened to expand to the compass of the whole of human history. He chose to research the Western psyche, on the assumption that its unique history accounted for its structural differences from, for example, the Eastern psyche. This led Jung to the last great expression of mythological material in Western civilization, the medieval and Renaissance alchemical tradition, which beside the Bible and the German mystics, is the central source for Böhme's theology. Alongside pioneer interpretations of ancient Gnosticism (especially Basilides) and Renaissance alchemical texts (above all Gerhard Dorn), Jung studied Swedenborg, Paracelsus, Böhme and Saint Martin, whom he saw as forerunners to the psychology of the unconscious.[10]

Jung's development of Freudian psychoanalysis into the Jungian art of individuation seems to be a total departure from psychoanalysis and a return to a romantic philosophy of the psyche. Nonetheless, the commonalities between the two systems of analysis emerge into visibility the more the unconscious is understood, not as a name for a concrete or ontic reality, a repository in the soul that is structured either sexually or mythically, but rather as a formal term: the unconscious describes a certain relationship of the whole of the psyche to consciousness. The Jungian unconscious is not an object; it belongs to subjectivity and is of the same being as the subject. Yet it is other: on the personal level, a stereoisomer of the conscious personality, constituted by counter-emphasis and compensation. For both Freud and Jung, the unconscious is dialogically related to consciousness: what consciousness represses, the unconscious expresses; what consciousness forgets, the unconscious remembers; what consciousness does not want to know or cannot see because of some hardened "ego-ideal," the unconscious dramatizes in dream, fantasy and myth. It was for Jung to see that the two, consciousness and unconsciousness, play off each other like light and shadow, Yes and No; they are a dialogical pair. Unconsciousness begins where consciousness ends. It is the self as other to itself, the un-appropriated (and perhaps at bottom un-appropriable) difference that divides the ego from the wider self of which it is only a part.

Jung's insistence on a prospective function to the unconscious breaks with Freud's Darwinian assumptions of psychological evolution, displacing the Freudian stress on childhood (the Oedipus complex) with an un-Darwinian emphasis on the importance of the future for psychological development. The psyche is not merely a product of past traumas, repressions and frustrated desires; it is teleologically oriented to balance, wholeness and health. It follows that dreams are not merely repetitions of denied desires, "wish-fulfillments"; they are also prescriptions of possible ways for psychological expansion and development. The psyche balances itself by unconscious compensations for conscious attitudes with a view to a certain ideal of psychological health, much as the body regulates itself with a view to an ideal state of internal equilibrium. The individual stands to the whole of psychic life, the *prima materia* of the personality, as a task of self-differentiation or individuation. The unconscious in Jung has a strange intelligence, a self-regulating center, that balances psychic disequilibrium with a view to future integration. "Everything psychic is future directed (*zukunftsträchtig*)" (Jung, 1977b, p. 57).

The psyche's ideal of wholeness may not in fact be possible for the ordinary man or woman. The fact that the archetype of the self is represented in God-images, (i.e., in the Christ figure in the West or the Buddha in the East), shows that it is a transcendent ideal, a goal that may not be achievable in this life and is at best approximated. The ideal remains no less determinative of all normal and abnormal psychological developments. The psyche cannot tolerate one-sidedness but endeavors to include within itself as much polarity as it can manage. It seeks a union of opposites, the *coincidentia oppositorum*: the masculine balanced by the feminine, consciousness balanced by unconsciousness, light balanced by dark, reason balanced by emotion, etc. Jung calls this ideal of wholeness through the balance of polarities the *syzygy* or archetype of the self. He finds indications of it in alchemical literature under the trope "the chemical wedding," the marriage of the white queen with the red king, or the union of sun and moon.

In Paracelsian alchemy, which was one of Böhme's primary sources, the self is represented by the figure of Mercurius, the quasi-divine spirit in nature who combines in himself the opposites, the two alchemical principles of sulfur and salt, found in every material and immaterial being. Sulfur is flammable, aggressive and corrosive, an active or masculine principle, without which a substance lacks the energy to actualize its potentialities. Salt is sustaining and receptive, a passive or female principle, the "matter" of the substance, that which receives the informing energies of sulfur, tempers them and gives consistency to being. Mercurius mediates the two poles, making of them a unity. Böhme describes Mercurius as "fiendish and poisonous," but paradoxically also "the primal cause of life and stirring." "This form [Mercurius] is agitation (*Unruhe*) but also the seeker of peace (*Ruhe*); with his search he creates agitation" (Böhme, 1997, pp. 524–25). Mercurius is not only the one who unifies opposites; he also generates the opposites, dividing and creating the conditions that make new unifications necessary. Psychological upheavals—personal crises, neuroses, even breakdowns—are in Jung's view often necessary to psychological development. Without the "stirring" Böhme speaks of, there would be no opposition, no struggle, and being would never be revealed to itself. As Böhme puts it, "If this [agitation and opposition] were not, there would be no nature, but rather an eternal stillness ... so would an eternal peace reign in the divine nature, but this nature would not be revealed, only in struggle is it revealed" (Böhme, 1997, pp. 519–20). Jung's positive appraisal of the psychological necessity of opposition, struggle even submission to what the ego regards as "evil" is an explicit repetition of Böhme's theogony.

Böhme's Theogony in Outline

In defense of his attribution of duality to God, Böhme references passages in the Hebrew Bible where the wrath and anger of God are revealed. Jehovah is a "jealous God" (Exod. 20: 5), a "consuming fire" (Deut. 4: 24). For Böhme these are not merely metaphors: God has the passion of egoistic anger within him, even if it is always mastered and subordinated to love. The same Biblical revelation testifies to God as merciful and loving (Deut. 4: 31). How is this apparent contradiction to be resolved, Böhme asks? It is not as though God is evil or wills evil. The duality in God has a single root: the *Ungrund*.

The *Ungrund* is the abyss of divine potency and freedom that precedes all actual existence and from which God as a self-conscious personality, aware of himself and capable of love, emerges. The *Ungrund* stands originally in need of being, desiring the fullness of manifestation, which it can only have insofar as it has another to whom it can show itself. The *Ungrund* must negate itself, allow for another, if it is to come to know itself. The primal Yes or will that constitutes the *Ungrund* spontaneously generates a No in the interest of achieving the fullness of selfhood. The affirmation of self that is the beginning of personality is only complete in a negation of self, a diremption and limitation of self that allows for another self to emerge and through the generated second self, the possibility of relatedness. For Böhme, God's coming to be is the genesis of difference out of identity for the sake of making self-knowledge possible. The notion of spirit as self-mediation through otherness, so central to German Idealism, begins here.[11]

The *Ungrund* is not God but an abyss of potency within God. It stirs with a longing to be revealed to itself. It does not think or reflect—this is not possible without self-revelation: it rather moves unconsciously toward self-differentiation. Within it a will arises, an impulse to let something be so that the will can "find, feel, and behold itself" (Böhme, 1997, p. 521). The *Ungrund* is possessed by what Böhme calls *Trieb* (appetite / *libido*); it churns with a desire for a relation to itself; it seeks itself. What it finds is nothing other than its own seeking for a self, "the hunger, which is itself" (Böhme, 1997, p. 521).

Without this duality, an eternal peace would reign in the Godhead, but it would be the peace of lifelessness, and the eternal nature would not be revealed. Difference irrupts in the night of undifferentiated pre-existence: a will moves toward the light of knowledge and revelation, while a counter will resists and holds back; out of the tension between the two personality emerges. The night of divine pre-existence bifurcates into a Yes and a No and then trifurcates into a three-fold play of counter-balancing drives: a dark principle of contraction, a light principle of expansion, which opposes it and sublates it, and a precarious stasis, which effects a fusion of the two. The first principle is a centripetal force, sometimes described by Böhme as an "astringent" (*herbe*) "hardness" (*Härtigkeit*). It holds itself within itself and contracts into a hidden center. The first principle is opposed by the second, a centrifugal force described as a "bitter" (*bittere*) "attraction" (*Ziehen*), which expands outward. The strife between the two gives rise to a third, a circumambulatory movement, a balance of contraction and expansion suspended between two opposing drives. Böhme describes it as "anguish" (*Angst*) (Böhme, 1997, pp. 521–22).

The first principle is the inward self-assertion of the *Ungrund*, the principle of narcissism. Without the opposing influence of the second, the expanding principle of altruism, which negates and sublates it and directs it out of itself, the first principle would be darkness, obscurity and obduracy. The second principle is originally negative; it does not have a substantial and independent being but exists only as a relation to the first. It is the outwardly directed kenotic movement of self-donation, which negates the egoism of the first principle and makes possible a different way of being: being as self-given. The third principle mirrors the dynamic balance achieved through the conflict of the first two principles: it reflects creative and life-giving tension, the unity in difference or the coincidence of opposing drives without which nothing can live.

The first psychological point to be made here is that according to Böhme, narcissism is more original than altruism. The primal Yes to self is the root of the personality. Altruism is originally negative, a No to the totalitarian tendencies of the first principle. Altruism allows for difference, pours itself out, by resisting the centripetal and ego-centric tendencies of the first principle. There is no love without narcissism, no self-donation without a seed of self-assertion. Love is not narcissism—self-assertion without self-donation is the essence of evil. But without the dark ground of narcissism, sublated and transformed, there would be no self to be given away. The three principles constitute the architectonic structure of the Holy Trinity: the Father, the point of gravity, which grounds everything in itself; the Son, the kenotic diffusion of being outward; the Spirit, the attractive / repulsive stability of relatedness between Father and Son. The Father is fully revealed in the Son; the Holy Spirit continues the revelation that has already occurred between the Father and the Son.

The three principles further exfoliate into the seven forms of eternal nature (*die Sieben Gestalten der Natur*), also referred to as the seven divine spirits (Böhme's version of the Sephirot of Kabbalah): harshness (*Herbe*), bitterness (*Bittere*), angst (*Angst*), fire (*Blitz*), light (*Licht*), sound (*Ton*) and figure (*Corpus*). The seven forms are divisible into two sets of three, with one mediating between them. The first three—harshness, bitterness, angst—represent the wrath of God; the last three—light, sound, figure—represent his mercy, the right hand of God. Fire, the alchemical agent of transmutation, unites the two sides of God. Böhme thus fuses the triadic structure of Christianity with the dark-light dualism typical of Gnosticism (Koslowski, 2001, pp. 214–16). The seven forms constitute God's original other: They are psycho-genetic structures by means of which the Triune God eternally (and with no need of material being) mediates itself to itself. In Böhme's metaphor they are a sphere of seven wheels, eternally revolving around a single center in the heart of God.

The metaphor of the seven interconnected wheels allows Böhme to unite the opposites of eternal movement and eternal rest, eternal difference and eternal identity, endless rotation circumambulating a still point. Böhme's thinking is essentially dialectical: Everything is to be understood in relation to everything else. No form exists in isolation; all exist for the sake of the others. The seven forms cannot be separated from the divine nature; they *are* the divine nature. However, God is not reducible to the seven forms; rather the seven radiate out of a single center. In the still point at the center, God is neither this nor that, neither *Herbe* nor *Bittere*, neither *Licht* nor *Ton*. The seven wheeling spirits are each separate from one another but identical at their root. The movement of each depends upon the movement of the others; all seven movements preserve the stillness of the center (Böhme, 1997, pp. 231–32).

Lacking the knowledge of Latin requisite for a study of Scholastic metaphysics, Böhme appears to have developed his notion of personality through artless introspection and projected this psychological experience onto God. One might want to say that this is his ultimate theological error: to attribute to the mind of God what is only properly true of the human mind. On the other hand, we must ask ourselves what would personality be if it did not include a process of unifying diversity, overcoming difference and returning to itself through the other? Ultimately, Böhme's concern is to remain true to the Biblical revelation and describe God as a person, not a metaphysical principle. If Böhme posits movement in God, it is not to deny the fullness of being of Him but to affirm it of Him. For Böhme, as for Hegel and the late Schelling, higher than the undifferentiated unity of *simplicitas* is a unity that unifies duality. The fullness of being, in Böhme's view, is personality, and without difference, relation and process, it cannot be.

The Question of Evil

Böhme's concept of evil is built of two insights that are constitutive of his original vision and central to all his theology. The first insight concerns the mixed nature of the created order. We cannot with Augustine simply say, being is good, evil is a mere privation of being, a *privatio bonis*. Everything in this world, Böhme says, is a mixture of good and evil. For Böhme it is not enough to follow the scholastics and distinguish moral evil from natural evil, attribute the former to the abuse of freedom and dissolve the latter into the privations necessary so that every grade of being might be filled. The world strikes Böhme as both a wonder through which the glory of God shines in the most insignificant things and a harsh and cruel place, a world of pain and unjustified suffering, which no moral God could directly will. Böhme is troubled by the discrepancy between the evil that men do, pride, wrath, greed, etc., and the evil that they suffer, sickness, natural disasters, old age and death. We find ourselves not only in a morally fallen order of existence, but also in an ontologically disordered creation. The fall of Lucifer, which preceded creation, infected everything subsequent to it. As Schelling argued, in a metaphysical defense of Böhme's position, evil has its own diabolic perfection; it is not an expression of inferiority, a mere symptom of a low grade of being. On the contrary, only the highest of beings is capable of evil (Schelling, 2002, pp. 245–46). Evil is the moral law inverted and is as such a free act of spirit, not a mere privation of goodness.

Böhme's second insight is to find in moral evil an energy or spirit that is in itself divine. This is going further than saying that the being of the devil, insofar as it is created by God, is good. Böhme says, with the Kabbalists, that God has within him a terrible power, a darkness and a wrath, that stands eternally tempered and transformed by mercy. If it were not, if it somehow broke loose, horror and destruction would follow. This dark power in God is essential to being. In the language of medieval philosophy, it is the *principium individuationis*. In the angelic and human sphere, the dark side of God is potentially cut off from the tempering qualities; through an anarchic act of senseless rebellion, it becomes willed for its own sake. God has within him a "tart, terrible sharpness," the first of the seven forms, harshness (*Herbe*). Considered alone, it is a horrible and cold negation of life, like winter without the promise of spring (Böhme, 1997, pp. 227–28). This "quality" is in fact never separated from the other qualities; it is one radii in the wheel of divine nature. But considered in itself it is terrible: self-consuming narcissism.

Because divine wrath is balanced by mercy there is no evil in God. But in his creation, which is in its angelic and human tier free, a one-sided upsurge of wrath over love is possible. In the first creation, the creation of the angels that preceded the creation of the earth, the angels were given a choice, to join the harmony of heaven and mirror the divine personality by participating in "the play of love" (*Liebe-Spiel*)—or not. The choice was in fact between order and chaos, life and death, for there is no other way to be a person than to mirror the personhood of God. The fallen angels' refusal to submit to the divine order was ultimately a decision to self-destruct. By tearing the wrathful qualities out of alignment with the merciful qualities, they created a self-imploding anti-nature and became sub-personal. The three forms in the demonic realm do not issue into the second triad, which tempers and transforms them: rather the fire of transformation becomes a destroying blaze; everything conflicts with everything else and "a perpetual Enmity" (*stette feindschafft*) irrupts within creation (Böhme, 1997, pp. 228–29).

In Böhme's reconstruction of the myth of Satan, he describes Lucifer as one raised above all angels, ennobled with the most beautiful and powerful body in all the heavens. He was "the morning star," singled out by the Father to be his perfect image, the pinnacle of his self-revelation. Lucifer was the first Son of God. Seeing how beautiful he was, Lucifer became entranced with himself (Böhme, 1997, p. 223). He fell in love with himself and desired nothing but that he alone should be all in all, that there should be nothing above him. He willed only himself, and the principle of darkness, the perpetually sublated narcissism of the Father, possessed him, upsetting the balance of his own nature and disrupting heaven. The dialectic of the three principles was truncated and became demonic; the principles clashed with each other in such a way as to produce not a harmony but a terrible discord, the sound of a being at war with itself. The result was not an aggrandizement but a shrinking:

Lucifer became less than what he was. He lost his divine stature and became a shadow of his former self. His very nature was changed, distorted, rendered sick, uncoordinated, insane, hating God and hating himself, lashing out in rage at all that is good and true. This act of the finite destroying itself by willfully asserting itself against the infinite is Böhme's figure for evil. It is not merely the assertion of contraction over expansion; it is rather the two principles eternally at war with each other, never coming into harmony, a self-imploding narcissism refusing the otherness without which they cannot be free.

Böhme's Lucifer is the first psychotic. When the order of the principles is inverted in him, he loses his sense of reality. The good appears to him as bad, the bad as good. Rendered unconscious of others, he is incapable of empathy. He lashes out against himself, like one trying to break free from a cage. The dark fire that when tempered makes possible love and life becomes in him a source of pain and torment. He understands everything incorrectly. In his distorted view, it is God who has wronged him; he is innocent. Seething with resentment, he becomes a shadow of what he was and therefore assumes a new name. Satan in Böhme is a failed personality, a soul that has lost touch with reality. That he brings the doom upon himself does not alter the fact that this is the appearance of the first psychosis. Hereafter creatures will involuntarily suffer the pathology of soul that Lucifer brings upon himself.

One sees from a close reading of Böhme's description of Lucifer's devolution from archangel to devil Böhme's sensitivity for what we have come to call the psycho-dynamics of the soul. At the foundation of the devil's personality is a disavowal. The devil refuses to recognize God and denies what on one level he knows intimately: the divinity of God. He rejects a God above him because he has inflated himself into God. This puts him at odds with reality, a reality that he can no longer understand but that threatens him and fills him with shame. In truth, God is the condition of the possibility of Lucifer's being. Even in rebellion, Lucifer dwells in God, but the indwelling now takes the form of denial.

> And so we understand also why the wicked soul as well as the devil sees not and knows not God, namely because their will will not unite itself to God, it will itself be lord. It remains accordingly without God, only in itself, and God remains also in himself, and so one dwells in the other, and knows nothing of the other, for one turns its back to the other, and sees not the face of the other … the devils know nothing of the world of light, save only this, that they were once in it. … It terrifies them; also they are ashamed about it.
>
> (Böhme, 1620, 67)

The result of Lucifer's rebellion is ignorance, where previously there was knowledge, obduracy, where before there was love, terror and shame, where previously peace and self-acceptance reigned. The devil's soul is split among parts or potencies that in a normal soul function together for the sake of health. "The fallen morning star willed to bring forth the light from out of himself, he did not wait on any positive command, as did Saul, he did not want to recieve the light from God. Therefore he disturbed the co-orindation of one potency over another, and the darkness broke forth in him, tainting and diminishing him" (Oetinger, 1920, 63)[12].

The inner plurality that is constitutive of personality gives rise to internal war in the devil, a constant torment and psychological dualism that does not resolve itself, as it should, into a higher unity. Because the devil refuses to recognize God, the principle of unity, he is doomed to interior fragmentation. The three principles that ought to be ordered and co-inhere into a higher unity fall asunder into discord. They hate one another but are fastened to each other and so cannot flee each other, cannot escape that which torments and antagonizes them.

> In the darkness there is in the essence only a perpetual stinging and breaking, each form being enemy to the other—a contrarious essence. Each form is a liar to itself, and one says to the other, that it is evil and adverse to it, that it is a cause of its restleness and fierceness. Each thinks in itself: If only the other form were not, thou wouldst have rest; and yet each of them is evil and false.
>
> (Böhme, 1620, p. 99)

The form of reason that takes shape in the demonic personality is the lying consciousness. It is not only that the devil lies to those whom he enslaves; he lies to himself. He makes the one he has rejected into his tormentor; he holds the one whom he knows to be guilty (himself) to be innocent. "Hence it is, that all that is born of the dark property of wrath is lying, and is always lying against the other forms, saying they are evil; and yet it is itself a cause thereof, it makes them evil by its poisonous infection" (Böhme, 1620, p. 99). Disavowal, projection and unreality are the devil's lot. And yet the devil is no weakling. On the contrary, only because of his perfection, only because of his power in the hierarchy of being is he capable of rebellion. Evil for Böhme is not privation, weakness and inferiority, but power, strength and supremacy. Nevertheless, the power of evil becomes comical when it tries to act as a substitute for God. In the light of God, the devil posturing as divine appears foolish, a juggler, a pauper who thinks himself a king.

> There is no faintheartedness in him, but a constant will to kindle the poison-source more, that his fierceness may become greater. For this fierceness is his strength, wherein he draws his will to mount above the thrones and inflame them. He would be a mighty lord in the poison-source, for it is the strong and great life. But the light is his misery and dread; that checks his bravery. He is terrified at the light; for it is his true poison, which torments him. Because he abandoned it, it now resists him. Of which he is ashamed, that he is thus a deformed angel in

> a strange image. He would be content with the source of wrath, if only the light were not so near him. Shame is therefore so great in him that he grows furious and kindles his poisonous source more and more, so that his figure becomes increasingly horrible, and the divine image is not recognized in him. He aims only at how he may storm and rage against God, as if he were a foreign thing, or a foreign power, as if he had a foreign kingdom; whereas he is poor, and the dark kingdom is not his, but he is only a prisoner in it. It is God's abyss; he is only a creature therein. He would be lord therein, and yet he is but a juggler with the fierceness; although he must according to the property.
>
> (Böhme, 1620, pp. 102–103)

What comes to actuality in evil are principles that when ordered to the good prove essential to it. Hence the possibility of a devil cannot be ruled out of a universe that is ordered, that is, a universe that is a unity in multiplicity. "But the dark cannot be abolished, for without it no light" (Böhme, 1620, p. 100). Evil is an exteriorization of the dark principles that make light possible. When ordered to the light these principles are not in themselves evil but give matter its subsistence and solidity and add the tension in the organism without which it would not grow and so not live. "If the dark kingdom were to be kindled with the light, the light would have no root to its nature and property, no fire could be generated, neither were there any light, nor any power, but all were a nothing. Hence the Kingdom of wrath must be, for it is a cause of the fire-world and the light-world, and all is God's" (Böhme, 1620, p. 100).

In contrast to the Augustinian tradition, Böhme insists on the ontological nature of evil. Without making God responsible for evil, Böhme posits a substantial material structure to evil. The inversion of the three divine principles in the free-falling creature gives rise to an alternative nature, a being that on some level should not be. For Böhme this catastrophe is the source of not only sin but pestilence, sickness, natural abominations and disasters, and we would add, mental illness. Evil is more than a moral negation of God; it is also an ontological negation of harmony. Böhme explains this by recounting how Lucifer's rebellion and Adam's fall change the structure of nature itself (Koslowski, 2001, p. 209). God's first creation, the angelic order, which was free of ontological evil, was destroyed through Lucifer and the rebel angels; God's second creation, the earth, was disfigured from the beginning through the interference of Satan in the process of creation. Adam was intended to take Lucifer's place, to become the new morning star, the image of the Father. He succumbed to the temptation of the serpent, and the tragedy of the first fall repeated itself. Christ redeems both orders: first, he does what Lucifer ought to have done and becomes the true Son of God; second, he redeems material creation and restores humanity's lost image of God.

More original than *logos*, self-consciousness and reason, the *Ungrund* becomes in creation the source of the difference, darkness and conflict in being. The harshness of the father, the first of the seven forms, is the principle of individuality in things. Without it a thing could not hold itself together and be differentiated from other things (Böhme, 1997, p. 228). Not all egoism is evil: If things did not assert themselves over and against God and against all other created things they could not be. God invests his creatures with a will to selfhood, a contracting principle that protects the being from its environment and encloses it around a center, a pulsing middle point that animates the whole organism with an overpowering hunger to live, to preserve itself, to be what it is and nothing else. The difficulty arises from the apparently inevitable conflict of individual essences with one another (not only individual beings with other individuals but also principles within a single being). Sickness, pain and death have their roots in a conflict of wills, a collision of self-asserting forces. Health is a precarious, ultimately unsustainable detent between the warring elements, a momentary realization of the balance between contraction and expansion, which is eternally achieved in the heart of God. At the center of everything is strife and struggle. If there were no such oppositions nature could not be, for only in movement is there life, and only in opposition is there movement. Nature is only made manifest in war (Böhme, 1997, pp. 519–20).

Böhme's largely neglected works are proof that the concept of the unconscious, typically traced back to Charcot, Breuer and the early Freud and, if earlier sources are needed, van Hartmann and Schopenhauer, is in fact theological. For Böhme, there can be no divinization without passion and will; the first principle—harshness / narcissism—is integral to the realization of the good. Sanctity cannot be achieved by a simple negation of self will; it requires, rather, its transmutation. Böhme's greatest psychological insight is this identification of the seed in love that otherwise sown becomes evil, or better, the seed of evil, which, with cultivation, blossoms into love. Against the emasculated Christianity that preaches love without self, sanctity without self-assertion, Böhme argues that the loving personality has at its heart a flame of narcissism—overcome, self-donated, but undeniably alive.

Acknowledgment

This chapter is a revision and augmentation of matters I treated in *The Dark Ground of Spirit* (McGrath, 2012, 44–81).

Notes

1. On Böhme's influence on Schelling, see McGrath (2012), Brown (1977) and Mayer (1999). On Böhme's influence on Hegel, see O'Reagan (1994), Magee (2001) and Mills (2002). Ludwig Feuerbach noted that the power of Böhme's thinking lies in the depth of its psychological insight. "Jakob Böhme is the deepest, most unconscious and most unlearned psychologist. What he says about the essence of desire, about the anguish of passion, about the longing for freedom and self-identity, the emotion of the emotionless, is as deep as it is true, as poetic

as it is stirring—stirring because he feels what he thinks and says. His metaphysics is nothing other than esoteric psychology" (Feuerbach, 1981, 226).

2. Koyré sums up the Böhmian theory of personality as follows: "For [Böhme] to be means to realize one's potentialities actively, dynamically, and realization means manifestation, uncovering one's essential nature and deploying all inherent possibilities. The perfect being is the one in whom this self-realization is most complete. Essential nature becomes conscious of itself within us in order to be revealed. Being as personal is thus the highest form of being because it achieves self-realization and self-revelation. Only by defining itself and manifesting itself is self-realization and self-revelation fully achieved" (Koyré, 1929, 36).
3. On the Kabbalah, see Scholem (1974) and Drobb (2000). According to the Renaissance Kabbalist Isaac of Luria, whom Böhme may or may not have been aware of, the infinite, *Ein-Sof*, contracts its being in order to create the nothing in which the finite can emerge. The contraction is initially a negation, a withdrawal into self, a self-limitation and self-concealment. The negation is also an implicit affirmation, for it happens for the sake of letting another be, or better, letting otherness itself be. Before the contraction or the *Zimzum*, the divine is a one without another. After the contraction two opposed sets of divine principles (the *Sephirot*) come into being. In Böhme, the opposites that succeed the *Ungrund* are the principle of selfhood or ipseity, the wrath of God—a self-assertive or narcissistic drive, on the one hand—and the principle of love or alteritity, the mercy of God, a self-negating or altruistic drive, on the other. The two principles depend upon one another as the positive and negative poles of a magnet and between them a field of possibilities opens up. Among these possibilities is evil, the assertion of self in place of other, or wrath untempered by mercy and love, the assertion of the other in place of the self. While Böhme left no notes on his sources, the parallel between Böhme's notion of the original negation of the *Ungrund* and the Lurianic understanding of *Zimzum* seems to be too close to be accidental. The degree of the Lurianic influence on Böhme is, however, in dispute. On Böhme and the Kabbalah see Schulze (1955), Häussermann (1966–1972), and van Ingen (1997). Schmidt-Biggemann (2013) denies a direct influence of Luria on Böhme.
4. Ellenberger (1970) is still the standard work on the evolution of dynamic psychiatry from exorcism.
5. On the influence of Schopenhauer and von Hartmann on Freud see Young (2014).
6. On Fechner, see Heidelberger (2004). On Freud's romantic and mystical roots see Schott (1983) and (1985). Schott has also written extensively on Anton Mesmer, who stands at the centre of the romantic and medical traditions out of which Freud and Jung emerged.
7. See Jung (1989), 333–34, 338, Uhrig (2001), and Jaffé (1950).
8. See Dufour (1998); Koyré (1929).
9. See Jung (1989, pp. 338, 329; 1970).
10. On Jung's sources see Rode (1982) and Shamdasani (2003).
11. Koslowski argues that Böhme is the first philosopher of revelation, opening up a way of thinking that is perfected by Schelling and Hegel. See Koslowski (2001), p. 210.
12. Oetinger (1702–1782) was a founding father of the Speculative Pietist movement in Germany (the religious tradition into which both Hegel and Schelling were born) and the chief interpreter of Böhme in the eighteenth century.

References

Böhme, Jakob. (1620). *The Six Theosophical Points*. London, UK. This is the baroque English translation of Böhme's treatise. It was translated by John Sparrow and published in England with translations of all of Böhme's works between 1647 and 1661.

Böhme, Jakob. (1997). *Jacob Böhme Werke*, Ferdinand van Ingen (Ed.). Frankfurt, a.M.: Deutscher Klassiker Verlag. This text comprises critical editions of the original German versions of *Aurora* (1612) and *De Signatura Rerum* (1621).

Brown, Robert. (1977). *The Later Philosophy of Schelling: The influence of Boehme on the works of 1809–1815*. Lewisburg, PA: Bucknell University Press.

Drobb, Sanford. (2000). *Symbols of the Kabbalah: Philosophical and Theological Perspectives*. Northvale, NJ: Jason Aronson.

Dufour, Dany Robert. (1998). *Lacan et le Miroir Sophianique de Böhme*. Paris, France: Cahiers de l'Unebevue E.P.E.L.

Ellenberger, Henry. 1970. *The Discovery of the Unconscious*. New York, NY: Basic Books.

Feuerbach, Ludwig. (1981). *Geschichte der neuern Philosophie von Bacon von Verulam bis Benedikt Spinoza*. Berlin, Germany: Akademie Verlag.

Freud, Sigmund. (1994). *The Interpretation of Dreams*. Trans. A.A. Brill. New York, NY: Modern Library, 1994.

Häussermann, Friedrich. (1966–1972). Theologia Emblematica. Kabbalistische und alchemistische Symbolik bei Fr. Chr. Oetinger und deren Analogien bei Jakob Boehme. *Blätter für Württembirgische Kirchengeschichte*. In three parts. Württemberg, Germany: Verein für württembergische Kirkengeshichte.

Hegel, Georg Wilhelm Friedrich. (1965). *Vorlesungen über die Geschichte der Philosophie*. Georg Wilhelm Friedrich Hegel Sämtliche Werke. Hermann Glockner (Ed.). Stuttgart, Germany: Friedrich Frommann.

Heidelberger, Michael. (2004). *Nature from Within: Gustav Theodor Fechner's Psychophysical Worldview*. Pittsburgh, PA: University of Pittsburgh Press.

Jaffé, Aniela. (1950). Jakob Böhme. Der Gedanke der Polarität. In *C.G. Jung, Gestaltungen des Unbewußten*. Zürich, Switzerland: C.G. Jung Institute. 321–327.

Jung, C.G. (1966). The psychology of the tranference. *The Collected Works of C.G. Jung*. Vol. 16. Princeton, NJ: Princeton University Press. 163–323.

Jung, C.G. (1967). On psychic energy. In *The Structure and Dynamics of the Psyche. The Collected Works of C.G. Jung*. Vol. 8. Princeton, NJ: Princeton University Press. 3–66.

Jung, C.G. (1970). Answer to Job. In *Psychology and Religion: West and East. The Collected Works of C.G. Jung*. Vol. 11. Princeton, NJ: Princeton University Press. 365–474.

Jung, C.G. (1977a). Symbols of transformation. Revised version. *The Collected Works of C.G. Jung*. Vol. 5. Princeton, NJ: Princeton University Press.

Jung, C.G. (1977b). Mysterium Conjunctionis. *The Collected Works of C.G. Jung*. Vol. 14. Princeton, NJ: Princeton University Press.

Jung, C.G. (1989). *Memories, dreams, Reflections*. Aniela Jaffé (Ed.). New York, NY: Vintage Books.

Koslowski, Peter. (2001). *Philosophien der Offenbahrung. Antiker Gnostizismus, Franz von Baader, Schelling*. Paderborn, Germany: Ferdinand Schöningh.

Koyré, Alexander. (1929). *La Philosophie de Jacob Böhme*. New York, NY: Burt Franklin Publishers.
Lammers, A. & Cunningham, A. (Eds.). (2007). *The Jung-White Letters*. London, UK: Routledge.
Magee, Glenn Alexander. (2001). *Hegel and the Hermetic tradition*. Ithaca, NY: Cornell University Press.
Mayer, Paola. (1999). *Jena Romanticism and its Appropriation of Jakob Böhme*. Montreal and Kingston, Quebec: McGill-Queen's University Press.
Mills, Jon. (2002). *The Unconscious Abyss: Hegel's Anticipation of Psychoanalysis*. Albany, NY: State University of New York Press.
O'Regan, Cyril. (1994). *The Heterodox Hegel*. Albany, NY: State University of New York Press.
Oetinger, Friedrich Christoph. (1920). Kurzer Auszug der Hauptlehre Jakob Böhmes. In H. Kayser (Ed.), *Schrifften Jakob Böhmes*. Leipzig, CT: Insel. 54–94.
Ricoeur, Paul. (1970). *Freud and philosophy. An Essay on Interpretation*. New Haven, CT and London, UK: Yale University Press.
Rode, Christian. (1982). Jung und Seine Zeit. In D. Eicke (Ed.), *Individual Psychologie und Analytische Psychologie, Tiefen-Psychologie*, 4, 153–159. Weinheim, Germany and Basel, Switzerland: Beltz Verlag.
Schelling, Friedrich. (2002). *Philosophical Investigations into the Essence of Human Freedom and Related matters*. Trans P. Hayden-Roy (Trans.). In E. Behler (Ed.). *Philosophy of German idealism*. New York, NY: Continuum. 217–284.
Schmidt-Biggemann, Wilhelm. (2013). *Geschichte der Christlichen Kabbalah*. Volume Two. Stuttgart, Germany: Frommann-Holzboog.
Scholem, Gerschom. (1974). *Kabbalah*. New York, NY: Meridian.
Schopenhauer, Arthur. 1836. *On the Will in Nature*. Trans. E.F.J. Payne. New York, NY: Berg, 1992.
Schott, Heinz. (1983). *Sigmund Freud und die Entstehung der Psychoanalyse*, Freiburger Universitätsblätter 22, Heft 82.
Schott, Heinz. 1985. *Zauberspiegel der Seele. Sigmund Freud und die Geschichte der Selbstanalyse*. Göttingen, Germany: Vandenhoeck & Ruprecht.
Schulze, Wilhelm August. (1955). Jacob Boehme und die Kabbala. *Judaica. Beiträge zum Verständnis des Jüdischen Schicksals*, *11*, 12–29, 209–216.
Shamdasani, Sonu. (2003). *Jung and the Making of Modern Psychology. The Dream of a Science*. Cambridge, UK: Cambridge University Press.
Uhrig, Elizabeth. (2001). Gegenüberstellung einiger Aussagen Jacob Böhmes und des Schweizer Psychologen Carl Gustav Jung. In *Görlitzer Magazin. Beiträge zu Geschichte und Gegenwart der Stadt Görlitz und ihrer Umgebung 14/15*, 59–66.
Van Ingen, Ferdinand. (1997). Jacob Böhme: Leben und Werke. In F. van Ingen. (Ed.), *Jacob Böhme Werke*. Frankfurt, Germany: Deutscher Klassiker Verlag. 795–831.
Von Hartmann, Eduard. (1893). *Philosophy of the Unconscious*. W.C. Coupland (Ed.). London, UK: Kegan Paul, Trench, Trübner.
Weeks, Andrew. (1993). *German Mysticism from Hildegard of Bingen to Ludwig Wittgenstein: A Literary and Intellectual History*. Albany, NY: State University of New York Press.
Young, Christopher, and Brook, Andrew. (2014). *Schopenhauer and Freud*. http://http-server.carleton.ca/~abrook/SCHOPENY.htm.

Chapter 3

Demonic Consciousness as a Dynamic of Evil

Jungian Approaches to Understanding Evil

John Beebe

Jungian analysts do not tend to neglect the discussion of evil in either their theoretical or their clinical work. Yet it is difficult to define the Jungian position on evil and to distinguish it from the more general Jungian discussion of "the shadow" as the dark side of the ego. Especially because Jungian thought has refrained from demonizing the shadow, it is hard to be sure what Jungian psychology considers to be evil. Jung puts the matter very well early in his book *Aion* (1951/1968), when he says, "... it is quite within the bounds of possibility for a man to recognize the relative evil of his nature, but it is a rare and shattering experience for him to gaze into the face of absolute evil" (§19).

More than 40 years ago, at the beginning of my career as a psychiatrist, I encountered a case that touched on this problem as it emerged in the soul of a woman patient of mine. I was actually prepared for what I would encounter by an odd dream I had the night before I saw the patient for the first time. In my dream, I was talking to Eva Braun, Hitler's mistress. Braun, in my dream, had survived him. She was speaking of Hitler with great nostalgia. "But," I was saying to her, "wasn't he a terrible dictator?"

The patient I met the next day was a Jewish woman who had lived in Germany for a brief period of her childhood before Hitler came to power. A parent had fortunately seen to it that she was able to get out and come to America. Here, she had been a successful university student, married well and had begun to explore a creative career. Often plagued by anxieties in her younger years, around the time she entered menopause she fell into an agitated depression, the great feature of which was that she was constantly summoning help that she couldn't use. Mine turned out to be no exception. Whatever I did in the therapy seemed to make little difference.

One of her children dreamed that there was a lady fireman trying to cope with a lake that was on fire. She was using a fire extinguisher that, the more she sprayed it on the fire, the higher the flames rose. The dream was shared by the boy's father who was on the verge of leaving his wife. Not long after her unsuccessful therapy with me had resulted in the kind of impasse the dream had predicted, she committed suicide. After her death, I met with the husband who showed me a dream my patient had never shared with me. It had preceded the onset of the depression that I, like other analysts before me, had not found a way to help. In the dream, which was written in the patient's own hand, the Devil appeared to her. He said, "I will give you my beauty, if you will give me your power. "I have no power," she answered, "but I will accept your beauty."

Reading this summary of the dream brought a moment in the analysis to my memory. I had asked her if there was any "sin" that she could recall committing for which she might be unconsciously punishing herself. There was none, she said. Yet this dream suggested that she had in effect sold her soul to the Devil. It was not hard to link this dream of hers with my own about Eva Braun and Hitler. The patient, who tyrannized others with her relentless insistence on getting their help, always asserting that she had no one else but the person she was talking to, and never admitting to finding any solace in the help given, had in the part of herself Jung called the *animus*[1] become quite a dictator, indefatigable in demanding that others serve her.

What she was not willing to explain to anyone was what had happened to her own power to bring change into her life. Attempts at pharmacological interventions had proven as useless as analysis in releasing her from the agitated, importuning state of mind that she brought to all her relationships, a display of helplessness variously described as histrionic, masochistic and passive aggressive that was so oppositional that it seemed more characterological than psychiatric in nature. The way she presented herself in her frequent phone calls summoned up the picture of crazy-making interpersonal demandingness that has been described in the Jungian literature as "animus possession" (e.g., Jung 1917/1953, §337; 1954/1959, §223; von Franz 2002, pp. 36, 39–40; Wheelwright 1984, pp. 16–24).

I would like to refine that diagnostic formulation that was once so popular among analytical psychologists, which in practice has often depreciated the animus originally described by Jung as a woman's healthy spirit (1951/1968, §33). It would be better, I think, for the Jungian analyst resorting to metaphor to speak not of a possession of the woman by an unconscious animus complex, but of a possession of the healthy animus by a demonic spirit that brings evil into her psyche, as it were, from outside her usual psychic apparatus. We might examine the role of such invading demonic consciousness in the dynamic developments that can lead the animus to be not a source of strength for the woman—an indomitable spirit—but a conduit for dominating others and in the process quite undermining herself, that is, becoming a source of evil. The "fire extinguisher" in my patient's son's dream would be an image of the now ineffective, because possessed, animus, and its paradoxically flame-inducing contents would represent the demonic, goal-undermining energy that was destroying this woman's life. That this represented a hideous example of identification with an aggressor of her childhood past, symbolized by Hitler, did little to explain away the fact that she had now made a Holocaust of her own inner life (the reservoir of consciousness that was her "lake").

I offer this archetypal outline of the dynamic I encountered in this patient, whom I was not able to help enough, because it opens the subject of the role of the demonic in the truly evil clinical syndromes that sometimes find their way into psychotherapy. In analyzing evil within depth psychological analytic work, we have to consider that there may be limits to what we can do. This helps to avoid blaming the patient, a principle enunciated by Jung's close associate Marie Louise von Franz (1972):

> One should realize that even if you consider the patient to be completely wrong and possessed by evil, possessed by blindness of some kind, that is not deliberate on his part. It is not his evil will, nobody is possessed voluntarily. It is a tragic fate which should be respected in silence. So it is better to say that the treatment cannot go on since we are blocked. Obviously if I cannot help the analysand any more I am wasting my time, and the analysand is wasting time and money, so it would be better to separate in peace. (pp. 179–180)

When treatment is possible, it is essential to remember, following von Franz, that the thoughts, emotions and behaviors the analysand brings to our attention and finds particularly disturbing because they are indicative of malign agency, are not consciously chosen by the patient. Even in the dream of my middle-aged patient who allowed the Devil to take her power so that she could have his beauty, the Devil approached *her*, and she assumed she had the best of the bargain because she believed that she had no real power to give him. That is why she accepted, not imaging that the Faustian bargain would fatally compromise her ability to stand up to the demonic energy that soon began to flood her soul. The "beauty" that she won from the Devil expressed itself as an uncanny ability to attract and seduce dozens of people into wanting to rescue her psychologically, assuring each that he or she was the only one she could turn to and keeping each one engaged and motivated even as she systematically rejected his or her help.

In a case of this power and gravity, we have first to distinguish whether what has become so troubling has arisen from a conscious or unconscious source. Conscious evil accompanies the differentiation of effective will, and there is little to say about it that ethicists and moral philosophers have not already articulated. To have consciousness at all is to be capable of doing quite a bit of damage, effectively, and we are all (as the late James Hillman once put it to me) "damagers" (1993, personal communication). That does not mean, however, that all evil is enacted by conscious choice. The choice we have concerns holding onto the integrity that, as our lives proceed, we will need to deal with something outside ourselves trying to take a foothold in us.

Answer to Job

Jung illuminates this point in his analysis of the biblical Book of Job (1958) where he takes up the question of God's "Answer to Job" when Job asks why God has visited so much evil upon him. God's answer is to remind Job that he has little right to question the Almighty, saying, in effect, "Who do you think you are?" (God's exact words, in the unsurpassed King James translation, are, "Where wast thou when I laid the foundations of the earth? Declare, if thou hast understanding" [Job 28:4]). Job demurs, recognizing that his integrity is no match for God's authority. Jung, however, dares to answer, and his book could almost have been titled *Answer to God*.

Jung's view is that one of the foundations of the earth on which God's creatures dwell is the psychological ground that is a condition of every human creature's being. This ground is the reality of the psyche (Jung, 1933/1960, §742–48), and it has certain givens. One of these is that God himself, like any Creator, is incomplete and needs his Creation to complete Himself. That God made humans in His image did not mean that he was finished with them. The *integritas* he gave his creatures was given for a divine purpose. He needed the quality he had graced them with, an original moral wholeness, to process His own nature. Integrity of their sort was not in him to draw upon, any more than the artist has in himself the perfection and beauty and wholeness he can impart to a work of art. Jung's view of God is that, perfect as He may be as a Creator, He is still in search of a solution to his own imperfections. This need to complete Himself, which in Jung's view is not really conscious—consciousness being a human characteristic—God chooses to resolve by entering His own Creation.

That is Jung's interpretation of the Christian story, in which God becomes a man by impregnating a virgin, symbol of integrity, with His Spirit. This Holy Spirit, Jung explains, contains not the purity of God's intention as is so often assumed by Christians, but the opposites of Good and Evil that God Himself still has not resolved or even made wholly conscious. God, in Jung's view, is a *complexio oppositorum* (1958/1980, §1640),[2] meaning that far from being only and purely Good, God is a complexity, a still unconscious mix of Good and Evil. For that reason when the Spirit of God enters an actual woman or man, the Spirit presents to that person a conflict of good and evil[3] that God himself has neither reflected upon nor attempted to transcend and which only the integrity of a human being's capacity for consciousness can resolve. As Jung sees it, this is what Job glimpsed: God's problem had become his, and Job's virtue lay in respecting and accepting the burden. Similarly, according to Jung, Christ brought to the world not just God's capacity to bring peace but the violence that prefigures an apocalypse. For Jung, the Christian Apocalypse described in the Book of Revelation reveals that even Christ is accompanied by Antichrist.

Jewish, Catholic and Protestant theologians have all challenged Jung's perception of God (Buber, 1952, pp. 78–92, 133–37; Jung, 1958/1980; Jung and White, 2007) as being as evil as he is good, and resist his view of the Holy Spirit as carrying the problem of God's opposites into the soul of man where it can more readily be examined, tested and perhaps faced as it is not in God, who is "not subject to any ethical laws" (Jung, 1958, §605 and §600, note 13). But for Jung, that the Spirit of God has indeed done so is supported by the evidence he finds in both the Old and New Testament amplified from his depth psychological explorations of individuals in conflict. Sooner or later, when one goes as deeply into one's religious background as Jung did, such conflicts touch on the soul's struggle with a problem of good and evil the origin of which seems to be outside the "personal" psyche yet is so deeply lodged there that its resolution becomes an urgent psychological problem. Jung is arguing as a psychologist that all of us who are led to look as profoundly into our inner lives as we do in analysis will come to realize that we are under strong pressures to be both good and evil, from a source of energy that seems, phenomenologically, to arise from beyond our personal histories. We need to discriminate the entry point of that energy more precisely to be able to discover a more conscious way of resisting its ability to flood and overwhelm our moral psychological integrity.

Demon and Daimon

What is the nature of the consciousness that creates such pressures, and what is the consciousness that can resolve them? I am going to argue here that what undermines us and what heals us are not the same consciousness, calling the former *demonic* and the latter *daimonic*. To understand how we can relate to the discomforting discontinuity involved, we have to make a distinction not unlike the one Jung makes in his amateur's theology between a human being's 'soul' (*anima* or *animus*) and the 'Spirit of God' that might be trying to incarnate its *complexio oppositorum* within that soul. Within such a model we can understand that the Self, as the organ of the complexity that derives from God, regularly presents the human soul with a choice between demonic and daimonic energies that only a soul with integrity (Beebe, 1992) is organized to make. The term *demonic* speaks for itself and is easy to identify in a case like the one I have described. I am using the perhaps unfamiliar term *daimonic* to mean a more benevolent inspiration that can make all the difference to a soul that has had to face absolute evil.

As we readily discover in Jungian analysis, as analytical work proceeds with the investigation of states of mind through the invaluable lens of dreams, there is a big difference between the gendered soul figures (anima/

animus) and the energy states demon/daimon. The latter pair *channel,* more than they contain, uncanny psychological experience. Quoting Auden, James Hillman[4] said in one of his final lectures, "We are lived by powers we pretend to understand." This is more than a realization of our "daimonic" inheritance as creatures made in the image of God, it recognizes a "demonic" inheritance as well and takes the point God made to Job, as he had also made to Adam and Eve, that much of what we experience is not ours to understand. Some people imagine God as a kind of 'voice' (whether of reason or of conscience) that can advise us as Socrates' *daimonion* advised him. If so, they can accept the daimonic grace of God as an ongoing guide to their integrity, but the term 'demonic,' speaking to the dark side of the *daimonion,* implies something many of us know and fear more often—possession by a darker power advancing evil ends, like the Devil in my patient's dream.[5]

With Jung, I share the conviction that God's decision to go on incarnating in human beings is, overall, a well-founded one, because in us what is unconscious can, at least potentially, be made conscious. If Jung is right, the shadow in which God in all His unconscious ambivalence may be discovered is not just a dark Presence about which we may say whatever we like as if that Presence had no say in the matter. That Presence has chosen us through whom to say his piece about good and evil; therefore it cares about what we choose to say in that regard.

For most of us, however, projection of the shadow of the observer regularly occurs when we approach this moral realm. I believe, therefore, in distinction from Jung, that we are truly justified in describing an aspect of our own or another's psychological performance as "demonic" only if that aspect, whether intrinsic or an introject, regularly operates in such a way as to fundamentally undermine others. We can know that is so when they can justifiably begin to feel that evil has been visited upon them. In the course of a therapeutic analysis, it is possible for an analyst in intimate contact with the psyche of a patient to experience firsthand all the kinds of interpersonal influence the person is capable of exerting and thus to identify any particular unsettling influence, which in the case of the evil transmitted by the demonic truly is like no other. In clinical circles, this undermining area of a patient's mind is sometimes spoken of as "pathological narcissism" or "unanalyzed superego pathology." A Jungian analyst recognizes it as a peculiar type of consciousness that has made its unwelcome appearance in a precise location, the very soul of the person (that is, the anima or animus) that is normally the access point to the energies of the Self. In such cases, the possessing spirit demands that the soul choose between good and evil aspects of the unconscious with all the consequences for the outcome of the treatment of such a decision. Most therapists who have wrestled with a case of possession like the one my patient suffered recognize how dramatic an individual case of suicidal depression can be.

Insights from Jung's Study of Types of Consciousness

Jung is not a fatalist. He gives a decisive edge to what the human being can bring to bear on this drama of the incarnation of godlike opposites. Humans have the capacity that God cannot seem to fully develop without them: consciousness. Human consciousness, as understood by Jung's analytical psychology, is not one thing, but a plurality of eight 'types' of consciousness, which organize themselves into pairs of opposites (Jung, 1921/1971, §556–671) and which are distributed in markedly uneven and qualitatively distinct ways through a variety of complexes that make up an individual's ego and shadow. The pattern of the consciousness that emerges through these complexes is spoken of in Jungian circles as the individual's 'psychological type. ' Jung asserts four basic functions of consciousness—'sensation,' 'intuition,' 'thinking' and 'feeling,' each of which can be deployed with either an extraverted or introverted attitude, thereby comprising a total of eight types of consciousness.

Sensation and intuition form a pair of opposites: They represent two quite different ways of taking in information. When we take in information using 'sensation,' we notice and pay direct attention to the detailed data that come to us through our five senses. By contrast, if we rely on 'intuition,' we do not pay close attention to individual grains of sensory data but instead process them more unconsciously, gaining a general sense of the data's overall trends or perhaps having our attention called to quite anomalous data, but otherwise tuning out the details to focus on the bigger picture.

Thinking and feeling likewise form a pair of opposites as two different ways to make rational evaluations and choices. If we rely on 'thinking' to analyze, organize and decide then we are privileging logic; if we rely on 'feeling,' we are guided primarily by our values including especially the values that we apply to human relationships.

Within each of Jung's four functions of consciousness—sensation, intuition, thinking and feeling—the extraverted and introverted forms of the function also form a pair of opposites. When applied in an extraverted way, the consciousness is directed toward some object or Other that exists in a space that is shared or public, and tends toward action. When applied in an introverted way, the consciousness is directed inward toward a space that, although archetypal, is private and tends toward reflection. Here, an example will help. Upon encountering an unusual butterfly, an extraverted sensation consciousness might notice each detail of the insect's color, pattern, shape, size, texture and motion, remaining curious and attentive as long as there is significant new information to notice and as long as something even more striking does not draw its attention away. By contrast, an introverted sensation consciousness, encountering the same butterfly, might form an inner image of what it has seen and then gradually withdraw its attention from the real butterfly to 'interrogate' the inner image, asking questions such as, "What have I seen before that this butterfly reminds me of? What is similar to that earlier experience and what is different?" In the personal space of introverted sensation consciousness, an individual might recall another stunning butterfly that she saw 20 years earlier, musing over the details of the earlier experience, or she might make a connection to some other surprisingly beautiful thing she once encountered that made her heart leap in exactly the same way the butterfly did today.

Although each of us has some access to all eight types of consciousness that Jung first observed and then defined, we each tend to be most comfortable using one form of information-gathering consciousness—introverted or extraverted intuition or sensation—and one form of rational, choice-making consciousness—introverted or extraverted thinking or feeling. A natural balance seems to obtain in the psyche, not only between taking in information (sensation or intuition) and using it to analyze, evaluate and choose (thinking or feeling), but also between introversion and extraversion. Thus, if the form of consciousness that we are most comfortable with is introverted, then our second most preferred form of consciousness tends to be extraverted and vice versa.

To be able to recognize the eight types of consciousness in actual experience is not instantly grasped, but it need not require years of study. The types, or 'functions' of consciousness are described first by Jung (1921/1971, esp. §556–671) but also by Jungian analyst Daryl Sharp (1987), and, in their most conscious manifestations, by various type practitioners who work with applications that derive from Jung's type theory, such as the Myers-Briggs Type Indicator, including, most generously, Leona Haas & Mark Hunziker (2006); see also Beebe (2014).

If we are to get a handle on the greatest source of unconsciousness, and therefore danger, in us we must begin to identify where the demonic side of ourselves, and that of others, can be found. To the best of my knowledge, no system of thought other than typology is quite capable of making this contribution. Therefore, I beg the reader's patience as I explore just a bit further the dynamic implications of what might seem, so far, like a rather static, and even pedantic, presentation of the types of ego-consciousness.

Building on Jung's work and on that of his immediate students, especially Marie-Louise von Franz, I have pointed out that within a given individual each of the functions of consciousness is associated with a particular archetypal energy. This energy is like the "genius loci," the genius of the place in which the consciousness is found. In the case of the most preferred type of consciousness, called the 'superior' function, that archetypal energy is the well-known hero or heroine, the energy that wants to rise to life's challenges, to master each situation and, when necessary, to save the day. Its opposite is the 'inferior' function, the subject of one of von Franz's greatest essays (1971).[6] For each of us, the inferior function is a type of consciousness that we idealize but also tend to feel vulnerable, touchy and ashamed about because we are never able to wield it with consistent mastery.

To be very clear as to what I mean by 'opposite' here, I will provide a table that shows for each possible most-preferred type of consciousness what the inferior function would be:

If the superior function is	*The inferior function will be*
Extraverted sensation	Introverted intuition
Introverted sensation	Extraverted intuition
Extraverted intuition	Introverted sensation
Introverted intuition	Extraverted sensation
Extraverted thinking	Introverted feeling
Introverted thinking	Extraverted feeling
Extraverted feeling	Introverted thinking
Introverted feeling	Extraverted thinking

To reach the heart of the problem of evil in this approach, we must go one step further. The inferior function is a place in the psyche where we all tend, through clumsiness and unconsciousness, to do damage, but it does not tend to be intentionally destructive. The darkest and most undermining place in the psyche—what I call the demonic, but which can also be a benevolent, daimonic part of the personality, is the type of consciousness that has the same function but the opposite attitude from the inferior function:

Superior Function (Hero/Heroine)	*Inferior Function (Anima/Animus)*	*(Demonic/Daimonic Personality)*
Extraverted thinking	Introverted feeling	Extraverted feeling
Extraverted feeling	Introverted thinking	Extraverted thinking
Extraverted sensation	Introverted intuition	Extraverted intuition
Extraverted intuition	Introverted sensation	Extraverted sensation
Introverted thinking	Extraverted feeling	Introverted feeling
Introverted feeling	Extraverted thinking	Introverted thinking
Introverted sensation	Extraverted intuition	Introverted intuition
Introverted intuition	Extraverted sensation	Introverted sensation

This location and identification of the demonic personality within the psyche is one that I have reached not primarily from theory but rather from 50 years of observing and analyzing the types and qualities of consciousness expressed by my patients, my friends and myself. Others who have subsequently joined in this study have observed the same pattern.

My particular way of using the term 'demonic personality' is not entirely the same as Jung's occasional use of the term 'demonism' to describe a person's state of mind when possessed by a complex (Jung, 1945/1980, p. 648), James Hillman's use of the term 'daimon' to describe the psychic source of 'character and calling' (1996) and Donald Kalsched's use of the term 'daimonic' to describe dissociative defenses in traumatized patients (1996), let alone the use of the term 'daimonic' outside analytical psychology, for instance by Rollo May (Diamond, 1996). Nevertheless, I feel *demonic* is the best term for what I have in mind and that the contributions of these theorists and, more recently, that of Thomas Singer (2004), who has spoken of "daimonic defenses of the group spirit," can actually be clarified by the specificity with which I use the term in relation to the typology of the individual. The place of the demonic, for me, is as the natural shadow of Jung and von Franz's "inferior function." In my observation, of all the eight types of consciousness, the demonic, though still a consciousness, is the one that operates most outside the awareness of the individual and thus is able to act in the most insidious ways, as if energized by the Devil to undermine not only others, but the person him- or herself.

In the language of fairytales, perhaps the most natural expression of the way the psyche arranges itself archetypally, the relation of the inferior function to the demonic function, is described as the relation of Beauty to Beast. In a man's psyche, Beauty is a signifier of the *integritas* that is the anima's highest value and potential. The figure of Beast, kind and cruel at the same time (Henderson 1968, p. 138), perfectly conveys the essential quality of the demonic/daimonic function.[7] I have argued elsewhere that Beauty's task in the story, to relate to Beast in such a way that his essential value, his *daimon*, can be redeemed from his demonic presentation, is what the psyche's capacity for integrity (Beebe, 1992) is intended for (Beebe 1998).

Here I would like to comment on the way the Beast shapes the expression of the different types of consciousness that find themselves in his position, without regard to whether that demonic expression has been tamed or transformed in any way by an anima or animus. I present 'worst case' scenarios in the understanding that there have always been people who do not take responsibility for the beastliness and that therefore their demonic side is never able to become the occasion for an infusion of a transformed spirit (Beebe, 2000), but simply acts to undermine others and themselves. Indeed, the demonic, once enacted, regularly sets off a demonic counter-reaction in others, resulting in a chain of evil. Thomas Singer (2003) has perfectly expressed the cultural situation that emerges when the demonic consciousness of one group touches off the demonic consciousness of another, using here the term 'daimon' instead of my 'demon':

> It is precisely at this intersection—where the daimons or archetypal defenses of the spirit of one group's cultural complex trigger the daimons of another group's cultural complex—that I think we can most accurately locate "the axis of evil," be it the daimonic forces of Sharon aligned against

> the daimonic forces of Arafat, or the daimonic forces of Bush aligned against the daimonic forces of Saddam Hussein. These negative alignments truly form an "axis" in the sense that a direct line or connection is drawn between the daimons of one group, protecting their sacred center, and the daimons of a rival group, protecting their sacred center." (p. 204)

We need to understand that a consciousness in the demonic position, from the standpoint of the typology of the individual (or possibly group) is *normally* defensive, protecting the sacred center of the individual (or group) in a beastly way, to see the importance of identifying the place of the demonic in any possible system of consciousness. Then we can more easily identify which consciousness in ourselves is the one we use regularly in a demonic way. If it knows this, our integrity can begin to recognize what it must attempt to contain if we are not to go on defending ourselves in evil ways.

It behooves us, therefore, to try to learn the place of the demonic for at least our own superior function type, because this is exactly where we are most likely to terrorize others. We should recognize, moreover, that our place of greatest demonic defense is likely to be our place of greatest vulnerability (if we did not have so great a vulnerability we would not need to resort to so great a defense) so that when we learn something about our demonic ability to undermine we are also identifying something about our vulnerability to being undermined. It is humbling to recognize that we are capable of being most terrorized in the very part of our consciousness where we are most demonic. But finally, if we can learn the type of terror someone else is addressing us with—that is, the consciousness type of that person's Beast, we will have gone a long way in understanding how and why we are feeling undermined and threatened by that person. So let us explore the eight types of demonic consciousness one by one.

In its conscious form, extraverted thinking is goal-oriented thinking that helps us to plan the steps to achieve a goal and to persuade others with the clarity of our logic so they will join in the plan. In the demonic place, however, extraverted thinking tends to be ruthlessly *opportunistic* in the plans it develops. In *The Wizard of Oz*, the Wizard embodies demonic extraverted thinking. When Dorothy seeks his help in a way that is likely to expose him as a humbug, he callously instructs her to go and capture the broomstick of the Wicked Witch, figuring to dispose of her permanently in that way.

Extraverted feeling, in its conscious form, is focused on validating, affirming, and staying in relation to others. In the demonic place, extraverted feeling tends to be *insensitive* and even brutal, interpersonally, even as it goes through the forms of being appreciative. For example, the appreciation expressed may be exactly for the one trait that the other person does not want to be valued for. In the film *As Good as It Gets* (1997), the character of the obsessively obnoxious Melvin (Jack Nicholson) who initially manages to offend and upset everyone, personifies demonic extraverted feeling.

As we have noted earlier, conscious extraverted sensation is the kind of consciousness that notices the most salient details of what is presented to the senses. In the demonic place, however, extraverted sensation tends to be *grossly inattentive* to immediate realities and to introduce confusing or distracting new elements so that important details are missed. Such demonic extraverted sensation is often found in the intuitive person who fails to listen when information is being communicated and distracts others when they are trying to orient themselves.

Extraverted intuition, when consciously deployed, shows itself as a keen sensitivity to future possibilities that inhere in the shared, public space. An individual with heroic extraverted intuition, for example, tends to scan the horizon for promising new ideas and developments, to know about new books, movies or music before others do and in general to approach change with optimism, envisioning numerous opportunities that can make life better for everyone. When in the very unconscious, demonic place, however, extraverted intuition, in the name of focusing on the positive, tends to *turn a blind eye* to an emerging risk that everyone else can see—for instance, a relationship with an exciting new partner who has little more to offer than possibilities.

Introverted thinking is a consciousness that is above all concerned with understanding situations. To this end, it takes time to assign the correct names to things and approach problems with a kind of careful analysis that seeks to find the truth. In the demonic place, however, introverted thinking tends to define things in a lazy, *reductionist* way that disavows the actual experience of others, particularly those who are suffering. Misidentifying the reason for the suffering, demonic introverted thinking puts the worst possible construction on it. This is the consciousness of the "Job's comforter" who tells you that you have brought the problem you are complaining about upon yourself, 'adding insight to injury.'

Conscious introverted feeling is focused on staying true to one's most deeply held values. This kind of consciousness can quickly evaluate a situation and, with innate graciousness, know what is an appropriate response for a given situation from the point of view of upholding values. In the demonic place, introverted feeling is subtly *depreciative*: It tends to assign values to others in such a way as actually to blur their value: the husband who tells his wife how grateful he is to her for "representing the feminine" in their household, a valuation that undercuts and blurs her real identity as a woman.

Introverted sensation, when conscious, is very reactive to sensory stimulation. It is good at mastering many details and is attentive to involuntary reactions of the body. It avoids being wasteful in its use of money, materials and energy. In the demonic place, introverted sensation tends to *wrongly concretize* what should be left more metaphoric. Religious fundamentalism that insists on applying ancient, sacred texts literally and concretely, heedless of the consequences, is an expression of demonic introverted sensation.

Introverted intuition, when conscious, is a function that perceives archetypes symbolically and in so doing organizes information around a vision that is religious even though it is well-nigh intangible. This kind of intuition can be a reliable, if mysterious, inner guide, even though the person who uses it may not be able to articulate *how* he or she comes to the intuitions. In the demonic place, however, introverted intuition tends to *distort* the archetypal ideas it transmits so that they become both seductive and undermining. Hitler's backing up his ambition for a German nationalism that could prevail on the world stage with notions like the "master race," together with his use of imagery and rhetoric evoking the old Northern European god Wotan (in the distorted form of a demanding deity of storms, stripped of the balancing attributes of natural wisdom and justice that were part of this god in the original Germanic myths) created what might be called a 'bad faith' that misguided the German people under his rule. Like a virus in the collective unconscious, this demonic introverted intuition contained some potent nuclear mythological material but in a culturally pathogenic form. The mythologem led many Germans during the Nazi era to go along with, or even replicate, a ruthlessness that their reception of the actual image of this god would not so one-sidedly have sanctioned.[8]

These are specific examples of how the type of consciousness that is demonic for a given individual will affect the way in which that person undermines self and others. Because Jung himself has cast this problem in theological, and therefore theistic, terms I will now turn to an example of how typological insight might have illuminated the case of an atheist.

The Case of Mersault

My example is that of the character of Mersault, in Albert Camus's *L'Étranger.* The French title, which at one time was generally translated *The Stranger*, has recently, and I think more accurately, been translated by Sandra Smith (Camus, 1942/2013) as *The Outsider*, which shifts our understanding of the theme of the novel. It is less about the strangeness, or even the estrangedness of Meursault, than about his status as an outsider, living beyond the bounds of so many cultural assumptions, including belief in God. He is a totally modern man, a 30-something Frenchman working in an office in the French colonial city of Algiers, who in an impulsive, unexpected way kills an Arab on a beach. Earlier in the day, in a sudden fight, the Arab had inflicted a very minor injury on one of Meursault's French friends.

In telling the lead-up to Mersault's murder of the man, which begins in the psyche with the fact that Mersault himself has just suffered, rather passively, the death of his mother in a nursing home, the novel shifts its theme to what is depicted as outside of Meursault's psyche. It moves from the self-consciousness that accompanies grief to its hero's lack of awareness of any duty to the Other at the moment of the murder. This is an unconsciousness of basic compassion, for which Mersault will have to pay according to a French justice system in which he will be punished not only for what he did but because he cannot credibly explain why he did it.

Meursault's point of view, throughout the novel, is organized by introverted sensation. Mersault is not someone who thinks before he acts. Nor does he feel the value of what he does or doesn't do or foresee in an intuitive way what the consequences of his action or inaction may be. Rather he is primarily sensitive to the physical discomforts inside of his body and unwilling to give anything else, including the moral implications of his existence, any more energy than necessary. The reason he gives the magistrate for committing the murder is that the sun was unusually hot that day.

That this "hot sun" could be the infusion of the Divine Spirit in all its ambivalence would not have escaped Jung, the author of *Answer to Job*, had he read *L'Étranger*. In Camus's novel, however, the protagonist experiences this irrational perception of an infusion in purely sensate ways, even as it drives him to murder. The way Mersault takes in the evil in the sun is by having to experience, physically, its inescapable, undermining hotness. This in itself, as he begins to swelter past all endurance, becomes an impetus to discharge himself of that undermining energy with the same mercilessness that the sun has shown him. What is not as obvious is that what has been undermined is the agency of Meursault's soul. The anima, or soul, of a man with superior introverted sensation is normally extraverted intuitive. Lacking all connection to his intuition, Mersault has no effective spiritual center, just a blind presumption that the disagreeable overstimulation has come to him randomly and therefore need not be tolerated; its annoying charge can be dispatched just as randomly—by forcing a bullet into the body of the Arab.

Those who know the work of René Girard (1977) will recognize his emphasis on mimesis in such acts of violence, the tendency we all have to pass along whatever hits us and even to imitate the apparent desire of others to hurt, resulting in scapegoating. Such mimetic currents can come from political, social and family influences on the unconscious such as cultural complexes (Singer & Kimbles 2004), phantom narratives (Kimbles 2014) and blood feuds (Salman 2003). But they can also come from the archetypes of the collective unconscious. The term *archetype* means "prime imprinter," suggesting that archetypes invite us to act out patterns of behavior for which they provide the model. In Meursault's instance, the mimesis is of the hotness of the sun itself, which carries with it Jung's point, in *Answer to Job,* that God seems to want human beings to process his violent side. Camus's character conveys the poignancy of finding oneself put in this position without choosing it.

What makes this a demonic possession of Mersault's soul is that there is *nothing but* mimesis. What is absurd in nature (the way it holds unconsciously opposites of good and evil) has become a motive for the human absurdity of random destructiveness. When human consciousness does not realize the opposites of good and evil any more than nature does, the ego is left to enact copycat violence, sacrificing without consciousness the lives of others. Wisdom is eclipsed.

Writing about Sophia, the figure of wisdom in the Book of Proverbs and later Gnostic texts, Jung (1954/1967) makes clear how catastrophic it can become for the anima to be "cast out as a bait into the darkness." What is hooked are all the shadow desires of others, especially within one's own cultural group (Girard, 1977, pp. 143–68). As Jung puts it, "Sadness, fear, bewilderment, confusion, longing" flood the lost Sophia, and an entire new world is created by her illusions. Describing the impact on a man of dissociation from the anima, Jung explains:

> In a case like this the unconscious usually responds with violent emotions, irritability, lack of control, arrogance, feelings of inferiority, moods, depressions, outbursts of rage, etc., coupled with lack of self-criticism and the misjudgments, mistakes and delusions which this entails.
>
> In such a state a man soon loses touch with reality. His spirituality becomes ruthless, arrogant, and tyrannical. The more unadapted his ideology is, the more it demands recognition and is determined to gain it, if necessary by force. (§452–55)

Clearly, this is the proto-fascist state of mind—a collective attitude of his time—that has overtaken Mersault in *L'Étranger.* We see it today in young men who are tempted to engage in terrorist acts through identification with political desires they scarcely understand.

The paradox of the anima, once it is uncovered and can become part of the working psychic apparatus of the person, is that it brings a consciousness of the face of the Other to the ego, allowing one potentially to return good for evil. One might wish to give the Other the comfort that has eluded oneself. Meursault's absence of soul means that he has no brake on his own precision; he is able to set no limits on his fascist way of directing an aggression equal to that he has felt the otherness of this world to have visited upon him.

Mersault never experiences the compassionate, daimonic spirit that can enter a soul. His extraverted intuitive anima, if not so dissociated, might have been able to see how the situation, though temporarily intolerable, could change for the better. The healthy godlike daimon that would have infused it with respect for the Other, however, could only have been an *introverted* intuitive consciousness. Such a consciousness, would be religious in character. Its presence could have enabled Mersault to consider the situation he encountered on the beach less concretely and to imagine the possibility of sparing rather than killing the person who had come, for him, to personify harassment itself.

Mersault's story suggests that to recognize when we are ourselves in the grip of the demonic would take us a long way toward relating to the hostile behaviors of others. Negative reactions from others are sometimes our final chances to look inside to see where we have been alienating and undermining. Those, like Meursault, who can recall discomfort but are not sufficiently self-reflective to consider how it might be discharged by other means than mimetic efforts to induce an equal measure of discomfort in another, cannot come to know how self-scrutiny, if it suffuses a soul, can lead to self-control. They cannot imagine how reflection, the soul's most characteristic activity, reduces the tendency we all have, in the face of the relentlessness of the world we sometimes must live in (its very hot sun) to mobilize demonic consciousness. Instead, liked Mersault, many of us under extreme stress surrender to the heat of demonic consciousness.

Clinical Example

To contrast to the unhappy case of Mersault, I would like to close by citing a more hopeful case of a patient being treated in a very ordinary, contemporary Jungian way, for depression.[9]

> At the outset of my psychiatric career, I had as a patient a 55-year-old plumber with chronic depression, who at that time was seeing me in an outpatient clinic only for refills of an antidepressant. During our monthly sessions, I kept hearing from him how his wife was always "on him." Asked for evidence, the patient could only report a mildly sarcastic remark she had made. But asked if he ever dreamed, he responded with more animation: "Why yes. Last night I had a dream about my little dog. I was holding him up in my arms, and he was looking up at me ever so tenderly, when suddenly he seemed to droop his head like he was going to die."
>
> I asked the patient to tell me about his dog. It turned out that he loved his pet above all other things because the dog was always sweet and cheerful. I then asked the man if this dog might not be his own cheerful disposition, which had faded into despondence after his wife's sarcastic remark. My patient seemed to like this idea.
>
> At the next monthly session, the patient related another dream. "The dog was there again, sitting at my feet and looking up at me. As I watched, its face turned into a vicious wharf rat." The patient told me that he had seen wharf rats in his younger days when he often worked on the harbors "around people that were hardly better than wharf rats they were so mean." Pursuing the lead of the previous month's session, I asked my patient if he was ever mean, if he ever lashed out. "Well if you put it that way, doctor, I guess I do. Oh I don't like that dream. I hate to think my little dog would turn into a wharf rat."
>
> "Yet that's what seems to happen to a good disposition when a person gets mean," I responded.

It was not easy to confront this patient, already depressed, with the reality that he could be the perpetrator as well as the victim of meanness, but this is what the dream seemed to be saying. This was the first picture this patient ever had of his mood problem, and he marveled at the insight it gave him. Then, for the first time, he allowed himself to tell me that he launched nightly into verbal attacks against his wife, not unlike the content of his monthly sessions, when he would belittle her to me. His wife's occasional barbed remarks turned out to be her weak defenses against the things he said.

"I can be pretty cruel, doctor," my patient admitted.

The following month, the patient brought his wife to the medication clinic with him. She turned out to be a nice, quiet, somewhat timid woman, frightened of her husband. She reported that he upset her with his critical remarks but lately there had been some improvement. For the first time, she had been curious to see his doctor, and my patient had been willing to bring her. This contact opened the door to some much needed couple work.

In this case example, the little dog can be seen as a symbol of the man's anima. When it turns into a wharf rat, it is being overtaken by a masculine meanness that the patient has observed in men working on the docks. It seems to me now that he was channeling this meanness the way the anima does when it becomes dissociated rather than that the meanness was essential to his own character. Once he felt that he needed to protect and stay aware of the vulnerability of the little dog to a demonic transformation, his ability to deal more fairly with his wife began to emerge.

Notes

1. In Jung's terminology, *anima* and *animus* are the names given to the image of the soul of the man and woman, respectively (Jung, 1921/1971, §808, also §803n80).
2. This Latin phrase meaning "a complex of opposites" originates with the German philosopher, jurist, and theologian Nicholas of Cusa (1401–1464) and was appropriated by Jung, who explains what it means for his psychology of good and evil thus: "I have never (as you state) understood from my study of the Fathers that God is the highest good *with reference to man*, no matter what he is in himself. ... If one assumes him to be a *complexio oppositorum*, i.e., beyond good and evil, it is possible that he may appear equally well as the source of evil which you believe to be ultimately good for man. I am convinced, as I have seen it too often to doubt it, that an apparent evil is really no evil at all if you accept and obediently live it as far as possible, but I am equally convinced that an apparent good is in reality not always good at all but wholly destructive" (Answer to a question from the Rev. David Cox (Jung, 1958/1980, §1640).

3. "Anyone who takes up the question of the Holy Spirit seriously is faced with the question whether Christ is identical with the Holy Spirit or different from him. With dogma, I prefer the independence of the Holy Spirit. The Holy Spirit is *one*, a *complexio oppositorum*, in contrast to YHWH after the separation of the divine opposites symbolized by God's two sons, Christ and Satan. ... It seems to me to be the Holy Spirit's task and charge to reconcile and reunite the opposites in the human individual through a special development of the human soul" (Jung, 1954, §1553).
4. Sonu Shamdasani, in his Preface to Dick Russell's *The Life and Ideas of James Hillman*, New York: Helios Press, 2013, p. xi) has pointed out the originality with which Hillman "took on Jung's daimonic inheritance." (The last three words echo the title of an article by Hillman in *Sphinx*, 1, 1988, pp. 9–19).
5. That this can be a pernicious oversimplification of a psychiatric tragedy was made clear in a recent lecture posted online by Jeffrey A. Lieberman, MD, "Robin Williams' Suicide Had Nothing to Do with Demons" (2014).
6. The reader who doubts the relevance of typological analysis of the real problems of living should read von Franz's monograph.
7. See also *Hamlet,* Act III, Scene 4, lines 175–180: "... but heaven hath pleas'd it so, To punish me with this and this with me, That I must be their scourge and minister. I will bestow him, and will answer well The death I gave him. So, again, good night. I must be cruel only to be kind."
8. See Sandner and Beebe (1995, pp. 329–30) detailing the evidence for my view that Hitler was an introverted sensation type and began to function out of his demonic introverted intuition in the course of his 12-year reign as Third Reich Chancellor. This type assessment is derived from von Franz (1971, p. 68). The way his demonic introverted intuition led him to "bedevil" Germanic mythology is revealed in Margrit Burri's 1978 essay "Repression, Falsification and Bedeviling of Germanic Mythology."
9. This case is presented in my essay "Archetypal Aspects of Masculine Adaptation" (2011) where my emphasis was more on the personal shadow than on the mimetic currents in the merchant seaman culture to which the patient fell prey when depressed.

References

Auden, W. H. (1939). In memory of Ernst Toller. In E. Mendelson (Ed.), *W. H. Auden: Collected Poems*. New York, NY: Vintage International, 249–250.

Beebe, J. (1992). *Integrity in depth*. College Station, TX: Texas A & M University Press.

Beebe, J. (1998). Toward a Jungian analysis of character. In A. Casement (Ed.), *Post-Jungians Today: Key Papers in Contemporary Analytical psychology*. London, UK and New York, NY: Routledge, 53–66.

Beebe, J. (2000). The place of integrity in spirituality. In P. Young-Eisendrath and M. Miller (Eds.), *The Psychology of Mature Spirituality*. London, UK and Philadelphia, PA: Routledge, 11–20.

Beebe, J. (2011). Archetypal aspects of masculine adaptation. In C. Blazina & D. S. Shen-Miller (Eds.), *An International Psychology of Men*. Hove, UK and New York, NY: Routledge, 289–314.

Beebe, J. (2014). Unpacking the eight function-archetypes. *TypeFace, 25*(4), 10–12.

Brooks, J. L. (1997). *As Good as it Gets* (Producer & Director, Motion picture). USA: Tri-Star Films.

Buber, M. (1952). *Eclipse of God.* New York, NY: Harper and Row.

Burri, M. (1978). Repression, falsification and bedeviling of germanic mythology. *Spring Journal, 78*, 88–104.

Camus, A. (1942/2013). *The outsider* (S. Smith, Trans.). London, UK: Penguin Classics.

Diamond, S. A. (1996). *Madness and the Daimonic: The Psychological Genesis of Violence, evil, and Creativity.* Albany, NY: SUNY Press.

Girard, R. (1977). *Violence and the Sacred* (P. Gregory, Trans.). Baltimore, MD: Johns Hopkins University Press.

Haas, L., & Hunziker, M. (2006). *Building Blocks of Personality Type.* Huntington Beach, CA: Unite Business Press.

Henderson, J. L. (1968). Ancient myths and modern man. In C. G. Jung, M-L. von Franz, and J. Freeman (Eds.), *Man and His Symbols.* Garden City, NY: Doubleday, 104–157.

Hill, G. (1998). Men, the anima, and the feminine. *The San Francisco Jung Institute Library Journal, 17*(3), 49–62.

Hillman, J. (1996). *The Soul's Code.* New York, NY: Random House.

Hillman, J. (1998). Jung's daimonic inheritance. *Sphinx, 1*, 9–19.

Jung, C. G. (1917/1953). *Two essays on analytical psychology.* In R. F. C. Hull (Trans.). *Collected Works of C. G. Jung,* volume 7. Princeton, NJ: Princeton University Press.

Jung, C. G. (1921/1971). *Psychological types* In R. F. C. Hull (Trans.). *Collected Works of C. G. Jung,* volume 6, Princeton, NJ: Princeton University Press.

Jung, C. G. (1933/1960). The real and the surreal. In R. F. C. Hull (Trans.). *Collected Works of C. G. Jung,* volume 8, Princeton, NJ: Princeton University Press, 382–384.

Jung, C. G. (1945/1980). The definition of demonism. In R. F. C. Hull (Trans.). *Collected Works of C. G. Jung,* volume 18. Princeton, NJ: Princeton University Press, 648.

Jung, C. G. (1951/1968). Aion: Researches into the phenomenology of the self. In R. F. C. Hull (Trans.). *Collected Works of C. G. Jung,* volume 9, 2nd ed. Princeton, NJ: Princeton University Press.

Jung, C. G. (1954/1959). Archetypes of the collective unconscious. In R. F. C. Hull (Trans.). *Collected Works of C. G. Jung,* volume 9. Princeton, NJ: Princeton University Press, 3–41.

Jung, C. G. (1954/1967). The philosophical tree. In R. F. C. Hull (Trans.). *Collected Works of C. G. Jung,* volume 13, Princeton, NJ: Princeton University Press, 251–349.

Jung, C. G. (1954/1980). Letter to Père Lachat, 27 March, 1954. In R. F. C. Hull (Trans.). *Collected Works of C. G. Jung,* volume 18, Princeton, NJ: Princeton University Press, 679–691.

Jung, C. G. (1958). Answer to Job. In R. F. C. Hull (Trans.). *Collected Works of C. G. Jung,* volume 11. Princeton, NJ: Princeton University Press, 355–470.

Jung, C. G. (1958/1980). Jung and religious belief. In H. L. Philp, (Ed.), *Collected Works of C. G. Jung,* volume 18. Princeton, NJ: Princeton University Press, 702–744.

Jung, C. G. and White, V. (2007). *The Jung-White Letters.* In A. Lammers, A. and C. Cunningham (Eds.), London, UK and New York, NY: Routledge.
Kalsched, D. (1996). *The Inner World of Trauma.* London, UK and New York, NY: Routledge.
Kimbles, S. L. (2014). *Phantom Narratives: The Unseen Contributions of Culture to Psyche.* Lanham, MD: Rowman & Littlefield.
LeRoy, M. (Producer) & Fleming, V. (Director) (1939). *The Wizard of Oz.* (Motion Picture) USA: Metro-Goldwyn-Mayer.
Lieberman, J. A. (2014). Robin Williams' suicide had nothing to do with demons. *Medscape.* Sep. 04, 2014. http://www.medscape.com/viewarticle/830614.
Russell, D. (2013). *The Life and Ideas of James Hillman.* New York, NY: Helios Press.
Salman, S. (2003). Blood payments. In J. Beebe (Ed.), *Terror, violence, and the impulse to destroy.* Einsiedeln, Switzerland: Daimon Verlag, 235–261.
Sandner, D., and Beebe, J. (1995). Psychopathology and analysis. In M. Stein (Ed.), *Jungian Analysis,* 2nd ed. Chicago and La Salle, IL: Open Court Publishing, 297–348.
Shakespeare, W. (1603/1998). *Hamlet* in *The Arden Shakespeare: Complete Works.* Walton-on-Thames, Surrey, UK: Thomas Nelson and Sons, 291–332.
Sharp, D. (1987). *Personality Types: Jung's Model of Typology.* Toronto, ON: Inner City Books.
Singer, T. (2003). Cultural complexes and archetypal complexes of the group spirit. In J. Beebe (Ed.), *Terror, Violence, and the Impulse to Destroy,* Einsiedeln, Switzerland: Daimon Verlag, 191–209.
Singer, T., and Kimbles, S. L. (Eds.). (2004). *The Cultural Complex: Contemporary Jungian Perspectives on Psyche and Society.* London, UK and New York, NY: Routledge.
Stein, M. (Ed.). (1995). *Encountering Jung on evil.* Princeton, NJ: Princeton University Press.
Von Franz, M-L. (1971). The inferior function. In M-L. von Franz and J. Hillman, *Lectures on Jung's typology.* New York, NY: Spring Publications, 1–88.
Von Franz, M-L. (1972). *Problems of the feminine in fairytales,* New York, NY: Spring Publications.
Von Franz, M-L. (2002). *Animus and anima in fairy tales.* D. Sharp (Ed.), Toronto, ON: Inner City Books.
Wheelwright, J. H. (1984). *For women growing older: The animus.* Houston, TX: C. G. Jung Educational Center of Houston.

Part II

The Psychology of Perpetration

Chapter 4

Breaking Bad and the Rhetoric of Evil

Ronald C. Naso

It was not until 17 years after our initial consultation that Nick entered treatment on a twice-weekly basis. When he called to schedule his first appointment, he asked if I had seen a recent newspaper article about him and suggested that I read it prior to meeting with him. Nick was living at home without a job or any apparent source of income. He had been charged with possession of narcotics and accused of a serious assault. I struggled to reconcile my memory of this impressive, promising young man with the story I read in the paper.

Nick provided the following account of what happened: After a series of disappointments in the world of investment banking, he left Wall Street still clinging to the hope that he might start his own company. With virtually no regular income, he bartended and relied heavily on his parents to make ends meet. By the end of his stay in New York City, Nick was selling drugs. He began by supplying co-workers, gradually expanding his activities to include their friends and acquaintances. He rationalized his actions as temporary, but necessary. He said he had every intention of discontinuing illegal activity once he was back on his financial feet. Unfortunately, the money and the lifestyle it afforded were more than he could resist. He brokered several large deals and, for a time, established and ran a small gambling operation. During this time, he drank heavily and abused narcotics and anxiolytics.

Approximately one year before consulting me, Nick was approached by a friend whose business was failing. He had known this man for many years and said he felt sorry for him. Danny had exhausted his financial resources and had nowhere else to turn. He knew Nick had money and connections to people with money. He asked for a loan, promising a handsome return on the investment. He explained that he was having cash flow problems that were temporary and would once again flourish when some renovations were made. Nick agreed to help because, as he explained, he loved Danny and trusted him completely. He added, "loyalty means everything to me and Danny is family." Nevertheless, no one's fool, he structured a deal with very favorable terms.

As the months passed, Danny's business languished. He did not repay Nick and did little to assuage his concerns. Nick was frustrated and upset. Two weeks before the assault, he warned Danny that continued nonpayment would be a "problem." Emboldened by Nick's restraint, Danny did not heed the warning. As they argued one evening, Nick remembered him saying, "you're not going to do shit about it because I know where your family lives." Unsure what happened next, Nick believes his first punch knocked out Danny's front teeth. His next memory, only seconds later, was of Danny laying bloody and unconscious on the floor. Fortunately, Nick had not killed him. When the police arrived, they arrested Nick and rushed Danny to the hospital. A search of Nick's car uncovered a substantial amount of narcotics. With a bond of almost $500,000, he spent several days in jail before his parents posted his bail.

Nick exemplifies the phenomenon of what I shall call "breaking bad," a form of instrumental evil that begins abruptly, typically in response to a dramatic reversal in fortune. It is a response that can have irreversible, life-altering implications. Importantly, its dependence on situational factors and on chance invalidates the claim that it follows directly or necessarily from personality as a whole or existing psychopathology. I shall formulate breaking bad more specifically as an effort to cope with trauma, conflict and adversity notable for the selective deactivation of moral commitments. Like other forms of instrumental evil, it is a destructive, but expedient, compromise that satisfies needs and reduces inner conflict.

Narcissism, paranoia, splitting and projective identification play prominent roles in breaking bad as they do in virtually all forms of instrumental evil. However, recent psychoanalytic investigations of mass violence underscore how powerfully group processes can induce regression, undermine moral judgment and unleash unimaginable destructiveness. That apparently well-established commitments are so facilely deactivated signals the need for an integrative approach to understanding evil.

In this chapter, I shall argue that evil is formulated more aptly as a moral judgment than as a complete or comprehensive psychological explanation of transgressive behavior. This should not be interpreted to mean that it is misapplied to instances of horrific wrongdoing and depraved indifference to others. Rather it is to appreciate the rhetorical function of evil, which is to condemn, ostracize, and segregate those who violate rules and norms. Paradoxically, the mechanisms productive of condemnation are isomorphic with those of heroic idealization, of course with a very different affective valence and evaluative judgment. Both rest on projection, dissociation and splitting. When ascribed to individuals, these mechanisms promote the demonization of perpetrators who, as a result, are regarded as inhuman or monstrous, inhabiting an inner world devoid of human values and respect for the dignity of others.

In contrast to a perspective that uncritically accepts pure evil as a motive, I shall argue that the phenomenon of breaking bad confronts us with behavior whose aims and purposes are recognizably human, however much its consequences may be disproportionately harmful or horrific. Lust, greed, jealousy and revenge figure prominently among its motives. Rather than issuing from unimaginable sources, breaking bad discloses the ever-present potential for good and evil in all of us.

Breaking Bad as Character Pathology

One might argue that Nick's actions were nothing more than a straightforward expression of greed. He wanted to live the good life, to be a player surrounded by an entourage of admirers, and dedicated himself to these goals. He sought a life that was sexy and grand and actively cultivated his image as someone proficient in gaining access to powerful, wealthy people. Contemptuous of those who did not share his values, he reacted immediately, sometimes violently, to those who threatened his security or beliefs. He insisted on receiving the respect he believed he deserved, whether out of fear or love.

Nick enjoyed this fearsome image ambivalently. He was divided in his identification with "thug life" and wished to be seen as a good person who was loyal, generous, fair and forthright. He believed himself to be a principled person who cared about others. He had a wide circle of friends, many of whom he loved and helped in various ways. Yet, in breaking bad, Nick knowingly did wrong. He gratified needs in ways that created conflict and caused pain. He engaged evil instrumentally, which is to say that, at least initially, he might have refrained from wrongdoing if he believed his goals were achievable by morally acceptable means (Svendsen, 2010, p. 85). He never believed his actions were entirely justified by an objective good.

Kernberg (2004a; 2004b) focuses on the role of aggression in the varieties of antisocial behavior observed in breaking bad. He anchors inclinations to violence in the idealization of destructiveness and unconscious identification with a grandiose, transgressive self. Under their sway, the infliction of suffering is intentional rather than inadvertent, expressing a need for power fulfilled only when others fall under one's complete control. The pleasure of victimization follows from an enactment of the unconscious hope that early experiences of helplessness can be magically undone. When victimization transpires in the absence of integrated values, the malignant narcissist delights in his perverse accomplishments (Kernberg, 2007). Violence is a ubiquitous possibility in an individual identified with his own sadistic aggression, who idealizes a vengeful, controlling, repetitively aggressive self immured in a dehumanized subjective world.

One is inclined to see the malignant narcissist as capable of doing evil for evil's sake—that is, of inflicting suffering for no reason other than the destruction itself. However, psychoanalytic investigation establishes how rarely wrongdoing is so motivated. Even when primitive aggression is a prominent aspect of personality, few offenders fully occupy an "anal universe" (Chasseguet-Smirgel, 1984) in which one is completely free to dominate others because all values have been abolished. Typically, morality and transgression coexist, permitting some preservation or appearance of normalcy. With sufficient narrowing of perception, one also can preserve a sense of oneself as principled, even good. While transvaluation is capricious and defies logic, affecting some spheres of life rather than others, it implicitly reflects a continuing recognition of moral authority. One must not confuse selective or even gross failures to honor norms with indifference to their reality requirements (Kernberg, 2007). Effective deception and manipulation depend on accurate appraisal.

Shame frequently catalyzes instrumental evil. As a moral emotion, it powerfully regulates behavior through the unexpected exposure of one's flaws and diminished standing relative to others. To feel shame is to recognize the authority of rules, norms and goals (Lewis 1991) but always within the (fantasized or real) presence of an audience experienced as a source of critical judgment. In this context, morality is contingent rather than universalized and internal. Hidden from "public" view, trangressions may not activate shame. In contrast to guilt, shame is based on the reflexive avoidance of exposure. The shattering sense of powerlessness and defectiveness makes reputation management by any means a compelling motive. It makes the choice between acceptance of one status as a helpless victim or the pursuit of revenge no choice at all.

Grand (2000) focuses special attention on the impact of early, horrific trauma in the histories of individuals who have broken bad. Inspiring shame and dissociative efforts to preserve sanity, its legacy is a kind of psychic death, leaving some victims unable to connect emotionally with others except through the imposition of suffering (Grand, 2000, p. 26). The need to reverse early experiences of helplessness and victimization can unleash horrendous destructiveness. Consider the following diary entry:

> The Petit family passed through their fear and into the calm waters of abject terror, like mesmerized rabbits cornered by a springing predator. To see that fear, that emotional pain I feel inside every day manifested on anothers [sic] face, validates that this pain in me is real; that it exists not only as an apparition in my mind but is reality as well.
>
> (Bennett, 2008)

In 2007, Joshua Komisarjevsky and an accomplice invaded the Petit home in Chesire, CT. After assaulting Dr. Petit and leaving him for dead, they raped and murdered his wife and two daughters. Komisarjevsky sought validation of his suffering by recreating it in another, knowing full well that he was doing wrong and that he could have acted otherwise. Torture was integral rather than incidental to his goal. Freed for several hours from conventional moral prohibitions, he acted without regard for his victims' humanity. Although later expressing regret, Komisarjevsky experienced an intoxicating sense of validation from their reactions. Dissociation and splitting allowed him to take pleasure in the perpetration of evil and, later, to disavow, rationalize and diminish its harm. Stripping the Petits of their humanity made him feel less alone in a world inhabited by dehumanized objects. Yet, despite the overwhelming evidence of his depravity, Komisarjevsky reinterpreted his sexual assaults as consensual, conversations with these desperately frightened people as evidence of intimacy and concern, thus preserving an image of himself as good. His murderous impulses locked away, he regarded himself as someone who respected (and, one suspects, should benefit from) the moral laws he violated. In short, he wanted to be seen and to feel both human and humane.

Breaking Bad and Unconscious Compromise

While narcissism and dissociative defenses figured prominently in Nick's behavior, they did not rise to the level of malignant narcissism. He maintained close relationships with friends and long-term relationships with at least two women he had cared deeply about. Importantly, he seemed capable of commitment to others, particularly to his immediate family where he also demonstrated some capacity to regulate his behavior on the basis of guilt. Caring for others was a source of pride and pleasure. Hence, it is more accurate to say about his antisocial behavior that it reflected a selective deactivation of conventional morality rather than a thorough corruption of it.

The coexistence of other-advancing and self-interested motives within Nick's personality complicated his turn to evil. Rather than following necessarily and inevitably from character, his breaking bad followed from the undoing of a delicate balance that had been established among conflicting forces within him. Part of him desired to *be* good, another to *feel* good—in the latter self state, without particular regard for means. So long as Nick imagined himself as successful, he did not feel diminished by others. He was comfortable with who he was and felt neither temptation nor pressure to engage in criminality. All of this changed when he felt his career deadended. He was devastated by the realization that he could no longer sustain his spectacular lifestyle. Yet he refused to relinquish the fantasy of being a player, of achieving spectacular success. He oscillated between rage at the injustice of his situation and taking comfort in achieving success by whatever means necessary.

Increasingly, the gap between conventional, prosocial strivings and recklessness widened. On the one hand, Nick talked insightfully about his life and the devastating impact of his impulsivity. He acknowledged the destructiveness of his addictions and reckless thrill-seeking. For days and weeks at a time, he was open, tolerant of ambiguity, emotionally placid, and able to countenance the coexistence of love and hate, and to mourn the loss of his previous life. On the other hand, criminality made it possible for him to eat in the finest restaurants and to enjoy VIP status in some of the most exclusive nightclubs. He took great pleasure in outsmarting the authorities, playing them like fools.

When court dates approached or he was confronted with minor disappointments, Nick's presentation changed dramatically. He was visibly shaken rather than self-assured, bubbling over with rage at the idea that a "scuffle" was being treated as such a serious matter. He spoke of the numerous fights he had been in that had never been reported to the police. Real men settled their disagreements directly and physically if necessary; they never involved the police.

For a period of months, Nick also grew more paranoid, fearful that the individuals with whom he had had conflicts might do harm to him or his family. Persecutory anxieties washed over him like a rogue wave. Under their sway, he was incapable of meaningful self-examination and obsessed with how to insure his safety—"let them come after me" he would say. "I'm ready for anything and they'll regret it." Pitted against malevolent forces, he felt he had no choice but to defend himself. In his view, he was not the aggressor, but merely reacting to threats like any other reasonable person would do. "Doc, who wouldn't do the same thing if they were in my shoes?"

The Relevance of Group Psychology

Freud (1921) noticed that the perceptions of group members are deeply influenced by identification with and idealization of their leaders. Members are bound to leaders on the basis of the same feelings of love and loyalty a child feels for its father. Consistent with this relationship, the leader and his values can replace the ego ideal of the individual in a process of regressive dissolution, with disastrous consequences for critical thinking and moral judgment.

Rangell (1980) also emphasized the importance of the individual's identification with charismatic leaders. However, he focused on conflicts arising among moral imperatives and their integration within personality and character. He distinguished reprehensible conduct derivative of superego weakness from chronic failures in moral problem-solving. Evil may result from failures to identify, generalize, extend and sustain one's commitments as easily as it follows from excessively strong desires. Conflict and moral ambiguity contribute to failures of restraint, destabilizing repressions, unleashing aggression, deactivating moral restraints or, more troublingly, reinforcing group interpretations of destructiveness as permissible or praiseworthy. Ethical action requires continuous negotiation internally as well as between self and a wide array of situational factors.

Zimbardo (2008) acknowledges the importance of identification with authority, but argues that individuals are vulnerable to misconduct whenever situations permit diffusion or displacement of responsibility. Evil need not be sanctioned or reinforced by authority. Rather, anonymity often plays a vital role. According to Zimbardo, anonymity explains why unhurried passersby are six times more likely to help someone in need than their hurried counterparts (Darley & Batson, 1973); five times more likely for one to help an apparently injured man who drops his books when ambient noise is at normal rather than at high levels (Matthews & Cannon, 1975) and less likely to intervene during an emergency in the presence of bystanders (Latane & Nida, 1981). The latter finding is particularly disturbing: absent a direct and inescapable personal confrontation with another's distress, most individuals look to others to take action. While these findings do not establish Zimbardo's (2008) sweeping conclusion that there are no "bad apples ... [, only bad] ... barrels" (p. 10), they are consistent with the hypothesis that morally arbitrary situational factors dramatically influence conduct. They suggest that conscience is neither decisive for nor predictive of moral behavior.

The thinking of Rangell and Zimbardo has particular relevance to an understanding of Nick's behavior. Without a devastating series of job losses and the ensuing financial difficulty he experienced, it is unlikely that he would have chosen as he did. Nevertheless, it is difficult to imagine breaking bad as a viable option were it not for his personal history, motives, aspirations and identity. The clinical material strongly suggests that the latter set the stage for transgression and made it possible for Nick to reinterpret his immoral actions as moral. In other words, rationalization, advantageous comparisons and euphemistic descriptions of his behavior permitted him to retain an image of himself as a "good guy" while gratifying forbidden wishes (Bandura, 1990). For a time, he seemed to experience an escape from the oppressive demands of conscience described by Rangell as an "intrapsychic dream come true" (p. 28).

Misconduct is more likely when one (a) finds ways to justify it morally; (b) minimizes the perception of harmful consequences; and/or (c) blames or dehumanizes the victim (Bandura, 1990 p. 27). When these cognitive strategies operate in tandem with personality as a whole, particularly under the pressure of paranoid or narcissistic states, the impact on behavior can be dramatic. Separately or jointly, they offer ways of processing and appraising information, including that which Zimbardo and others describe as situational variables. Ultimately, situational impact will be determined by how these influences aref transformed by the individual, both consciously and unconsciously, in a way that maintains self-continuity. Evil flourishes when cognitive dissonance and identity diffusion are forestalled.

There has been a growing appreciation of these cognitive strategies by psychoanalytic investigators concerned with human rights abuses, mass atrocities, terrorism and trauma (Kernberg, 2003a & 2003b; and Volkan, 2006). For example, Bohm (2006) links normal oscillations between the depressive and paranoid positions to those processes identified by social psychologists as productive of "blind-patriotism" (p. 24). Unable to entertain complexity, and/or empathize with views other than their own, these individuals are threatened by difference, inflexible in processing information contrary to their perspective and capable of selective and nonveridical interpretations of reality. Remarkable about Bohm's thesis is its portrayal of these oscillations as normative, representing perspectives or self states alternately inhabited and abandoned without any necessary connection to moral conduct. Varvin (2005) focuses on the role played by regression in promoting fluidity among self states, particularly in bringing about a pathological outcome described by Bohm as the "closed" mind (p. 24). Regression blocks access to critical thinking, empathy, and trust. It sets the stage for wholesale embrace of radical ideology and demonization of individual differences. Absent judgment and the capacity for critical evaluation, biased perception readily crystallizes into paranoid-autistic inner reality.

The psychoanalytic perspectives are unified by their recognition of the fluidity of human mental states and the role played by trauma in the regressive activation of paranoid thinking. When individuals or groups feel disenfranchised, oppressed, powerless and afraid, the emergence of more primitive mental states and destructiveness are the rule rather than the exception. While those with sadistic trends are most likely to succumb, the real problem of evil resides in "bystanders" who remain passive in the face of gross inhumanity. Passivity out of fear of reprisal is understandable; all too often, however, it mediated straightforwardly by the degree of anonymity afforded by the situation. Evil is more likely when potential responses are supported by group expectations. The data overwhelmingly support the conclusion that few individuals resist group pressures and most willingly relinquish their knowledge or what they believe to be true when it is not shared by the group (Asch, 1955). It is the exceptional individual who takes a stand in the face of strong conformity pressures.

The social psychological and psychoanalytic perspectives on evil converge in a deeper way in recognizing the primary role played by narcissism. While this term is rarely employed outside of psychoanalysis, its multifactorial structure encompasses traits of social desirability, impression or reputation management as well as self-efficacy, self-esteem, and mastery experience. Transgression may satisfy destructive wishes and enhance self-efficacy, bringing one closer to others whose respect and admiration is highly valued. Preservation of identity and positive self-appraisals are powerful reasons to deceive oneself into believing that one's actions are justified. Sadly, sometimes the appearance of morality trumps the reality of being moral. The latter entails greater sacrifices and can bring one into conflict with others as well as with oneself. Rationalization and self-deception relieve attachment insecurity.

Deconstructing Nick

Nick entered the job market after college fired by ambition but was unable to find anything but entry level positions at second tier firms, doing work that was completely uninteresting to him. He wanted to broker multimillion dollar deals, but was relegated to the back office where he provided technical data to more senior associates. The first two firms he worked for folded within six months; another let him go almost as soon as it hired him. Not that it mattered, because his salary never covered his expenses. Sadly, without parental support, he could not afford to remain in these positions. After a fourth position imploded, he felt something change inside him. Angry rather than depressed, he was consumed by the idea that he would prove those who fired him wrong. The man who imagined he could do anything could not find or sustain an "ordinary" job. Enraged at his lack of power and control, he refused to acknowledge fear or failure.

Precipitously, he decided to jettison his banking career. As he put it, "I just said, 'fuck it!'" He said he could make more money bartending than he had as a banker and would use his free time to secure investment capital for several business ideas he had. He did not plan to sell drugs but found that it was an easy way to make money. Besides, "I was really good at it. People wanted to buy from me and hang out—it got to the point that I rarely had to pay for drugs. My buddies just gave it to me."

For a time, Nick was living large. He spoke excitedly and with a sense of pride about suitcases filled with cash, mounds of cocaine, and parties lasting for days at a time. As his addiction deepened and friends died or went to jail, he recognized that he was in trouble. In more lucid moments, he thought about sobriety but, surrounded by friends or feeling the pangs of withdrawal, desire prevailed. In sessions, he acknowledged having confused happiness with money, pleasure with reckless thrill-seeking and the nightmare he had created. Alone and feeling empty, he now admitted that the 'good life' had been no good for a long time.

In treatment, Nick struggled with the realization that he was ill-suited for life on Wall Street. He was far too restless to sit in front of a computer monitor all day. Bright, handsome, and charismatic, he was a people person. Women loved him, and he seemed to be a man's man—athletic and unflinching in the face of adversity. Attention to detail, sitting through team meetings and memorizing procedures were painful. At a more basic level, he struggled to rouse himself from sleep before 9:00 am. His white collar literally was suffocating him, making it impossible to breathe. He took no comfort in the hope that he might work his way to the top, nor could he invest himself in anything he imagined would bring less than immediate and spectacular success. The job losses had been devastating on a number of levels but perhaps most poignantly because they confronted him with the possibility of being ordinary. Failure was not an option.

Nick also felt paralyzed by his legal troubles. He wanted to travel, do "big deals" but was unemployable because of the very public criminal charges he faced. At times, the tension he felt was so great that he could barely refrain from slamming his fist on my table. He proclaimed that he didn't care what happened. He wanted to go to jail immediately so that he could just "get this over with," claiming he was sure he could "do the time." "I can handle myself if I have to; I'm not afraid of anyone" he said. At the conclusion of such rants, his mood typically softened. With sadness in his voice, he described how devastating this ordeal was on his parents and reiterated his determination to cause them no further pain. Unconcerned about consequences or his own welfare, he was mindful of the potential impact of his actions on those he loved.

As the criminal case against him languished in court, Nick became convinced that he was the subject of a federal investigation. He based this conclusion on curious clicking sounds discernible on his cell phone and on cars he was certain followed him about town. On one occasion, he angrily pursued one of these vehicles, following its occupant several miles to a shopping center and into a retail store. There he locked eyes with an unidentified man, explaining to me that he wanted him to know he was neither afraid of nor intimidated by this harassment. Fortunately, he did not confront the man. It was a frightening moment when I feared that violence was a real possibility.

While I was concerned about his paranoia and anger, Nick's past activities and ties to individuals in organized crime made it possible that he might be part of a larger investigation: unlikely, but possible. Hence, I decided to address the striking omission of fear in all that he reported. I said to Nick that, on the one hand, he presented himself as a warrior: battle-ready, committed, and without fear; on the other hand, as someone who felt powerless and afraid. Rather than reacting angrily, Nick sighed and sat silently in reflection before speaking. He said that he hated feeling helpless but recognized that this was the reality of his situation. He was being persecuted for a matter that should have been settled man to man.

More than frustration, Nick struggled to speak of his fears. It was an emotion he could not avow, let alone talk about with others. "Being a man means never showing weakness—and, let's face it Doc, fear is weakness." When queried about how he came to this view, he simply shrugged. Later, as I pressed him about seeking comfort when he felt fear as a child, he seemed to drift off into deep thought. He spoke of his father's temper and the displays of violence so frequent among the male members of his extended family. Family gatherings often involved excessive drinking, arguments, and physical altercations. "Boxing" matches among the cousins were encouraged, sometimes for sport, sometimes to resolve disputes. He found himself as the main event, frightened, unprotected, and completely on his own.

In a particularly intense session, Nick tearfully confided that he had been regularly abused by a paternal uncle between the ages of 6 and 12. Out of fear he had never told anyone. Addicted to alcohol and drugs, his uncle regularly lost his temper and beat his children and Nick with whatever he could get his hands on: kitchen utensils, belts, shoes and, if all else failed, his fists. He was a big, powerful man with a reputation for violence. Frightened beyond description, Nick made a point of never letting on that he was afraid, never backing down and, on occasion, taking blows to protect his female cousin from her father. Increasingly, he disconnected what he showed to others from what he felt.

From Nick's perspective, there was simply no way to communicate to his parents what was happening. He made the conscious decision to countenance occasional beatings in order to spend time with his cousins, whom he adored. More selfishly, he refused to relinquish the unsupervised freedom he enjoyed at his uncle's house. In a stuporous state, his uncle sometimes handed the kids hundred dollar bills, instructing them to "get lost." He and his cousins walked to town to "get lost" for the entire day.

At a deeper level, Nick struggled with the realization that his father had failed him profoundly. He was therefore not entirely the man Nick had imagined him to be. Nick's bruises were quite noticeable and hard to explain. His father knew better than anyone what his brother was capable of. He knew of his substance use and proclivity for violence; certainly he was aware that his brother had physically abused his ex-wife. Knowing this, how could he let Nick spend unsupervised time there? How could he let him go there at all? What was he thinking? What did he make of the bruises he saw on Nick's body, the occasional swollen lip or blackened eye? How could he not be suspicious?

Because men act like men, Nick's father seemed to accept the situation at face value. The kids had been roughhousing, doing what kids do. Nick did nothing to clarify matters. He idealized rather than resented his father despite this catastrophic failure. Consciously, he could only speak of their special bond. He asked rhetorically: "How could I show weakness to someone whose love and admiration I so desperately needed?" To show weakness was to risk everything, and Nick learned rather quickly to unleash all of his anger, disappointment and frustration on his adversaries. To take down a bully, stand up for himself or others, and right a wrong was "better than any drug."

The Rhetoric of Evil

Prominent in Nick's personality were a keen sense of justice and propensity to aggression. Vigilant to unfairness and others' efforts to control him, he remained loyal to friends but no longer experienced their distress as a call to action. After entering treatment, he no longer felt obligated to make their problems his own. He cared deeply but recognized that his feelings were likely to place him in jeopardy.

Nick's life had changed for the better, and he worked hard to distance himself from high risk situations and destructive relationships. He resisted the lure of danger and made a conscious effort to evaluate the corrupting influences in his life, slowly learning to negotiate more constructive compromises. He took pride in a newfound sense of self-control and ability to choose good over evil. Curtailing his substance use facilitated self-regulation.

At a deeper level, Nick glimpsed the possibility that idealization had blinded him from a more realistic assessment of his father and of himself. Ultimately, it reinforced the belief that the qualities he admired were beyond his reach. Only spectacular success, however achieved, might fulfill his dreams and transform him into the heroic figure he imagined his father to be. When this core fantasy was threatened, he did whatever was necessary to keep it alive. He experienced the means as regrettable but ultimately as something he had no choice about. As Grand (2010) so insightfully notices, Nick's perception of his father and of his own possibilities emboldened him by immunizing him against fear. Heroic idealization protected him from uncertainty as long as he believed his vision could be realized, despite his growing awareness of his father's and his own flaws. Through idealization, Nick transformed his father into what he wanted and needed him to be; a powerful, protective figure who tacitly took pride in his son's breaking bad.

Is Nick evil? The answer to this question clearly depends on how one defines it. Construed as profound immorality, wickedness and depravity, evil involves harmful actions and the intentional infliction of suffering, whether perpetrated by an individual, group or institution. It involves actions that are repetitive or persistent, not commensurate with provocation and produce extreme harm (Staub, 1999). That being said, it is also the case that evil actions need not be the worst imaginable. Albeit extreme and disproportionate, evil often arises from normal rather than pathological psychological and social processes (Staub, 2012); it is observed in otherwise normal, moral individuals.

To be sure, Nick's assaultive behavior, drug trafficking and other nefarious activities caused foreseeable and substantial harm. It is therefore reasonable to describe them as evil. Yet, it would be incorrect to claim that Nick engaged in these activities *because* he was evil. As a descriptive term, evil makes a moral claim. It expresses attitudes, inclinations and emotions toward actions one believes are impermissible. It is as if one is saying that certain actions are wrong and "you should feel this way too!"

In contrast to its moral or emotive function, evil also is used to explain wrongdoing. It is pressed into service as if it were a sufficient condition of perpetration. Used in this way, the concept of evil embroils one in what Bernstein (2002) describes as the "black hole" problem (p. 235). Simply put, the black hole problem reflects the inherent incompleteness of causal accounts of evil, no matter how thoroughly one inventories the motives, intentions, circumstances and character of the agent. As Bernstein suggests, "there is much we can say about someone's background, training, education, character ... [, and] ... circumstances(,) ... [b]ut it never adds up to a complete explanation of why individuals make the choices they do" (p. 23).

Rather than closing the gap in one's understanding, reliance on the concept of evil widens it and exposes its status as a category error.

The most serious consequence of mistaking evil for a cause is its diminishment of the vital role played by agency. Moral responsibility depends on the fact that one makes choices about what one does, especially in circumstances in which one could have chosen otherwise. Saying one's actions followed from character and/or situation as if unmediated by choice, causes individual history, motives and beliefs to become both incomprehensible and unnecessary because they are regarded as operating outside the scope of human intentionality. Just as idealization robs the hero of his real human interior (Grand, 2010), the misappropriation of the term evil demonizes and renders its object unrecognizable as a *human* subject, driven by *human* motives. We may condemn one's actions in the strongest possible way without relinquishing Sullivan's (1930) insight that "we are all more simply human than otherwise" (p. 32).

Evil is not an empirical property that can be verified like a nonmoral property. When one says "murder is wrong," one makes a decidedly different claim than one does in saying that "John's hair is black" or "Carmelo Anthony scored 35 points in his last basketball game." Not only is the former opaque to verification in the same way as hair color or points accumulated during a competition but also may be false. For example, it is factually incorrect that murder or torture is universally wrong despite one's general disapproval of these practices. Why? Because one can imagine circumstances that might justify such actions (murders sanctioned during the course of war; "one-off" instances of torture to save the life on an innocent child, etc.), revealing the fact that moral permissibility varies according to time, place and culture.

Should we dispose of the concept of evil altogether? Can it be replaced by terms like "very bad, horrific or egregious?" I do not think so. Despite its difficulties, evil plays a vital role in moral discourse and our moral deliberations. It focuses attention on the nature and extent of wrongdoing and frames our perception of those who violate norms and cause harm to others. The real danger is not its meaning but rather its use as a rhetorical device that demonizes a wide array of wrongful acts and explains them as products of natural, nonagentic, nonhuman forces. It reinforces the perception of evil as an action perpetrated by monsters, solely on the basis of inclinations that cannot be shared or empathized with. They are not like us, but rather inflict suffering for its own sake rather than to fulfill a comprehensible, if misguided, human end. For this reason, they are not part of our moral community, instead occupying a world we imagine as devoid of human values.

Is there an alternative to the pure, causal notion of evil that does not undermine one's ability to condemn, punish and make every effort to prevent it? I think there is. Simply put, it requires that one resist the temptation to dissociate the traumatic reality of evil's consequences and the very human motives and intentions that inspire wrongdoing. This, in turn, requires acknowledgement of the fine line between good and evil as well as of one's inherent vulnerability to wrongdoing when inner restraints are not activated for a variety of reasons. To resist dissociation involves a courageous confrontation with the implications of actions, both imagined and real, that are painful to avow because they cast one in an unfavorable light. Only by critically evaluating oneself in light of what one does can one's moral center be preserved. It is also how one can begin to understand the processes that undergird engagements with evil.

Conclusion

I have argued that Nick's early family experiences laid the groundwork for a perspective in which he felt unable to choose a course of action that made him feel anything less than a man. He could not countenance fear, disappointment or anything less than spectacular success. Hence, to forgive the money Danny owed him amounted to being played for a fool. It rendered him powerless to right what he perceived as a wrong. The experience of helplessness unconsciously reproduced the traumatic abuse he suffered at the hands of his uncle and resurrected the bind he experienced with his father whom he felt would not respect him if he did not take care of business. His reactions were immediate and unformulated. More broadly, his breaking bad, his turn to evil, represented a compromise among these forces and influences, one that reduced inner tension and preserved his identity as moral and good.

Taken to the extreme, this argument might be construed as validating the claim that Nick's actions were shaped by factors beyond his control. Indeed, once it is acknowledged that evil is not a property, essence or element preprogrammed within personality, but instead reflects one among myriad potentials nurtured over the course of one's life, one must acknowledge that Nick had no control over influences that were likely decisive in shaping his behavior. These influences include, but are not limited to, family, interpersonal relationships and social/cultural experiences, as well as his biological makeup. If his character is a product of such forces, are we justified in holding him accountable for the actions that followed from it?

Although highlighting tensions between psychological and moral evaluations of evil, this argument draws a false dichotomy between understanding and exculpation, explanation and personal choice (Cole, 2006). While it is true that people do not choose their character or the traumas shaping it, they are not compelled to break bad. The linkages between early experience and behavior are complex and multifactorial, and one rarely is without choices or alternative courses of action. Understanding all possible factors as well as options reasonably available places us in a better position to understand why the agent chose as he did (Cole, 2006). To act repeatedly on destructive impulses when one is not compelled to do so is worthy of condemnation, even if one can empathize and therefore place in a more human light the various forces that contributed to one's choices. However, to interpret any and all behavior in which chance plays some role as outside the realm of ordinary moral discourse is unwarranted. As Svendsen claims, "We can blame a perpetrator, but we can't blame a dysfunction—a dysfunction can merely be corrected" (Svendsen, 2010, p. 22). He argues that this kind of reductionism undermines moral standards and, importantly, any basis for personal accountability and guilt. It destabilizes the concept of agency altogether by suggesting that no one is ever fully responsible for anything.

While Nick struggled with revealing weakness and showing others how he felt, it is inaccurate to claim he could not have handled the situation differently. The very possibility of change and redemption rests on the reality of this capacity. To this point, it is significant that Nick ultimately confided that he never felt threatened by Danny, despite his being a formidable figure in his own right. Nick knew that Danny was not violent and was just "talking shit." Hence, what he conveyed as a dissociative act—as he later clarified, was more a figure of speech than an altered state of consciousness. In the end, he acted out of anger rather than fear; he wanted to teach Danny a lesson.

It will be recalled that Aristotle (1984) departed from the Socratic alignment of knowledge and ethical action. To know the good, to have a vision of it fixed clearly in mind, was for Socrates to do good. Evil was a form of error, an expression of ignorance or distraction from what one knows. Aristotle was more realistic about human nature in allowing for wrongdoing born of excessive desire or failures of restraint. For this reason, he emphasized the cultivation of evaluative skills that permit one to identify possible courses of action and choose judiciously among them. Motives, intentions and dispositions were important but not determinative. Rather, one strives to find the mean between extremes of excess and deficiency, knowing that one can never fully know in advance what the consequences of one's decisions will be.

This view resonates with contemporary views of morality that understand ethical conduct as a product of highly evolved skills that permit recognition, inquiry and playful reformulation of self as well as the creative management of adversity. These capacities are neither fixed dispositions nor modularized skills, but rather depend on an array of cognitive-affective processes that require the selection and implementation of problem-solving strategies. Character is creative because it depends on and transcends existing capacities, inspiring actions that often are unexpected and unscripted. In the ethical sphere, it is linked to situations in which one must take a stand. However, even knowing that one will be tested is not at all to know how and in what circumstances and what will be required.

Breaking bad is one possible response to adversity. It is a compromise that unfolds simultaneously at conscious and unconscious levels, integrating and sometimes failing to integrate or refashion these influences in a prosocial way. Conscience of course plays a vital role, but only when it is regarded as offering guidelines for moral conduct rather than representing a fixed disposition leading invariably to moral behavior. Standards and inner imperatives can be selectively engaged or disengaged. Moral standards that are not activated are essentially no standards at all. How these influences are refashioned may be productive of character pathology by virtue of being promoted and reinforced by influential individuals and family members as well as by groups, institutions or cultures. Viewed in this way, one can appreciate why evil often occurs only in selected spheres of one's life. It explains how it is possible to be a devoted father and loving spouse while torturing inmates by day, drug trafficking or reaping the rewards of a Ponzi scheme by night. One is most likely to do so when one believes one has no choice, is responding to a perceived threat or injustice, or believes one's enemies to be less than human.

Without agency and choice, one can have misfortune, even destruction, but not evil. Hence, to speak of character and of ethical life more generally is to privilege performances over dispositions, actions over reasoning or deliberation. Contrary to Socratic wisdom, moral conduct requires more than a commitment to fair, just and rational standards. It means doing the right thing—which is to say, fashioning choices on the basis of values like compassion, fairness, respect and human concern in a way that does not require conscious formulation.

References

Aristotle. (1984). *Nichomachean ethics*. In J. Barnes (Ed.), *The Complete Works of Aristotle* (Vol. 1). Princeton, NJ: Princeton University Press.

Asch, S.E. (1955). Opinions and social pressure. *Scientific American, 193*, 31–35.

Bandura, A. (1990). Selective activation and disengagement of moral control. *Journal of Social Issues, 46*, 27–46.

Bennett, H. (2008). CT State Police, Chesire triple homicide interview with Komisarjevsky, *Tape 1, side 1 of 2, State 189b, 9–22, Part 1, New Haven Register*, http://www.scribd.com/doc/66451297/State-s-189b-9-22-Part-1, downloaded 10/15/2013.

Bernstein, R. J. (2002). *Radical Evil: A Philosophical Interrogation*. Cambridge, UK: Polity Press.

Bohm, T. (2006). Psychoanalytic aspects of perpetrators of genocide: Experiences from Rwanda. *Scandinavian Psychoanalytic Review, 29*, 22–32.

Chasseguet-Smirgel, J. (1984). *Creativity and Perversion*. New York, NY: Norton.

Cole, P. (2006). *The Myth of Evil: Demonizing the Enemy*. Westport, CT: Praeger.

Darley, J., & Batson, C. D. (1973). From Jerusalem to Jericho: A study of situational and dispositional variables in helping behavior. *Journal of Personality and Social Psychology, 27*, 100–108.

Freud, S. (1975/1921). *Group psychology and the analysis of the ego. The Standard Edition of the Complete Psychological Works of Sigmund Freud,* Vol. XVIII, 67–144. London, UK: Hogarth Press. (Original work published, 1921).

Freud, S. (1975/1930). *Civilization and its discontents*. In J. Strachey (Ed. & Trans.), *The Standard Edition of the Complete Psychological Works of Sigmund Freud, 21*, 59–148. London, UK: Hogarth Press. (Original work published 1930).

Grand, S. (2000). *The Reproduction of Evil: A Clinical and Cultural Perspective*. Hillsdale, NJ: The Analytic Press.

Grand, S. (2010). *The Hero in the Mirror from Fear to Fortitude*. New York, NY: Routledge.

Kernberg, O. (2003a). Sanctioned social violence: A psychoanalytic view, Part I. *International Journal of Psychoanalysis, 84*, 683–698.

Kernberg, O. (2003b). Sanctioned social violence: A psychoanalytic view, Part II. *International Journal of Psychoanalysis, 84*, 953–968.

Kernberg, O. (2004a). The concept of drive in the light of contemporary psychoanalytic theorizing. In *Contemporary Controversies in Psychoanalytic Theory, technique, and their Applications*, 48–59. New Haven, CT: Yale UP.

Kernberg, O. (2004b). Hatred as a core affect of aggression. In *Aggressivity, Narcissism, and Self-destructiveness in the Psychoanalytic Process*, 27–44. New Haven, CT: Yale UP.

Kernberg, O. (2007). The almost untreatable narcissistic patient. *Journal of the American Psychoanalytic Association, 55*, 503–539.

Latané, B., & Nida, S. (1981). Ten years of research on group size and helping. *Psychological Bulletin, 89*, 308–324.

Lewis, M. (1991). Self-conscious emotions and the development of self. *Journal of the American. Psychoanalytic Association, 39*, 45–73.

Matthews, K. E., & Cannon, L. K. (1975). Environmental noise level as a determinant of helping behavior. *Journal of Personality and Social Psychology, 32*, 571–577.

Rangell, L. (1980). *The Mind of Watergate: An Exploration of the Compromise of integrity*. New. York, NY: Norton.

Rangell, L. (2000). A psychoanalytic view of the impeachment process. *Psychoanalytic Dialogues, 10*, 309–313.

Staub, E. (1999). The roots of evil: Personality, social conditions, culture and basic human needs. *Personality and Social Psychology Review, 3*, 179–192.

Staub, E. (2012). The psychology of morality in genocide and violent conflict: Perpetrators, passive bystanders, rescuers. In M. Mukulincer & P. Shaver (Eds.), *The Social Psychology of Morality*. Washington, DC: APA Press.

Stein, A. (2007). *Prologue to Violence. Child Abuse, Dissociation, and Crime*. Hillsdale, NJ: The Analytic Press.

Sullivan, H. S. (1930). *Schizophrenia as a Human Process*. New York, NY: Norton, 1962.

Svendsen, Lars. (2010). *A Philosophy of Evil*. (K. Pierce, Transl). Chicago, IL: Dalky Archive Press. Originally Published, 2001.

Varvin, S. (2005). Humiliation and the victim identity in conditions of political and violent conflict. *Scandinavian Psychoanalytic Review, 28*, 40–49.

Volkan, V. D. (2006). *Killing in the Name of Identity: A Study of Bloody conflicts*. Charlottesville, VA: Pitchstone Publishing.

Zimbardo, P. (2008). *The Lucifer Effect: Understanding how Good People Turn Evil*. New York, NY: Random House.

Chapter 5

Predatory Identity

Robert Prince

This essay approaches evil by hypothesizing a particular variant of identity, "predatory identity," as one of its sources and elucidating its manifestations, paradoxes and contradictions by looking first to a case study of characters from a fictional series. The main recommendation for this choice is its enormous current popularity; the second, the historical record, primarily from the last century. Predatory identity is proposed as a psychoanalytic framework particularly suited for understanding evil.

The formation and consolidation of identity is a crucial developmental task linked to creativity and the achievement of "the good." For Erikson (Erikson, 1950; Singer, 1965), identity formation supersedes successful identification, which in some ways is antagonistic to it, as the primary developmental task. However, the concept of identity, having had a moment in the psychoanalytic sun, has been cast off on the shoals of ego psychology, presumably having insufficient depth to merit psychoanalytic attention given competing concepts and eclipsed by interest in the concept of self to which it is intertwined and without which it cannot be defined. More modern conceptions of the self, with a de-emphasis on a unitary self, are particularly inhospitable to the exploration of identity. Ironically, as it presumably sits on the surface of consciousness, it has an outsized impact on lived life and human relations. Even Volkan (1997 & 2002), who relies on the concept of identity to explicate terrorism and ethnic violence by using the metaphor of a layer of clothing that covers the person, simultaneously demonstrates the power of identity and a reservation that deeper strata are the proper subject for psychoanalysis. In this regard, Levenson's (1980) application of Oscar Wilde's quip that only a superficial mind is not concerned with appearances, which explores the primacy of surfaces, is *appropriate* for consideration of the external manifestations that constitute identity. People often seem less aroused to actions on a grand scale by deep personal concerns and more moved and motivated by external definition of who they are, most obviously race, religion and ethnic heritage. Of paramount importance to identity, encapsulating many of these visible parameters, are beliefs, perceptions and cognitions that aggregate into belief systems. These are crucibles not only of individual identity but also of group identity. Often, to those outside the group, the shared beliefs seem incomprehensible, deluded or absurd. But what is seen to be true, or factual, is that which has been measured through the surveying instrument of individual identity within the group and group identity within the individual. The sociologist George Tilly (2006) shows that the explanatory principles we adopt arise out of our group affiliation. Both group and individual identity become what the cognitive psychologists call a "heuristic,"(Kahneman, 2011) arguably the most powerful one, through which the world is organized and understood. Heuristics may intertwine; for example, the heuristic of race or gender may be more or expressed in ideologies with any component more or less implicit, salient or saturated.

The inextricable connection of group to individual identity is foundational to consideration of evil because it is through identifications with group values, beginning with the family unit, that the superego forms. Erikson's conceptualization of identity, though it referenced the conscious and was located near "the social surface" (Erikson, 1970, p. 19) was anything but superficial. It was scaffolded on his developmental model; a lifelong developmental schema beginning in the earliest mother-child exchanges, reaching a crescendo during adolescence and proceeding throughout the life cycle. Central to identity is a consolidation of the experience of a central self that has cohesion, continuity and definitions that include gender and sexual orientation, as well as layers of group membership, beginning with family and including ethnic, religious and national affiliations.

Erikson (1970) uses the word *ideology* to describe belief systems and sees these as having a central role in organizing the world. It makes "facts amenable to ideas, and ideas to facts in order to create a world image convincing enough to support the collective and individual sense of identity" (p. 22). Thus, for Erikson, constructivism might be thought of as identity seeking a reality to support and reinforce itself. This lapidary insight reflects the primacy of identity in what we believe individually and collectively and unravels the mystery of the persistence and dominance of the most absurd, extreme and demonstrably false ideas. These are not discarded even when overwhelmed by evidence, because they are functionally entwined with the dynamics of identity. Thus, the most hideous prejudices persist and justify horrific acts because they support identity. The demands of practices, which might once have been instrumental, when they become incorporated into identity, threaten future adaptation and even transcend survival. Diamond's (2005) study of "collapsed" civilizations demonstrates that practices that have become catastrophic are maintained despite leading to the civilization's extinction because these practices have become part of its identity.

The concept of identity is distinctive in psychoanalysis precisely because it simultaneously involves the inner and outer dimensions of the person, a duality Lichtenstein (1977) identifies as "the dilemma" of identity, namely, that it has "the component of being objectified by itself and also by the others including the social world in which it is located. Thus, the self-sameness and continuity that defines identity also include the continuity of one's meaning for others" (p. 159). Central to Erikson's concept is group membership, belonging and affiliation as a key component of identity. This group component of identity differentiates the terminology of identity from the terminology of self, adding to it a second dimension. On an even larger scale, consideration of identity brings into psychoanalysis the dimension of the circumscribed lived reality of the person in connection to the grand reality of history. Erikson (1946) describes "the individual's ego identity in relation to the historical changes which dominated his childhood milieu." He goes on. "Men who share an ethnic area, an historical era, or an economic pursuit are guided by common images of good and evil. Infinitely varied, these images reflect the elusive nature of historical change; yet in the form of contemporary social models, of compelling prototypes of good and evil, they assume decisive concreteness in every individual's ego development. Psychoanalytic ego psychology has not matched this concreteness with sufficient theoretical specificity" (p. 359). Thus, to understand identity and to recognize evil requires understanding history.

Implicit in Erikson's approach is an absolutely extraordinary perspective: Human identity is temporally bi-directional. He looks at identity in terms of human self-sameness rooted in continuity from the past and also, in his attunement to historical crises, in terms of the human trait of self transformation—the ability and propensity to become something new, to undergo revolution. In other words, successful identity formation requires simultaneous preservation of the past and the creation of the future.

There are two other categorizations of identity to which predatory identity is being added and compared. Psychiatrically, identity diffusion, that is fragmentation and a failure of cohesion, is the pathology of identity most often attributed to destructive outcomes and personal breakdown. Other pathologies certainly have a bearing on it: frank psychosis, congenital psychopathy, impaired ego, executive or intellectual functioning and affective dysregulation. Other psychodynamics can provide a shape for identity; for example, obsessional structures can easily be seen as contributing to ideologies of purity. Predatory identity should be contrasted to Erikson's "negative identity," a complex concept that contains within it the potential for: (a) growth through differentiation from the group; (b) "criminality" through anti-social rebellion and rejection of group ideals; and (c) submission to destructive new group ideals fostered by historical contingencies. Erikson (1970) writes:

> Every person and every group harbors a *negative identity* as the sum of all those identifications and identity fragments which the individual had to submerge in himself as undesirable or irreconcilable or which his group has taught him to perceive as the mark of fatal "difference" in sex role or race, in class or religion. In the event of aggravated crises,

> an individual (or, indeed, a group) may despair of the ability to contain these negative elements in a positive identity. A specific rage can be aroused wherever identity development thus loses the promise of an assured wholeness: an as yet uncommitted delinquent, if denied any chance of communal integration, may become a "confirmed" criminal. ... In periods of collective crisis, such potential rage is shared by many and is easily exploited by psychopathic leaders, who become the models of a sudden surrender to total doctrines and dogmas in which the negative identity appears to be the desirable and the dominant one. (p. 20)

Erikson here is struggling with the vicissitudes of identity during normative "crises" and adolescent delinquency, and though writing during the particular counter-culture movement of the 1960s clearly referencing the "psychopathic" identity of the previous generation that saw the massive depredations wrought by totalitarian regimes. For him, negative identity contains both the threat of the evils on a mass scale and the promise of a leap into the future that would later be theorized by the historian Eelco Runia (2007 & 2010). The promise of negative identity as a step toward identity formation is that it constitutes, according to Singer (1965), "a type of identification process in reverse, i.e., a process of rejecting deeply established identifications for the sake of establishing new identifications" (p. 170). For Singer, the statement, "This is not I," is a potential step to the development of identity. He observes that there are also those whose identity is so tenuous and insecure that they reject the identity of others as an immediate threat to their own sense of self; describing a "negative and denying orientation ... [that] is all that can be mustered in support of a sense of identity. ... [They] behave as if they had experienced any agreement as so dangerous that they cannot afford mutually affirmative interaction with others. 'No' is their watchword" (p. 170).

There can be variants of insufficient identity. The articulation of any particular vector of identity, be it race, gender or religion can be overly rigid, stereotyped or conversely impoverished and devoid of content. They can be conflicted, as for example when a person strives to consolidate a particular dimension but cannot integrate other aspects. There can also be conflicts between identities; a classic one is the so-called Jewish Question of the nineteenth century that imputed the impossibility of having a simultaneous national identity and Jewish identity. Any dimension of identity can be flattened, narrowed or impoverished. This is true of any of the attributes by which we define ourselves but especially true of ideology, which can be so rudimentary that while it functions as a heuristic, it also fails as a successful one. Ideology can subsume all the others, e.g., an ideology of religion can have a bearing on beliefs about sexual orientation and thus conflicts between religious identity and gender identity.

Predatory identity may be thought of as a verb, adjective or noun; as an aspect of identity, more or less salient or as a distinct categorization. Its claim as a distinct type is its construction of itself by directing itself against the other. Negative identity can have an ultimately constructive or destructive course and may be on a continuum with, may be a specific variation of or even be distinct altogether from insufficient identity. In pure form, predatory identity has the defining character of destroying the identity of the other. Like an animal consuming its prey, it sustains itself by predation. Predatory identity is intolerant of any identity alternative to itself. It enunciates sentences like "To be me I have to destroy who you are," "If you are something other than I am, I cannot be me" or "for me to be me you cannot be something that is not me; I must transform you into who I am." And ultimately, "*my* destruction of you is who I am."

Predatory identity is a source of evil that may contain, express or emanate from well-known dynamisms including sadism, malignant narcissism and envy. It encompasses readily observable phenomenon, assaults an individual or group on the identity of others. Echoes of it are found in universal cognitive processes such as confirmation bias and cognitive dissonance. Specific examples of it are in the newspaper everyday from schoolyard bullying to racist actions or even rooting for a different sports team. Since belief systems are integral to identity, evidence of another belief system can produce rage and reactions ranging from a scotoma to cognitive filtering of dissonant perceptions to violent persecution of those who are "other." Religion provides the oldest and most obvious example of the extremes of violence in the service of promoting particular faiths and the viciousness of suppressing heresies even as extreme cruelty runs counter to the religious tenet.

Many candidates for predatory identity, individuals for whom predation on the identity of others takes priority over other motivations, suggest themselves from across the ages and include such as Caligula, Tamerlane, Torquemada, Rasputin, Stalin, Pol Pot, and Mao. Each of these exists in relation to particular cultural and historical circumstances that enable and color the evil he enables. The extraordinarily popular book and Television Series *Game of Thrones,* described by a reviewer in the estimable *London Review of Books* (Lanchester, 2013) as being "addictive," provides a fictional representation of the interplay among negative, diffuse and predatory identity and their enabling circumstance. *Game,* though set in an imaginary dystopia, located according to critics somewhere between the Sopranos' New Jersey and Middle Earth, convincingly evokes a broad range of actual *lieux de histoires* and as a reviewer in the very real and present *Foreign Affairs* avers (Carpenter, 2012) interrogates the complexity of identity, power and moral order. *Game of Thrones*, by consistently shifting point of view, leaves no shibboleth untested as it follows a host of characters through the vicissitudes of evildoing and identity.

Two linked characters, Ramsay and Theon, provide case studies that may illustrate the operation of predatory identity. Ramsay is the son of Rose Bolton, whose noble house has as its escutcheon a Flayed Man representing the preferred technique for terrorizing both its enemies and its subjects. Ramsay carries the last name Snow, designating him as an illegitimate son, thus unrecognized in his own right by the social order but who may be rewarded for his obedience and usefulness by the indulgence of his sadistic pleasures. One of these is giving chase to innocent, powerless girls whose situation is hopeless but who are allowed the brief illusion of escape and watching their terror as his vicious dogs hunt and tear them to pieces. His literal play is to prey on the helpless.

In the tangle of politics, shifting alliances, betrayals and characters, Theon Greyjoy is a somewhat more complex figure. The only surviving son of the ruler of the Iron Islands, a culture seemingly modeled after the worst imaginings of Viking marauders, he was "fostered" in their kingdom Winterfell by the ruling Stark dynasty 20 years before. Theon has simultaneously been a child hostage guaranteeing the submission of the Greyjoys and a foster child raised in kindly and kingly fashion as a foster brother, mostly second-class but occasionally equal to the Stark children. Theon, who has the hubris if not the stature of a Greek hero, stigmatized by the "Iron Born" for being raised outside of the Iron Islands, sullied by attributions of weakness, subject to his father's contempt for being soft, but always swaggering and self-important, is superseded by his war-like sister. Proud of his good looks and sexual appeal, Theon has a boldness and daring not matched by judgment. He seeks to prove his masculine identity by sexual rapaciousness and martial prowess, and then his loyalty to the Iron Islands by seizing an opportunity, when it presents itself, to conquer Winterfell and murdering the youngest surviving Stark children.

Roose Bolton, formerly a vassal of the Starks, has betrayed them as well for his own ambitions. He assigns Ramsay the task of expelling the Iron Island warriors under the command of Theon's sister. Ramsay disguises himself many times as the plot unfolds, first pretending to rescue Theon from captors intent on punishing him for crimes. He then undertakes a program of systematic torture having nothing to do with justice. He demands Theon first guess his identity and also state his name and corrects his assertion of name, lineage and role with, "your name is Reek" and proceeds to amputate another finger or toe joint with every failed guess of who Ramsay is or refusal to assume the name Ramsay wants to impose on him. The onomatopoeic name has been first given to the servant provided to him as an ironic "present" by his father, whose main feature was a congenital stench and whose interpenetration with Ramsay is signaled by his being Ramsay's only companion and then henchman, ultimately killed when mistaken in battle for Ramsay. Theon's sexual swaggering was portrayed as defining. His collapse comes after Ramsay makes a mockery of it by bringing women in to sexually arouse his tormented body and as he resists having an erection, amputate his penis, which is sent in an ornate box to the Iron Islands. Ramsay's demand of "What's your name?" is finally is answered, "My name is Reek." From that moment, Ramsay baits Theon who shirks in terror from even the temptation to express individuality, even to take a rat for company. Theon is reduced to an animal-like state, quivering in fear, steeped in filth, forced to live in Ramsay's kennel, inferior to the dogs. In this state he strangely becomes Ramsay's pet, replacing the original Reek, his primary attachment.

Ramsay's troops have besieged a strategic fort captured by the Iron Islanders and has the filthy Reek cleaned and dressed. He commands Reek to ride into the fort and *pretend* to be Theon Greyjoy and prevail on the Ironmen to surrender with the promise of safe passage to the Iron Islands. They are of course all hideously tortured, and Reek is returned to the kennel. The episode concludes with Roose Bolton conferring his last name of Ramsay whose pride is the only acceptably recognizable humanity we see in him.

While the themes here may not be subtlety rendered, the popularity of *Game of Thrones* attests to it touching recognizable, if atavistic psychological, chords. Theon is hardly a "good" character; he commits crimes, but he is portrayed as at least conflicted, the effectiveness of his criminal actions undermined by inhibitions and defenses, his behavior motivated by the drive to form a coherent identity, one that will be acceptable to his father and kinsmen, that is one that will be successful and respectable in his world. Theon strives for a masculine role the dimensions of which are consistent with his environment and an ideology that reflects the political, religious and social constructs of the people of his birth. Theon is torn between the Iron identity and the more civilized Stark identity. He commits evil deeds, but there is conflicted attachment to both. He doesn't want to hurt the Starks; he hurts them to be important. His value of loyalty forces him to choose betrayal.

Ramsay has a pure predatory identity. His motivation is not identity formation but the destruction of the identity of the other. The girls he hunts have adopted what otherwise would be conventional roles, but their defenselessness, docility and submissiveness is not allowed them; it will not save them except to the extent they give him good sport. Reminiscent of the Coliseum, he *may* then allow them a less painful death. Indeed, once in his clutches, a victim's fate is random and unpredictable, totally subject to his whim. One of Roose's reprimands is that victims know that submission will not offer any reprieve, so they are left no choice but to resist. Ramsay does not allow them any other identity (girl, daughter, citizen) but that of being his prey. Theon's insistence on remaining Theon is systematically assaulted until he is reduced to the sub human Reek. The depredations proceed at Ramsay's whim. As a key point of contrast for the understanding of different sources of evil, Theon, though guilty of crimes including betrayal and murder, is never directed at eradicating the identity of victim. On the contrary, as a would-be usurper, he affirms the identity of the Stark family even in the attempt to overthrow and reverse roles of the ruler and ruled.

In contrast, because Ramsay's sadism is so predictable, he spontaneously admits he tortures the innocent only to feel powerful; because it has such priority in his identity, he appears to be a less complex figure with a far more rudimentary ideological heuristic. The artistry of his character is that the audience, as evidenced by various reviews and on-line commentaries, more than anything else wants him to disappear like he "disappears" others, wants to turn its attention to other characters and plot lines. Unappealing in any way, possessed of no qualities beyond a primitive, feral cunning, he exists only through horrific acts. In the torture of Theon, he announces his approach by blowing a toy horn graphically illustrating that the suffering so real to Theon is to him only play.

Ramsey's back story is that he is the product of a *droit de seigneur* rape of a miller's wife whose husband is also gratuitously murdered. Disowned and isolated, his only companion is the foul-smelling servant given to him as an ironic "present" by Roose. Easy to despise, we readily perceive the narcissistic vulnerability stemming from illegitimacy. He is further raised by his mother in impoverished and feral circumstance until she urges him to go to the Bolton castle to claim his "rights." In contrast, Theon is given a more textured history to contextualize his attempts at narcissistic repair, criminal though they be. While Ramsay has a fleeting non-predatory moment when he experiences the bestowal of the Bolton name as a substantial reward, Theon was raised and educated as befits a highborn person and yearns for both respect and recognition, and struggles against guilt. Ramsay experiences rage with any reminder that he is a bastard and only experiences an identity of his own when preying on the identity of others. Ramsay's only attachment is to his Reeks, the first of whom he impersonates. The extent of his depravity defies reason and motivation beyond twisting the Cartesian maxim into "I destroy (who others are) therefore I am." Ramsay is more cruel than he is ambitious, Theon more ambitious than he is cruel.

Theon and Ramsay are also distinguished by the quality of their early identifications, an early psychic operation that Erikson constructs both as a precursor and, according to Singer (1965), an obstacle to identity. Theon, with whom the reader can have some identification, if only with his need to prove his worth, has a range, albeit limited, of identifications. In contrast, search as one might for Ramsay's identifications, the only one found is possibly with his father's sadism, and even here it is rudimentary because for the father sadism is not primary but a means to other ends. There is a contrast between identification and empathy; Theon's early identifications lead him to at least some degree of empathy along with his only partly predatory identity. Ramsay's lack of identification leads to a total inability to see himself in anybody else; this inability demonstrates that he can only find himself by negating the identity of others and that the absence of empathy is the major attribute of the pure predatory identity.

I had considerable ambivalence about the choice of Theon and Ramsay as case examples. The Grand Guignol character of *Game of Thrones* makes it an ambivalent subject for psychological exposition, if only because it is inconsistent with the identity of the putative critic. However Terrence Des Pres's (1975) observation, "extremity makes bad art" (p. 175), provides a paradoxically compelling rationale for overcoming the bad taste left by these characters. Des Pres posits that the extremity defies symbolism: No metaphor is possible, no representation beyond the concrete, and thus the acts of a pure predatory identity ultimately destroy meaning.

On this basis, Ramsay beyond the revulsion he induces, his reek, is actually uninteresting, a result of the flattened contours of his identity. In her controversial and highly contested (Lipstadt, 2011) formulation of "the banality of evil," Arendt (1963) may have intuited this aspect. The constriction of his own identity corresponds to the constriction of his ability to hold an image of an another in mind—beyond the predator's instinct for predicting how prey will try to escape and when it will collapse—and has two important implications. First, it is an enabling condition for atrocity, for example, Genocidaires proceed on the basis of the dehumanization of the victim; the preparation for the Rawandan genocide was the designation of its victims as "cockroaches." Second, it is extremely difficult to imagine the inner workings and contents of their minds, possibly because there is less there than meets the eye. The denouement of the National Book Award winning novel *Paris Trout* (Dexter, 1988) is the discovery, on opening the malevolent racist's safe, the contents of which is important to the plot, is that his carefully guarded, secret "treasure" consists of mason jars filled with his urine.

The concept of predatory identity, like the concept of evil, is paretic. The purpose here is to achieve an approximate description and ask psychological questions. What accounts for where one falls on a continuum from healthy identity to predatory identity? What is added by going beyond the explanatory and descriptive principles provided by core biological and developmental failures provided by extremes of psychopathology, paranoia, malevolent narcissism, grandiosity and the like? How does the fate of identity interface with other conceptions of personality organization and psychopathology? What can be untangled in the inner motivations of these individuals? What are the early origins of the need to "feed" on the carcass? What is their concept of themselves? It is extremely difficult to know their defining beliefs, which if barren or impoverished could be construed as but does not necessarily have to be a contradiction of the idea that extreme evil is linked to ideology. Perhaps the contradiction is resolved by understanding that lack of meaning or absence of meaning, in political terms, nihilism, is an ideology of its own.

Ramsay's father very clearly sees him as representing nothing more than a political and military weapon in the House Bolton armory. Ramsay accepts this role more as an instrumental necessity than with loyalty or commitment to structures of meaning. This lack of fealty, a trivializing matter-of-factness, is reminiscent of Claus Barbie, who as Nazi commander was known as the "Butcher of Lyons," and whose dismissive comment while interrogated after his capture, "I've already forgotten, if they haven't, it's their problem" (Ophuls, 1988). The ideology of evil can go to the extreme; its malignancy can result from its exact iteration or from its emptiness.

There is a contrast between Theon's criminality and Ramsay's. From the point of view of the expression of identity, the former is striving to meet ideals of strength and conquest, reinforce his identification and loyalty to the Iron Islands in repudiation of identification with the Starks'. He heroically resists becoming Reek until his traumatic collapse. Ramsay does have an identity as a Bastard, an alienating and ambivalent definition of self in a social order defined by lineage. His limited, shallow identity is explained by Daryl Bem's (1972) "Self-perception theory," which Eelco Runia (2007) depends on for his theory of historical action: Individuals do not have privileged access to themselves. They do not derive their identity from somewhere "within." Rather, they do so by examining their own deeds and by subconsciously answering the question: "What kind of person am I, that I could have done the things I did?" (Runia, 2007, p. 319). Ramsay's belief system is rudimentary and limited to the horrors he can create in others. He never gets beyond his impoverished and feral childhood, his highest level of structuralization is achieving psychological twinship with the actual Reek who is despised and avoided by all. The ultimate contrast between the Theon and Ramsay characters is that Theon tries to hold on as long as he can before surrendering his identity while Ramsay goes on as long as possible to destroy. It is the conceit of *Game of Thrones* that the moral universe is random and unpredictable, and perhaps its appeal is that it asks if who we are matters, if there is a link between articulated ideology and outcome.

Using fictional characters for a case study is an epistemologically tricky business. To use Ramsay as a heuristic requires correspondence of the character to actual perpetrators. Can it be that such a identity exists outside of nightmares and cable television, representative of actual predators whose identities are dominated by the exercise of power, who have the primary aim of crushing the identity of their victims and some of whom have minimally articulated belief systems? Fortunately, or unfortunately, the evidence of their existence abounds. As one example, Shengold (1991) provides support for Ramsay's veridicality in his exposition of child and spousal abuse capturing the essence with the description "soul murder."

Perpetrators of domestic violence have a range of beliefs, varying in intensity and coherence. Ideas about gender and even quasi-religious justifications, which can be of any stripe, can be documented to produce a savagery that rivals Ramsay's. The difference is that while for Ramsay the violence is in itself the expression of his identity, for them there is a far more reciprocal relationship to violence as a means of protecting and enforcing adherence to other parameters of self-definition, particularly their beliefs. In this way, the group becomes integral to personal identity. Thus, while Ramsay has only an incidental relationship to a gang of henchmen who act as extensions of his will, Theon's actions serve as an expression of fidelity to group values; his attack on the Stark's Winterfell and attempted murder of the Stark children is a repudiation of the earlier Iron Born submission to the Starks and an assertion of martial ideology. For him, in a way very different than for Ramsay, individual and group identity is intertwined.

Analogous to the fundamental way beliefs organizing the self, even at the level of brain (Levin, 2011), beliefs give groups their coherence and cohesion and provide their members the "means of identity maintenance" (Lichtenstein, 1977, p. 173) and objectify the other criteria for membership, even persecutions based on racial or religious differences are under an ideological canopy of ideas that, whether distorted, loony, or counter-factual, are basic to or potentiate the evil that emanates from predatory identity. Protecting, supporting and promulgating them can take precedence over other needs. The range of their destructiveness is if anything only limited by the lack of justification by a belief system, an ideology, that is either fundamental to a robust identity or can engage and propagate latent predatory identity in others.

The Nazi's radical anti-Semitism provides an exemplar of an identity based on a precisely articulated ideology. Anti-Judaism constituted a powerful system for making sense out of the world (Nirenberg, 2013). As such, it did not have to correspond to any reality or even depend on the existence of real Jews. For the Nazis, the idea of a Jew was sufficient to provide a *raison d'etre,* one that required the extermination of Jews. Thus, Ramsay's reduction of Theon into Reek, only minimally supported by group belonging or ideology, could be repeated at least 6 million times by the Nazis for whom racial beliefs were at the absolute core of their ideology and for whom ideological indoctrination was a priority (Browning, 1998). It demanded an "excremental assault," (Des Pres, 1976) in Minz's (2001) words a "deliberate policy which aimed at complete humiliation and abasement" (p. 59). Minz's description provides an uncanny inverse of Erikson's description of identity formation. Premeditated, calculated atrocities disintegrated every aspect of humanity, constituting a "systematic annihilation of the individual's humanity before the final act of extermination. ... It is an experience in which human beings are stripped of all the integuments of identity, culture, solidarity and belief that clothe their nakedness" (Minz, p. 56). Further echoing the fictional Ramsay's assault on Theon, but with articulated ideology added, in the very real camps, individuals were wrenched out of communal and familial bonds and "the least individual expression." Elie Weisel documented the spiritual assault while Primo Levi documented the chemical decomposition of the person, as Roth (1995) puts it "the ways in which a man can be transformed or broken down and like a substance decomposing in a chemical reaction, lose his characteristic properties" (p. 181).

There is evidence that the promulgation of their racial theories and annihilation of Jews was the primary motivator, even more important that material gain. Indeed Goering called WWII a racial war (Fergusson, 2006). Vital resources were diverted from the German war effort, a madness that continued to the very end, which saw the continuation of their, in Staub's (1989) word, "feverish" (p. 149) extermination efforts. These included forced death marches, attempts to exterminate survivors and even hunting down individual Jews so they would not escape. "What possible explanation could there be?" Staub asks and answers, "Threatened with the loss of the war, their sense of superiority, and even their lives, many SS men reaffirmed their power and invulnerability by continued killing" (p. 149). The end illuminated the beginning; the Nazis came to power on a platform of elimination of Jewish identity and continued their project to their last breath. Alois Brunner, Eichmann's deputy, is reported to have said during his exile in Syria, that his only regret was not killing more Jews.

The claim is not that identity is the sole source of violence or destructiveness; it cannot be sufficiently stressed that the poly-causal conclusions characterizes the best historical research, but that it may have a greater or lesser role. Thus, Diamond's (2012) study of "traditional peoples" suggests that people with alternate identities, i.e., members of different clans or tribes, are not murdered when encountered because of identity intolerance, a psychological threat posed by their otherness, but because they pose actual physical danger. Pinker (2012) whose work is particularly compelling because of his application of empirical data analysis finds that through history war has had many causes but is particularly destructive and brutal when ideology and clashing belief systems are more salient than other sources of conflict. Chalk and Jonassohn (1990) develop a "typology of genocide" (p. 29). Granting genocide as the ultimate act of annihilation of the other, its motivation can be instrumental: eliminating threat, spreading terror among real and potential enemies, achieving militarily strategic advantage, acquiring economic wealth or territory. Their final category of genocide is linked to identity. It is defined by the motivation to "implement a belief, a theory or an ideology" (p. 29). In the four genocidal contexts that Staub (2009) studies, Armenia, Nazi Germany, Cambodia and Argentina, he concludes ideology was central. Similarly, Arendt (1966) describes ideologies of expansion, unity, superiority and purity as used to legitimize twentieth-century mass violence. Finally, Bauer (2004) attributes the quest for universal utopias, which can be attained only by a universal victory, to the probability of genocide. Identifying three such movements, German Nazism, Soviet Communism and radical Islamic fundamentalism, he writes, "The iron rule seems to be universal utopias kill; radical universal utopias kill radically" (p. 15).

The form predatory identity takes can further be refined into overlapping types defined by the dimensions that predominate. One form is portrayed by Ramsay's assumption of a sadism fueled primary identity. Many perpetrators took pride in representations of themselves as powerful, merciless and omnipotent. Still others see themselves as representing an ideology. Browning , whose study of the men of Reserve Police Battalion 101, 80 to 90 percent of whom participated in genocidal murder though they were given the option not to, portrays a sub-group "go getters," the men, like Ramsey, who threw themselves into the task with extreme gusto and cruelty. He then examines those who were reluctant killers, but who nevertheless committed atrocity without shirking to find the factors that evoked the acquiescence of these "ordinary men" in whom a predatory identity was evoked. To Browning's credit, his close examination of both conditions and individuals leads him to ascertain multiple factors. Rejecting the hypothesis of a psychopathic disposition, he finds these were the "least likely to be considered apt material out of which to mold future mass killers" (p. 166). Most relevant to them was first submission to first authority and then group norms. A consistent theme in studies of these perpetrators is their conformity in a situation of ideological justification and state legitimization.

A repeated question is what combination of internal and external conditions evoke the violent depredations of predatory identity. In his attempt to explain the acts of these "ordinary men," Browning turns to the well-known laboratory studies of Milgram and Zimbardo and goes into detail about variables that effected outcome. I serendipitously met one of Zimbardo's most notorious "prison guards" who had been nicknamed "Satan." A successful professional, he regarded his participation as a brief moment of fame. He had been sought after because of the notoriety of the study and had given several media interviews. Satan had thoroughly enjoyed his role but had an unexpected rationale. He had studied theater and was aware of the presence of an observing producer/director (the experimenter), aware that he was participating in a psychology study and regarded the "prisoners" and "guards" like himself as professionally obligated to play their roles to the best of their abilities. He felt those who did not were not earning their pay. He seemed a warm and friendly person from whom I could not elicit any evidence he enjoyed inflicting discomfort. He avowed pride in fulfilling his responsibility to Zimbardo's study and earning the money he was paid to participate. He is not completely like Theon, who saw himself as an exemplar of the ideology of his native land and people; he is not completely like Browning's ordinary men who did their duty no matter how distasteful, but not completely unlike them either.

Ultimately, these men can all be said to have superegos in the sense of having identified with social norms, even though they have, Theon and certainly Browning's policemen, committed atrocities. Their predatory acts were not impelled primarily by personal destructiveness but destructiveness in the service of the formation of personal, national or religious identity.

This is articulated by Omar Bartov (2002) who, trying to distinguish different causes for genocide writes:

> Moving to the larger context of these events, it must be pointed out that both the idea and the practice of genocide probably are as ancient as the idea and practice of war. Indeed, war and genocide have always been closely related, just as both are predicated on the existence of a certain level of human culture and civilization. The biblical concept of a war of annihilation or the destruction of Carthage by the Romans are two familiar instances of the manner in which the eradication of another culture during war, or in its immediate aftermath, serves as an important instrument in the assertion of group or national identity. Indicatively, in both cases—as in many others—destruction was not only justified, but also lauded as a noble act sanctioned by God (for the ancient Hebrews) or glorifying the republic (for the Romans). (p. 9)

Another aspect of predatory identity can be thought of as defensive, as in a reaction to threats to their identity or repair of their inadequate identity. Both Ramsay and Theon are narcissistically vulnerable, and compensation plays at least some role for both. Volkan (1997) describes "flawed personal identities" leading terrorist leaders to "use their ethnic identity as their primary identity" and "shore up their internal sense of self by seeking the power to hurt and by expressing their sense of entitlement to power" (p. 161). Bychowski (1948) unequivocally attributes an underlying weakness and inferiority to the tyrants who are the subject of his study.

Thomas Kohut (2013), who studied a German generation as a historian obviously influenced by his psychoanalyst father, suggests two predisposing factors in their participation in the Third Reich; the first is the losses they endured emerging from the first war and the second is the impairment of their ability to identify and thus empathize with its victims. Snyder (2012), in his study of *Bloodlands*, the name he gives to the location of the worst twentieth-century European atrocity, looks to the vacuum caused by the breakdown of authority. Ferguson (2006), also studying the extreme violence of the twentieth century, attributes it to empires in decline. He is anticipated by Bychowski (1948) who writes "Disintegration of a social structure creates not only general anxiety and thus weakens the collective ego but ... it also undermines the foundations of norms and ideals which form the basis of the collective ego ideal." Bychowski anticipates Kohut's interpretation of the inability of the "German generation" to put themselves in the shoes of the victims. Kohut's sample is homogenous, an iteration of the cost of having an excessively bounded identity. In contrast, Ferguson's observations foil too facile conclusions by remarking on the threat to established identity posed by diversity. The multi-ethnic composition of the area that both he and Snyder agree was the *Bloodlands* is counter-intuitive. Where the liberal humanist might have applauded multi-culturalism, this ideal of democracy was experienced as a threat to "purity" and the hopefulness about successful integration, even signaled by high rates of intermarriage, became preludes for violent conflict. The evidence of Europe and the more recent examples of the former Yugoslavia and Rwanda, both having experienced significant ethnic integration, supports his contention.

In his exploration of the fate of identity under duress, Czeslaw Milosz (1953) beautifully describes how these types of predatory identity oscillated and overlapped: "Murder became ordinary during wartime, and was even regarded as legitimate if it was carried out on behalf of the resistance. In the name of patriotism, young boys from law-abiding, middle-class families became hardened criminals, thugs for whom the killing of a man presents no great moral problem" (p. 26).

As he suggests, war is one of the circumstances that that evokes latent predatory tendencies. One the one hand it can be seen as Browning does, as primarily a phenomenon emerging from group dynamics. On the other hand, it is often seen as a creation of predatory leaders. One of the great psychological and historical questions concerns the base rate of pervasiveness of predatory identity: How many Ramsays who act on their own are there? How many are able to find a killing ideology and thus are able to lead or evoke latent murder in many more? Are followers predators in their own right, an extension of the leader or another kind of prey who fall under the leaders power or control and what are the enabling circumstances? Browning suggests that his subjects succumbed not so much to group pressure but to a need to belong; others for example put the locus of influence on malignant leaders. Pinker (2012), takes the position that a few "dedicated ideologues," he names Hitler, Stalin and Mao, supported by fanatical henchmen, are by far most responsible and assigns a more limited role to the great majority who are essentially passive bystanders. Bychowski (1948) in a psychoanalytic study of five historical dictators sees a "complete reciprocity" (p. 245) between leader and the led. Wangh (1974) also sees more of an interrelationship: He asks, "Why this 'crazy' man's oratory was so effective and why did the displacement of his personal unconscious needs onto the political state so inflame the minds of the German multitudes? Was it perhaps that he perceived their unconscious needs and that these were similar to his own?" (p. 130). Thus, where Pinker concludes that predatory identity is limited to a few Ramsey types who impose their will, Wangh clearly articulates the latency of predatory identity and a far more robust interrelationship between leader and follower. Kohut (2013) finds support for both the view that the majority of Germans were overwhelmed bystanders, at worst casual supporters, anything but lethal racists and Goldhagen's (1996) view of Hitler's "willing executioners" i.e., a belief in the deep cultural embeddedness of the genocidal impulse. The challenge of resolving these contrasting views is the challenge of understanding the degree to which and the conditions under which predatory identity becomes dominant.

Some puzzles of the emergence of predatory identity are only deepened by a realization there is a relationship of predator to prey. There is a bias to thinking of the predator as unrelated to prey in anything but basic definition, the marauding Cossacks coming from the hidden Steppes and returning as suddenly as they came leaving only trauma in their wake. But there are many instances of an intense bond as evinced by Ramsey's dependence on Theon not only for his sense of power and superiority but also for connection. It is in this sense that Sartre (1948) made his famous assertion that if Jews didn't exist, the Anti-Semite would have to invent them. Ferguson's and Snyders's observations, cited above, of the integration of ethnic groups as a precursor to unprecedented violence between them is also relevant. There is a comfort in attributing the worst depredations to strangers enabled by the anonymity of victims. Unfortunately, there is evidence to the contrary. The reassertion of ethnic boundaries after they have been softened is hauntingly evoked by Jan Gross (2002) who in his study of the massacre of one half the population of Polish Jedwabne, the Jewish half, by the other half. Poles who had traditionally lived with Jews harmoniously and thus might naively have been predicted to be immunized from a frenzy of savagery that exponentially exceeded ordinary killing. In Gross's description:

> ordinary Poles slaughtered the Jews ... very much as ordinary Germans from the Ordnungspolizei Batallion. no.101. ... They were men of all ages and of different professions; entire families on occasion, fathers and sons acting in concert; good citizens one is tempted to say (if sarcasm was not out of place given the hideousness of their deeds). ... And what the Jews saw, to their horror and I dare say, incomprehension, were familiar faces. Not anonymous men in uniform, cogs in a war machine, agents carrying out orders, but their own neighbors. ... (p. 78)

In post-war testimony, one Jerzy Laudanski, according to Gross the worst of the murderers, asks of his Stalinist captors, "Why do keep me behind bars if I was not a German sympathizer but rather a true Polish patriot? ... I was preoccupied only with matters related to my nation and my Motherland. As proof of it, I did not hesitate when there was need to give my strength for the good of the Motherland" (p. 76).

Laudanski's plea can be regarded as a pathetic rationalization, readily dismissible as self-exculpatory. However, it does fall into at least one aspect of the aftermath of the expression of predatory identity—the paradoxical need to repudiate, deny or hide it. Stalin was famously paranoid about Jews wanting to perpetuate the memory of the Holocaust. Examples of the protection of identity abound. Americans, for example, avoid consciousness of both slavery and genocidal practices toward Native Americans, historical realities that directly confound and undermine the values that define American identity. An outstanding example is the near hysterical proportions of the Turkish disavowal of the Armenian genocide. Danielian (2010) portrays Turkish atrocities of the type of identity described above as compensatory: assertions of superiority arising as compensation for identity insecurity developing from contemporary threats. Admission of those original acts would constitute a further stain and have been actually criminalized in Turkey as "insults" to the nation. In France the Resistance is glorified and the Collaboration denied. The Polish language publication of *Neighbors* in 2000 resulted in "... a long and, perhaps, the most complex confrontation with collective memory, and the need to revise it, that the Poles had ever faced" (Gross, p. 117). New instances seem to be reported daily, most recently with the Japanese right's attempts to intimidate and punish scholars and reporters documenting WWII atrocities. Interestingly, post-war Germany has perfected the art of Holocaust commemoration and used it as repudiation of predatory identify to promote a more positive one. Runia (2007), one of the most profound thinkers about commemoration, sees it as a means of saying: "This is not who we are."

Simultaneously maintaining multiple roles, ones of ruthless brutality, selfless patriotism, and even innocence, highlights a paradox of predatory identity. Is it possible to act out radically alternating identities, the trope of the killer by day, loving parent at night? Lifton (2000) in his study of Nazi doctors calls this phenomenon "doubling." It is by no means established that such alter egos can coexist without corrupting each other; many of Browning's ordinary men anesthetized themselves with alcohol after their killing sprees, and there is evidence that the so-called loving Nazi parent was in fact a sadistic tyrant at home. However, in the same way the predatory destroyer of one identity seems unable to imagine that the despised other has multiple parallel identities worth preserving (Goldman, 2014), it is possible that the immersion in an identity is so complete, for example patriot, that it totally occludes a negative view of the self or how one is seen by the other. Amon Goeth, the commandant of Plaszow concentration camp, while awaiting his war crimes trial, was reportedly bewildered that his former house slave was not eager to bring him his favorite meals. One is tempted to conclude that Goeth had to have a psychotic break with reality to have such a feeling, but there are many analogous examples, the devoutly religious whose conviction about the nature of goodness and avowals of love justify burning the heretic.

Many explanations are possible, but from the point of view of this essay, identity is the "heuristic" through which everything is understood and experienced. The men of Battalion 101 did not understand themselves as evil; they saw themselves as performing their duty. A last question about predatory identity going beyond *What is it? Is where it is?* That is, is it located within the individual or in some spaces in or between groups and history? To search for its location leads to a last paradox of identity: the same identity processes, the protection of the integrity and violent attack on any challenge to a defining belief system, may serve either good or evil. Certainly its ravages and consequential suffering are undeniable. However, in a social order valuing obedience and belonging, defiance is evil. From the point of view of the Nazis, the righteous gentiles who saved Jews deserved punishment for betraying the ideals of racial purity. In one of the defining moral statements of the Western tradition, Abraham privileges his identity as a servant of God over his identity as a parent. In arguably the most horrifying literary work in the Western canon, *The Book of Job*, God defines his identity by systematically stripping every layer of Job's identity. Exemplifying the assertion of absolute power by despots from antiquity to the present when challenged for an explanation, He denounces any option but total submission, in a prototype of the totalitarian despot. He delivers a thunderous rebuke: "Where wast thou when I laid the foundations of the earth? Declare, if thou hast understanding."

It would be a mistake to limit the instantiation of predatory identity in faraway times and places. Closer to our own professional identity, in the world of psychoanalysis, there have been numerous eruptions of predatory identity; those who promote ideas that have diverged from the mainstream have been responded to with "vehemence" and exclusion (Bergmann, 2004; Prince, 2014). In looking for understanding of predatory identity, simple explanations and conclusions are in Snyder's word, "fruitless" (p. 20). It is hard to improve on Yehuda Bauer's (2006) recommendation for, in each instance, close examination of local conditions.

The consolidation of the broad spectrum of identity is a developmental process that looks backwards and forwards, that preserves and protects what was and works toward establishing something new in a future. It defends itself from threats and at the same time is revolutionary. Identity defies facile generalizations; it is necessary to preserve for the sake of the good, but the effort to preserve it can lead to great evil. It is necessary to relinquish previous identities and establish new ones, a condition that offers great hope but risks another kind of evil. A lot may depend on the specific characteristics of the individual, which in turn depend on the specific characteristics of the era. What Erikson calls Historical Process becomes a force of both creativity and destruction. Neiman (2002) argues that the first trauma of modernity was the Lisbon Earthquake of 1755, an event forgotten today but cataclysmic for identity in its day. Occurring as it did in a devoutly Christian nation, it challenged the prevailing belief in theodicy that organized people's conception of who they were in the world. As a result, according to Neiman, the problem of evil became the guiding force of modern thought.

Erik Erikson asks of psychoanalysis: Who are we? Eelco Runia is a historian who asks of history, who are we that these things could have happened? Just as the psychoanalyst has a teleological idea of personal development, Runia's theory of history is that people "consume" their history and have an urge to create it. "People," he writes, "start to make history not despite the fact that it is at odds with—yes, destroys—the stories they live by, but because it destroys the stories they live by" (p. 320). From this perspective, all identity including predatory identity is ultimately a Manichean concept, its nature, to borrow the words Erikson (1970) used to describe identity conflict, depending on:

> the latent panic or, indeed, the intrinsic promise pervading a historical period. Some periods in history become identity vacua caused by the three basic forms of human apprehension: *fears* aroused by new facts, such as discoveries and inventions (including weapons), which radically expand and change the whole world image; *anxieties* aroused by symbolic dangers vaguely perceived as a consequence of the decay of existing ideologies; and, in the wake of disintegrating faith, the *dread* of an existential abyss devoid of spiritual meaning. But then, again, a historical period may (as, for example, the American Revolution did) present a singular chance for a collective renewal which opens up unlimited identities for those who, by a combination of unruliness, giftedness, and competence, represent a new leadership, a new elite, and new types rising to dominance in a new people. (p. 21)

References

Arendt, H. (1963). *Eichmann in Jerusalem: A Report on the Banality of Evil.* New York, NY: Penguin.

Arendt, H. (1966). *The Origins of Totalitarianism.* New York, NY: Harvest.

Bartov, O. (2002). From the Holocaust in Galicia to contemporary genocide: Common ground—historical differences. Joseph and Rebecca Meyerhoff Annual Lecture, *U.S. Holocaust Museum*, Washington, DC.

Bauer, Y. (2004). Contemporary research on the holocaust. In K. Kwiet and J. Matthaus (Eds.), *Contemporary responses to the Holocaust.* Westport, CT: Praeger, 3–17.

Bauer, Y. (2006). On the Holocaust and other genocides. Joseph and Rebecca Meyerhoff Annual Lecture, *U.S. Holocaust Museum*, Washington, DC.

Bem, D. J. (1972). Self-perception theory. In L. Berkowitz (Ed.), *Advances in Experimental Social Psychology.* New York, NY: Academic Press, *VI*, 1–62.

Bergmann, M.S. (2004). *Understanding Dissidence and Controversy in the History of Psychoanalysis.* New York, NY: Other Press.

Browning, C. (1998). *Ordinary men: Reserve Police Battalion 101 and the Final Solution in Poland.* New York, NY: Harper.

Bychowski, G. (1948). *Dictators and Disciples.* New York, NY: International Universities Press.

Carpenter, C. (2012, March 29). *Game of Thrones as Theory.* It's Not as Realist as It Seems – And That's Good. Foreign Affairs retrieved July 10, 2014, https://www.foreignaffairs.com/articles/2012-03-29/game-thrones-theory.

Chalk, F. and Jonassohn, K. (1990). *The History and Sociology of Genocide: Analyses and Case Studies.* Montreal, Quebec: Montreal Institute of Genocide Studies.

Danielian, J. (2010). A century of silence: Terror and the Armenian Genocide. *American Journal of Psychoanalysis, 70*, 245–264.

Des Pres,T. (1976). *The Survivor: An Anatomy of Life in the Death Camps*. New York, NY: Oxford University Press.
Dexter, P. (1988). *Paris Trout*. New York, NY: Random House.
Diamond, J. (2005). *Collapse: How Societies Choose to Fail or Succeed*. New York, NY: Penguin.
Diamond, J. (2012). *The World Before Yesterday*. New York, NY: Penguin.
Erikson, E. (1946). Ego development and historical change: Clinical notes. *Psychoanalytic Study of the Child, 2*, 359–396.
Erikson, E. (1950). *Childhood and Society*. New York, NY: Norton.
Erikson, E. (1959). *Identity and the Life Cycle*. New York, NY: International Universities Press.
Erikson, E.H. (1970). "Identity crisis" in autobiographic perspective. In E. H. Erikson, *Life History and the Historical Moment*. New York, NY: Norton, 1975.
Fergusson, N. (2006). *The War of the World: Twentieth-century Conflict and the Descent of the West*. New York, NY: Penguin.
Goldhagan, D. (1997). *Hitler's Willing Executioners: Ordinary Germans and the Holocaust*. New York, NY: Vintage.
Gross, J.T. (2002). *Neighbors: The Destruction of the Jewish Community in Jedwabne, Poland*. New York, NY: Penguin.
Kahneman, D. (2011). *Thinking Fast and Slow*. New York, NY: Farrar, Straus and Giroux.
Kohut, T. (2013). *A German Generation: An Experiential History of the Twentieth Century*. New Haven, CT: Yale University Press.
Lanchester, J. (2013). When did you get hooked? *London Review of Books, 35*(7), 20–22.
Langer, W. (1972). *The Mind of Adolf Hitler: The Secret Wartime Report*. New York, NY: Basic Books.
Levenson, E. (1980). More different than alike: Speculations on the uniqueness of the psychoanalytic experience. *Contemporary Psychoanalysis, 16*, 1–15.
Levin, F. (2011). *Psyche and brain*. London, UK: Karnac.
Lichtenstein, H. (1977). *The dilemma of Human Identity*. New York, NY: Aronson.
Lifton, R. (2000). *The Nazi Doctors: Medical Killing and the psychology of Genocide*. New York, NY: Random House.
Lipstadt, D. (2011). *The Eichmann Trial*. New York, NY: Random House.
Miłosz, C. (1953). *The Captive Mind*. New York, NY: Penguin.
Minz, A. (2001). *Popular Culture and the Shaping of Holocaust Memory in America*. Seattle, WA: University of Washington Press.
Neiman, S. (2002). *Evil in Modern Thought*. Princeton, NJ: Princeton University Press.
Nirenberg, D. (2013). *Anti-Judaism: The western Tradition*. New York, NY: Norton.
Ophuls, M. (1988). Director, *Hotel Terminus: The Life and times of Claus Barbie*. Motion picture.
Pinker, S. (2012). *The Better Angels of our Nature: Why Violence has Declined*. New York, NY: Penguin.
Prince, R. (2014). Balancing belonging and self-realization in psychoanalysis: The example of Sándor Ferenczi, *Psychoanalytic Inquiry, 34*, 135–144.
Roth, P. (1995). A conversation with Primo Levi. In Primo Levi, *Survival in Auschwitz*. New York, NY: Touchstone.
Runia, E. (2007). Burying the dead, creating the past. *History and Theory, 46*, 313–325.

Runia, E. (2010). Into the cleanness leaping: The vertiginous urge to commit history. *History and Theory, 49*, 1–20.
Sartre, J-P. (1948). *Anti-Semite and Jew*. New York, NY: Schocken.
Shengold, L. (1991). *Soul murder: The effects of Childhood Abuse and Deprivation*. New York, NY: Balantine.
Singer, E. (1965). Identity vs. identification: A thorny psychological issue. *Review of Existential Psychology and Psychiatry, 5*, 160–175.
Snyder, T. (2012). *Bloodlands: Europe Between Hitler and Stalin*. New York, NY: Basic Books.
Staub, E. (2009). *The Roots of Evil*. New York, NY: Cambridge University Press.
Tilly, G. (2006). *Why?* Princeton, NJ: Princeton University Press.
Volkan, V. (1997). *Bloodlines: From Ethnic Terrorism to Ethnic Pride*. Boulder, CO: Westview Press.
Volkan, V., Ast, G., Greer, Jr.,W. (2002). *The Third Reich in the Unconscious: Transgenerational Transmission and its Consequences*. New York, NY: Brunner-Routledge.
Wangh, M. (1974). The mind of Adolf Hitler: The secret wartime report. *Psychoanalytic Quarterly, 4*, 124–133.

Chapter 6

The Psychodynamics of Evil

Motives behind Acts of Extreme Violence in Peacetime

Michael Stone

My first task, before launching into a discussion about the motives underlying acts of violence that, in peacetime, rise to the level of evil—is to offer my definition of "evil." Throughout long periods in our history, the term *evil* remained the preserve of religion and philosophy—often enough of men who were religious leaders and philosophers at the same time, such as St. Augustine, St. Thomas Aquinas, Maimonides, Pierre Bayle, Spinoza and in our day, Reinhold Niebuhr. One of the most vexing religio-philosophic problems in the Judeo-Christian tradition was to answer the question: Why a good God permits the existence of evil? The answer was provided during the Enlightenment period by Leibniz, who coined the term *theodicy*—in which he attempted to reconcile the traditional view of God as omnipotent and benevolent with the obvious existence of suffering and evil in the world. Leibniz's 1710 essay was a responsum, in effect, to an earlier work by the Calvinist Pierre Bayle (1647–1706) in his 1696 commentary on evil. Bayle's criticisms, reminiscent of Epicurus' writings two millennia earlier, were framed as follows: "God is either willing to remove evil and cannot; or He can and is unwilling; or He is neither willing nor able to do so; or else, He is both willing and able." Bayle continues: "If He is willing and not able, then He must be weak—but that cannot be affirmed of God. If he is able and not willing, He must be envious—which is contrary to the nature of God. If he is neither willing nor able, He must be both envious and weak. If he is both willing and able—which is the only possibility that agrees with the nature of God as benevolent and omnipotent—then where does evil come from?" Bayle continued to believe in the divinity of Christ, whom he regarded as important for His moral example and His message of toleration. A radical thinker in his day, Bayle opposed the notion that unbelief led to immorality, since from what he could observe, there were many believers who were in no way deterred from cruel and destructive behavior out of any fear of divine punishment. And, *mutatis mutandis*, there were many atheists who, despite their freedom from fear of punishment in the Hereafter, behaved in a consistently scrupulous and moral manner. At all events, the Holocaust put paid to any idea that human suffering was somehow merited by our sinfulness as God's punishment, since the genocidal massacres of the twentieth century were obviously not prompted by the sins of the victims; rather by the evil actions of their oppressors. The Holocaust was bookended on either side—by the earlier massacre of the Armenians by the Turks, and by the Chinese in Nanking at the hands of the Japanese—and by the later massacres of the eastern Nigerian Ibos by the northern Moslem Nigerians, of the Bosnian Moslems by the Serbians, of the Tutsis by the Hutus in Rwanda. All this—preceded by still earlier pogroms, inquisitions and institutionalized massacres going back to the first days of our recorded history—has left theodicy an empty vessel and has shorn religious and philosophical explanations of evil of any utility and have rendered them airy and unconvincing. So how are we to understand evil?

As I have argued elsewhere (Stone, 2009) we can begin to make sense of *evil* if we recognize that the term, whatever overtones of the religious belief and philosophical speculation have adhered to the concept hitherto, is also a word in everyone's everyday vocabulary. Evil is a word answering to an *emotion*; specifically, the emotion of horror and revulsion when we hear of, or we witness, an action whose intention was to subject another person or a group of persons to extreme suffering, extreme humiliation, degradation and, often enough, dehumanization. When we witness or hear about such actions, we contort our face, we wince, we gasp, we express horror and often, we cry.

There is something excessive, over-the-top, way beyond what can ever be accepted in the body social—in our usage of the word evil. And this reflects its origin etymologically: our word is a latter-day version of the Anglo-Saxon *yfel* (pronounced the same way as our word), itself a cognate of the German words über ("over," "beyond") and übel ("ill," "evil," "sinful")—something, in other words, that tramples on the social bond that unites us.

I have chosen to focus on evil in peacetime, because it is clear from our history that in times of war, group conflict and struggles over vital resources in times of want quite ordinary people can descend quite readily to horrific actions of violence against persons "on the other side." Examples are legion. In fact what passes for human history is not much more than the meticulous cataloguing of nefarious and evil actions of the Xs versus the Ys. Here is one of the myriad instances: when Napoleon's troops attempted to conquer Spain in the very first years of the nineteenth century, they perpetrated all manner of torture and violence against the citizenry. This was not collateral damage, as when a bomb hits a building that happens to contain some noncombatants. This was willful butchery of civilians. But the Spanish civilians did not take this lying down. They formed mobs, who captured some of Napoleon's soldiers and pressed them between boards placed beneath huge boulders, slowly suffocating the soldiers. Once their revenge was exacted, the citizens, I assume, returned to their everyday activities ... just as the surviving soldiers at war's end returned to their quotidian lives back in France.

The capacity for ordinary people to become quite vicious in times of group conflict answers, it would seem, to an innate survival-related human disposition for avenging wrongs with such vehemence as to enter the realm of evil (i.e., to torture those who tortured us). This teaches us something (but nothing new!) about our species but is of little interest to the psychopathologist. Evil in peacetime is another matter.

Persons committing acts in peacetime that evoke the expression: Evil! have at the same time broken one or another law; what they have done is considered *criminal* in their own country. Furthermore, evil acts in peacetime are unprompted, in contrast to the vengeful acts of the Spanish civilians against their Napoleonic oppressors (which would be regarded as "evil" by the soldiers, but justified [albeit a bit excessive] by the Spanish). Acts that combine violence and cruelty are the ones we most readily and universally define as evil, especially if we react with horror. But there are gradations. Awareness of these different levels in evil is what led me to create a scale called Gradations of Evil (Stone, 1993). One might speak of the most outrageous examples under the heading, borrowed from the epilepsy term, *Grand Mal* (Great Evil). Beneath this are the cases of *Petit Mal* (Little Evil): less horrific, often more impulsive in nature, unlike the Grand Mal cases, where there is usually premeditation. Premeditated evil equates with what we call *malice*—the core feature of which is the *conscious plan* to inflict severe injury to another, whether in the form of humiliation, non-lethal injury, or death. Violent acts committed as clear-cut manifestations of self-defense are not evil; if death results, the act is one of (justified) homicide, not murder (murder implying *unlawful* killing). I purposely anchored my scale to self-defense homicide as Level-1, to define the boundary between evil and non-evil.

Since we are concerned here with the psychodynamics of evil, with the spotlight on *extreme* acts of violence, we will be dealing with examples from the higher numbers of the 22-compartment scale. In the lower levels of the scale (#2 to #8) the persons involved acted usually on impulse; some may also have had a few psychopathic traits (as outlined in the Psychopathy Checklist devised by Robert Hare and his colleagues [Hare, 1991]). Offenders placed in the higher compartments had scores on the psychopathy checklist that fell short of the "30" (out of a possible 40) necessary for the diagnosis of *psychopathy* proper or had scores well within the full psychopathy region (scores of 30 to 40). Since the essence of psychopathy as a diagnostic concept is a collection of narcissistic attributes, narcissism (usually in an extreme form) is the red thread that runs through the psychopathology we find in persons who commit evil acts. These attributes include: exploitativeness, pathological lying, callousness, lack of remorse, refusal to take responsibility for one's actions, superficial charm and glibness (the latter defined as insincere and facile speech meant to seduce or fool others for some nefarious purpose of the psychopath). Other characteristics at the more severe end of narcissistic personality disorder are arrogance and lack of empathy. By "empathy" is not meant *cognitive* empathy by which one can recognize correctly the emotion someone else is experiencing, but *emotional* empathy—by means of which we feel compassion and sympathy for other persons. As Baron-Cohen (2003) makes clear, even psychopaths often have cognitive empathy, but as to emotional empathy their level is close to or at the zero-mark (Baron-Cohen, 2011). Arrogance combined with "zero" empathy is the hallmark of ruthlessness, another quality noted in many persons we regard as capable of evil. We should make clear at the outset that persons given to one or more evil acts are much more common than the mercifully rare individuals whose tendency to commit evil acts (ones we also describe as heinous, depraved, atrocious, gruesome) is evident throughout out their lives. An *evil person*, otherwise put, is a rarity; a person who commits an evil act is not so rare.

In exploring the psychodynamics of evil we search for patterns and experiences during one's formative years that may predispose one to the later commission of evil. We also look for factors immediately preceding evil acts that may have ignited the transition from violent fantasy to violent behavior. Sometimes there is an obvious connection between early-life experience and the precipitating factors in adult life, as when a severely abused and vilified child grows up to explode with vicious behavior when threatened or when thirsting for vengeance. But there are still others whose commission of evil acts and whose underlying psychopathy have no "dynamics" in the usual sense; instead, inborn neurophysiological abnormalities set the stage for future psychopathic tendencies, thus greatly elevating the risk for future violence—even though the person in question came from a good and intact family, was of good intelligence and suffered no head injury or other adverse early experiences that could be held accountable for the subsequent acts of evil. As Stout (2005) mentions in her treatise on sociopathy: "sociopathy involves an altered processing of emotional stimuli at the level of the cerebral cortex. ... it is likely to be the result of a heritable neurodevelopmental difference that can be either slightly compensated for, or else made much worse, by child-rearing or cultural factors" (p. 125). Sociopathy is a synonym—of a kinder and gentler sort—for psychopathy. There are also similarities to the DSM definition of antisocial personality disorder (ASPD), which Stout estimates, affects about 4% of the population. Psychopathy as a full diagnostic entity (Hare score 30 to 40) is noted in perhaps 1.5% of the population. Either way, there will be a great male preponderance (between 5:1 to 8:1), which unsurprisingly equates with the great male preponderance in the murder rate (also estimated as between 5:1 to 8:1 or even 10:1: Craig & Halton 2009; Kellerman & Mercy 1992).

The foregoing remarks serve as a reminder that in our attempt to understand evil, we need to appreciate the impact of brain peculiarities and abnormalities stemming from: (a) genetic influences affecting corticolimbic structures that mediate empathy and impulse control, (b) fetal abnormalities in intrauterine life (as may be induced, *inter alia*, by maternal abuse of alcohol, cocaine, or other drugs), and (c) gender differences—all of which come under the heading of *pre-natal* factors, (d) psychodynamic factors as understood in traditional psychoanalysis, (e) head-injury and brain-disease, and (f) cultural factors—the latter three as *post-natal* factors. The persons we will be discussing below exhibit one or more of these factors, which, when several are present, can interact in various complex ways. Psychodynamics ordinarily embraces early childhood patterns emanating from parent-child, teacher-student, peer-related and other experiences that become interwoven into the emerging personality. These in turn affect what we may call *motivational* factors that in adult life more directly influence behavior (including evil actions), such as the motives policemen think of when confronted with a murder case: greed, jealousy, lust, hatred, envy and the like. In addition there are the *varieties* of criminal acts, reaching the level of *evil*, committed by the persons I will describe further on. I have already given examples of many of these varieties in a previous work (Stone, 2009), but here I will give attention mainly to what I call the "New Evil." I noticed in my survey of violent crimes over the past century, that the majority of the crimes we would call evil arose since the mid-1960s; some were all but unheard of until the mid-1980s. As with war, evil has always been—and will always be—with us. They are phenomena to which our species is strongly predisposed, but the forms in which these phenomena occur are colored to a certain extent by era and culture. Evil is not new, but the New Evil does appear to have taken shape within my lifetime.

Most of the examples I will provide involve crimes of violence: murder, rape, kidnap, torture, where cruelty and sadism figure importantly in the action, and where narcissism or (at the extreme of the narcissistic spectrum) psychopathy are key elements in the personality of the criminal. With few exceptions, the evil acts bespoke malice aforethought, which adds to the likelihood we would regard the acts as evil. These acts are *headline* material, not man-A in a barroom hitting man-B with a chair when B insulted him. The latter we may find repellant, but our jaws do not drop in horror. My original list for the New Evil was arranged alphabetically; here it is more appropriate to regroup them by category.

The New Evil

Bullying

There is nothing new about bullying, but what we have witnessed in recent years is a new type of bullying, relying on the Internet, Facebook, and other new forms of mass communication. One manifestation of this bullying that has captured widespread attention in the media is the organized derision of a highly attractive adolescent girl by her plain-looking and envy-smitten schoolmates, leading to the suicide of the attractive girl. One such victim was 12-year-old Rebecca Sedwick, who jumped to her death after the combined efforts at mockery by age-mates Katelyn Roman and Guadeloupe Shaw. One of them acknowledged that "I bullied Rebecca and she killed herself, but I don't give a fuck." We know little about the early lives of the perpetrators (other than that they were very plain-looking), nor can we with any confidence label them "psychopaths" or even "callous-unemotional youths" (Frick, 1998; Moffit, 1993). Psychodynamics aside then, we can only speak about motive. Here, the deadliest (or at least the least remediable) of the Seven Deadly Sins: Envy (aggravated in this case by the impulsivity of youth). Four other cases of school-girls in the last few years bullied for their beauty and who committed suicide were Amanda Todd (age 14), Audrie Pott (age 15), Phoebe Prince (age 15), and Rehtaeh Parsons (age 17), all victimized by envious schoolmates who, thanks to the Internet, were able to make their acid remarks go "viral" and thus have much greater impact than harassment confined (as in the old days) to one class, one school. A more well-known example of envy that culminated in outright murder is that of the Manson-follower Susan Atkins (Guinn, 2013, p. 107). Atkins grew up in a chaotic household, became promiscuous, got into alcohol and drugs—and robbery to pay for her habits—and was then mesmerized by Charles Manson into exacting revenge (his and hers) against the people who had everything. It was she, albeit a young mother herself, that stabbed to death Sharon Tate in August of 1969. To Tate's "three strikes against her": exceptional beauty, fame and wealth was added a fourth: she was 9 months pregnant. The late 1960s was a dividing line between the old and the new evil. We will have more to say about that in the discussion.

Child Abuse

There are many cases of child abuse that strike us as somehow different from what we witnessed in the earlier part of the last century. The diabolical torture of a child we regard as evil, regardless of whether the child survives or not. By diabolical I refer to especially depraved and carefully thought-out acts of violence that seem unparalleled in the annals of crime. An example: Mark Berndt, a Los Angeles elementary school teacher in his 60s. Berndt committed innumerable lewd and sadistic acts against his pupils, including putting cockroaches on their faces, feeding them cookies laced with his semen, exhibitionism, voyeurism, bondage, sexual molestation and photographing them in sexual poses. Convicted in 2013, he will spend the rest of his days in prison. We know nothing of his background. As to motive, Berndt's sadism and multiple paraphilias appear to have been in the service of exercising power in the sexual arena, as a compensation—in all likelihood—for impotence and failure as a man. Paraphilias in general, and of whatever sort, may be considered the last refuge, so to say, by which weak men can fancy themselves strong. The perverse behaviors of Berndt we experience as evil—because of their extreme repugnance, even though they fell short of murder.

Stepmothers are often reviled in children's fairy-stories, but none reach the depths of depravity of Jessica Schwarz—a Florida woman who tortured and eventually murdered her 10-year-old stepson, Andrew. The catalog of cruelties she inflicted on the boy make for uncomfortable reading. She would make him do all the chores at home: if he didn't clean the kitchen spotlessly, and if a roach were seen scurrying around, she would make Andrew eat it. Or she would push his face in the kitty litter and make him pick dog-feces up with his hands. He was forced to wear a T-shirt that said "I'm a piece of shit, don't talk to me," while she cursed at him with epithets like fuck-face, bastard's baby (Andrew was the illegitimate son of Jessica's husband by a prior union), or crack-head. Jessica forced Andew to walk around the house naked, and also locked him for long times inside his bedroom. She once struck the boy hard enough to give him two black eyes and a broken nose then told the school authorities he had "fallen off his bike." Finally when he was 10 in 1993 she threw him in the family pool naked and drowned him. We know something of her early life thanks to the research done by the authors of the true-crime book, Carol Rothgeb and prosecutor Scott Cupp (2005). Jessica née Woods grew up in a well-to-do home in Long Island, one of two daughters of an alcoholic shipping company executive. Jessica was considered "butch" (i.e., very masculine, though not gay), and once knocked her sister Stephanie out during a squabble. Jessica was "tough: you didn't mess with her," and was heavily into drugs throughout her adolescence: marijuana, alcohol, LSD and crack cocaine and was known for being foul-mouthed and uncouth. Indulged rather than abused while growing up, she wanted to be a truck driver, and her father bought her an 18-wheeler. Dave Schwarz, her second husband, was also a truck driver. The prosecutor at her trial said that her treatment of Andrew went beyond cruel; it was evil. Absent an early abuse history, perhaps her sadism and choice of a typically masculine line of work must be written off to constitutional factors that inclined her to grow up as a caricature of the worst of "masculine" traits (lack of empathy, harshness, master-sergeant-like toughness and intolerance). She will not outlive her 70-year sentence in Broward Prison.

Cruelty

Most of the cases I am describing involve uncommon levels of cruelty, but in some instances, an example seems to resist being pigeon-holed into any of the broader categories. In 2012 24-year-old Valerie Bartkey and, at the cusp of womanhood, her 17-year-old companion, Amanda Johnson, forced a high-school boy of 18 to drink their urine; they then twisted his penis with pliers because he refused to join them in smoking marijuana. To compound his uncooperativeness, he then refused to have sex when Valerie demanded it. When he threatened to complain to the authorities, Amanda said: "If you don't drop these fucking charges, we'll tell the police you did weed!" But charge them he did. At trial the women were given no more than a judicial slap on the hand: a few weeks in prison and an order to write the boy a letter of apology. Their biographies are not available, so we can only speculate that the women's movement in the late 1960s and *Roe v Wade* shortly after in 1973 gave women many freedoms that had hitherto been unjustifiably denied them. But for a few, freedom gave way to license to behave as badly (and in the same ways) as the worst of men.

Fetus-Snatching

A quarter-century ago Darci Pierce, née Ricker (D. Hughes, 1992), at age 20, inaugurated (if that is the correct word) an altogether new type of violent crime. It has as yet no official name, so I have called it fetus-snatching. Adopted into a blue-collar Oregon family, Darci hated her birth mother for giving her away and her adoptive mother for being fat. She had rage-outbursts at home, had intercourse with her cousins from age 6 to 13 and with an uncle and a large number of other men on the sly. She was taunted at school (where she was a straight-A student) for being an adoptee. Darci, described as narcissistic, grandiose, histrionic and antisocial, used her beauty to manipulate others. She entertained dreams of great wealth, living in mansions, taking fabulous trips and of having a baby, to prove how much better a mother she could be than her mothers. She conned a boyfriend, Ray Pierce, into marrying her, claiming he had gotten her pregnant. To keep the lie going as the days passed, she finally kidnapped at gunpoint a 9-month pregnant woman coming out of an obstetrics clinic. Driving her to a remote area, Darci slit open the woman's belly with a car-key, extracted the fetus and pretended it was hers. She is now serving a 30-year sentence. Here we have some good information as to psychodynamics: the fury at being given up for adoption, her disappointing "low-class" status, the taunting at school and her extraordinary sense of entitlement: killing without remorse a pregnant woman and using the baby as a bargaining chip in guaranteeing a marriage. Besides Darci's crime in 1987, there have been 17 other cases of fetus-snatching and two of stealing a two-day-old baby for the same purpose (to "prove" motherhood). All the cases have occurred in the U.S.

Home-Invasion

Until recently the most notorious crime involving home-invasion and murder was the 1959 execution-style killing of the well-to-do Kansas farmer, Herb Clutter, and his wife and two younger daughters. The story of the crime and its perpetrators, the two ex-cons, Dick Hickock and Perry Smith, was memorialized in Truman Capote's famous 1965 book *In Cold Blood*. Hoping to cash in on the moneys in the farmer's safe and live the good life afterward, the two men, whose motives were envy and greed, found no money at all. The story of the 2007 home invasion of Dr. Petit and his family in Connecticut was different. Envy and greed were of course factors, but lust played a role also. The team of two this time were psychopaths: Steven Hayes, 44, and Josh Komisarjevsky, 27—the latter an adoptee in a middle-class Connecticut family who had raised him in an atmosphere free from abuse, neglect or other adverse factors. Komisarjevsky was a "Bad Seed," a thief and burglar in adolescence and a drug addict who stole to support his cocaine and methamphetamine habit. After breaking into the Petit home, they knocked the doctor unconscious with a bat, tied up the daughters, and drove Mrs. Petit to the bank, forcing her to withdraw $15,000, warning her that they would kill her if she notified the police. Upon re-entering the home, they of course killed her (she could have identified them), and then raped the daughters, finally pouring accelerant, in hopes of destroying evidence of their crimes in the ensuing flames. Dr. Petit survived. The killers received the death penalty for what was the most ghastly crime in the state's history (though in Connecticut that means only life sentences without parole). At the court, a supporter of Dr. Petit said: "I came here to see what evil looked like."

Infanticide

I will focus here on *Infanticide* with uncommon cruelty. The term is used two ways: "infanticide" (with a little "i") when referring to killing a baby of less than a year old, and "Infanticide" (with a capital "I") to refer to killing children in general, though another term "filicide" is also used for the killing of children older than one. Killing newborns (another common term: *neonaticide*) goes back to prehistoric times, as a crude method of birth control; killing babies, especially females, is still widely practiced in Asia (Pakistan, China) either for population control or for avoiding having to pay a bride price later on (Stone, Krischer & Steinmeyer, 2005). But these cases did not involve torture or other varieties of evil at the Grand Mal level. The case of Dr. Deborah Green is quite different. Though class valedictorian with an IQ of 165, she was personally autocratic, abrasive, confrontational and given to foul language, fond of no one but her cats. She had three children with her physician husband Mike Farrar, whom she would call fuckhole or asshole in front of the children. She abused narcotics and benzodiazepines, becoming an abusive tantrumy harridan who set fire to the house when Mike first spoke of divorce. The insurance company failed to detect the fraud and gave her money, with which they bought an 18-room mansion. Mike began an affair with a sweet and attractive woman; when Deborah discovered this, she started poisoning her husband with ricin, which led to his being hospitalized 11 times before the correct diagnosis was made. He now sued for divorce in earnest and also custody, which led her to threaten that he would get custody "over our dead bodies." She once again burned the house down, this time with the children in it. One jumped to safety; the other two died in the fire while Deborah watched nonchalantly from outside. Her personality had many aberrations, meeting criteria for schizoid, borderline and narcissistic disorders. She pled to life without parole by way of avoiding the death penalty. As to her original family, her father was gregarious; her sister was quite normal, but her mother was described as "cold." The primary motive was of course revenge: The worst damage she could inflict upon her husband was to kill their children. The story is in every way a duplicate of Euripides' Medea where the barbarian wife (Medea) kills her children to punish Jason for leaving her to marry Glauké, a princess whom Medea also kills with the "gift" of a poisoned robe. I suspect Deborah had plotted how to get some ricin into her husband's fiancée, to complete the drama, but this scene did not unfold.

From the standpoint of torture, however, there are much worse cases of infanticide (as filicide) in the recent years than that of Dr. Green. In another work (Stone, 2009) I described two women, one of whom (Theresa Knorr) tortured and killed her teenage daughters out of morbid envy of their youthful attractiveness. Knorr (Clarkson, 1995) took one of her daughters in 1984 to a remote spot in California's Bay Area and had her son pour gasoline over the girl, burning her alive to the point where her charred body could not be identified. Another daughter she chained to a pipe in a closet, leaving her to starve to death. In 1965, Gertrude Baniszewski, was entrusted with the care of an acquaintance's 15-year-old daughter, Sylvia (J. Dean, 2008). Envy was again the primary motive: The girl was much prettier than Baniszewski's teenage (and already pregnant) daughter. The punishment she exacted for that "offense" was to have the girl burned, beaten, scalded, kicked in the groin, forced to ingest urine and feces and then branded with a hot needle in the abdomen with the words "I am a prostitute and proud of it." Sylvia was then tied to the bed and starved to death. Baniszewski, depicted as an embittered and impoverished woman, vengeful and sadistic, with six mostly illegitimate children of her own, had only this to say at her trial: "I had to teach the girl a lesson."

Jealousy-Murder

There is inevitably some overlap in the categories I have chosen here. Deborah Green, in her mimicry of Medea, is as noteworthy for jealousy as for infanticide, but the gruesomeness of burning her children to death makes the infanticide aspect even more prominent than the jealousy aspect. Jealousy affects the sexes about equally. Women are particularly susceptible to the loss of a husband's support during their child-bearing years; men fear a woman's infidelity as though they (the men) may get stuck toiling to support a child with another man's DNA. The child-issue is not the only ingredient of jealousy-murder. A passionate and all-consuming possessiveness of a lover is a common stimulus as well, as in the case of Richard Namey (Lasseter, 2006). Namey's parents divorced when he was young; he later became addicted to heroin. Possessively fixated on one woman after the other and abusive toward each, the first two fled to get away from him. He finally teamed up with Sara Rodriguez, toward whom he was also abusive. When she tried to leave for a nicer and more stable man, Namey stalked them and shot both (Sara died; her new beau was paralyzed from the chest down).

The evil in Namey's case is not so different from much earlier jealousy-murders, such as the murder of architect Stanford White by Harry Thaw, enraged by White's previous affair with the famous model Evelyn Nesbit, whom Thaw married in 1905. Dubbed "The Crime of the Century," it was one of many "crimes of the century" in America, all but one fueled by jealousy (the exception being the Leopold and Loeb case in 1924). Contrast these with some recent jealousy-murders that have a distinctly contemporary feel.

In 1990 Julio Gonzalez, an émigré formerly imprisoned in Cuba for military desertion, had a menial job in Queens, NY (from which he was fired) and a girlfriend, Lydia Feliciano, who had broken up with him. She was a hat-check girl in the Happy Land disco in the Bronx. Drunk and fighting with Lydia at the disco, he was thrown out by the bouncer. At that point he bought a dollar's worth of gasoline and spread it on the disco's only stairway and escape route. Eighty-seven people perished in the blaze; almost none escaped, although Lydia did through the back door at the hat-check box.

In 2009 Nasra al-Enezi in the Kuwait town of al-Jahra was enraged that her husband, Zayed Zafiri, was taking a second wife (permissible in Islamic law). At Islamic wedding ceremonies the men and women are gathered in separate tents. Pouring the same dollar's worth (approx.) of gasoline on the tent (which also had but one exit), al-Enezi, two months pregnant at the time, created a fire that killed 58 women and girls and wounded 90 others. Though the bride's mother and sister were killed, the bride survived. By Kuwaiti law, a pregnant woman cannot be executed, but to ensure that her death sentence could be carried out, she was forcibly aborted while in prison.

As a psychoanalyst I find it of interest that the otherwise "dead metaphors" in our language: "afire with passion," "aflame with jealousy," "burning up with rage" come alive (ironically) in cases of murders prompted by jealousy, a great many of which are committed via arson. Unlike Gonzalez and al-Enezi who *hoped* their intended victims would die in the blaze, some jealous killers leave nothing to chance. Daphne Wright, for example, was in a lesbian relationship with Sallie Collins and came to suspect (incorrectly) that Darlene VanderGiesen was trying to break up Collins' relationship with Wright. Adding a bit to the drama of the case: all three women were deaf-mutes. In a fit of jealousy, Wright killed VanderGiesen, cut up her body in pieces with a chain saw, and then, in keeping with the (not so) dead metaphor, *burned* all the pieces. I chose these fiery examples as part of the New Evil, since jealousy-murders in past times were rarely accompanied by this kind of wanton destructiveness.

Kidnap

Because of the public detestation of anyone kidnapping a child for ransom, and because the crime carries a death penalty that was almost certain to be carried out swiftly, kidnap-for-ransom has remained a comparatively uncommon crime. In the realm of kidnapping, demand for ransom was, in effect, the Old Evil. In the New Evil there was a new twist. A divorced parent abducting a child in a custody battle was a common situation in either era, but we now began to see kidnap for *sexual* purposes: rape, rape followed by murder, or creating a sexual slave via prolonged imprisonment. In my review of 1600 cases in my personal files, plus other cases from the literature, kidnap in the pre-1960 period was usually for ransom. The first in the U.S. was the celebrated kidnap of Charley Ross in 1874: the two-year-old boy of a prominent family near Philadelphia (Fass, 1997). The $20,000 ransom was not paid; the two kidnappers were later shot to death, but the boy was never found. There were other cases in between, but the next high-profile kidnap was that of 14-year-old Bobby Frank in 1924 by Leopold and Loeb, who demanded $10,000, although they had killed their victim. All previous cases were eclipsed in drama by the kidnap (for $70,000) of two-year-old Charles Lindbergh Jr., son of the most illustrious hero of the day, following his famous 1927 trans-Atlantic flight. The ransom was paid (considered a serious mistake at the time as encouraging other criminals to kidnap for money in the future), the child was killed, and one man was executed for the crime: Bruno Hauptmann, although the killer may well have been a different man: John Knoll. Then in 1953, there was the kidnap, famous in its day, in Kansas city of six-year-old Bobby Greenlease by Carl Hall and his accomplice, Bonnie Heady. (Heidenry, 2009). Both were psychopaths: the degenerate offspring of very wealthy families. Carl was an army deserter, alcoholic, disinherited by his mother. He persuaded Bonnie (by this time a prostitute) to go to Bobby's school, pretending to be his aunt offering the lie that he "needed to be taken to the hospital where his mother had had a heart attack." The two then demanded a $600,000 ransom ($5.3 million in current money), which was paid. They told the parents Bobby "didn't want to come to the phone," but of course they had already killed him, lest he identify his abductor. Their hope was to live happily ever after in California with the money. The pair, described as "evil and depraved"; their crime, "heinous," were soon caught and sentenced to death and executed three months later. Their speedy execution seems to have discouraged others from attempting kidnap for ransom as though it could be a profitable enterprise.

What we are witnessing instead in the last few decades is kidnap for sex (via rape) with or without subsequent murder or unlawful imprisonment of the victim as a sex-slave for long periods of time. The key dynamic, or better put, underlying abnormality is sexual inadequacy. The men (they are invariably men) are most often pathetic, socially awkward individuals; some however are violent psychopaths, also socially inadequate but endowed also with a penchant for sadistic control. Among the first were Burton Abbot, who abducted, raped, and killed Stephanie Bryant in 1955; Otis O'Toole, who killed and presumably had raped 6-year-old Adam Walsh in 1981; the abductor of 10-year-old Kevin Collins (never identified) in 1984; the kidnap and subsequent disappearance in 1989 of Jacob Wetterling; and the kidnap/rape/murder of Polly Klaas in 1993 by Richard Allen Davis (whose long series of violent crimes inspired California's "three-strikes" law).

Among kidnappers who kept their quarries as sexual slaves for long periods, the lengths of unlawful imprisonment vary over a wide range. John Esposito, for example, kidnapped nine-year-old Katie Beers, placing her in the underground bunker he had specially built in a place not far from her Long Island home. There she was molested sexually, but fortunately Esposito was captured 17 days later and Katie was released. A self-styled Mormon guru in Utah kidnapped Elizabeth Smart at knife-point in 2002, binding her in a remote spot, raping her several times a day, and holding her hostage for nine months before she was rescued. Mitchell, long known as a pedophile, molester of his stepdaughter, and an exhibitionist, was mentally ill (though considered legally sane at trial), imagining himself a "Davidic servant prepared by God as a Messiah, and summoned to acquire seven more wives" besides the one he had, a typical enough mind-set to "justify" having sex with any girl to whom he took a fancy. He is now serving a life sentence. In Syracuse, New York, a well-to-do man born in 1935, John Jamelske, who had always been an asocial "loner" in his youth, began, in what was called a "mid-life crisis" at 40, to dress like an adolescent, sport a pony-tail and capture a number of young women in his underground bunker, keeping them for periods from six months to several years. He was sentenced when arrested to life in prison. Depending on sexual orientation, kidnappers of this sort may capture either girls or boys. Michael Devlin in Missouri was a homosexual pedophile and an adoptee: a loner who kept to himself, well-liked at the pizzeria where he worked, though irascible with his neighbors. There were no clear "dynamics," as his adoptive parents were kindly, devoted, non-abusive and supportive, though his having been mocked in school for being fat (and perhaps for being gay) may have been a factor. In 2002 while trolling for boys of around 11, he waylaid Shawn Hornbeck at gunpoint and took him home. There he kept him for four years as a sexual slave, forcing him to refer to himself as Shawn Devlin, his "godson." The boy developed the "Stockholm Syndrome," somehow identifying with his captor to the point of not running away when given a bit of freedom to walk outside the house. He was rescued at age 15 and reunited with his parents. Devlin was sentenced to life without parole. It would appear that pre-natal factors were primary here: schizoid personality, homosexual orientation and perhaps also his pedophilic predilection, all presumably influenced by genetic factors in his biological parents, about whom we know nothing.

More mysterious as to dynamics and motives is the story of Cameron Hooker, whose parents were "salt-of-the-earth" types and who was not the product of an aberrant or abusive childhood (McGuire & Norton, 1988). Yet after his marriage, he became sadistic toward his wife, choking her to unconsciousness, subjecting her to bondage and acting out his fantasies of absolute power. In 1977, two years after his marriage, he abducted a 20-year-old hitchhiker, Colleen Stans, and kept her for seven years a sex slave, 23 hours a day in a coffin-like box he had built and placed underneath the marital bed, while he and his submissive wife carried on as a "normal" family with their two children. Colleen and the wife finally escaped. Cameron was ultimately sentenced to 104 years in prison, despite some initial puzzlement by the jury, given that Colleen (in another instance of Stockholm Syndrome) appeared to submit to intercourse willingly, in her effort to adjust to her intolerable situation. Evil prolonged becomes evil accepted.

In the still more startling case of Phillip Garrido (Glatt, 2010), we know a considerable amount about the origins of his enslavement for 18 years of Jaycee Dugard: the relevant factors here being biological and not the product of a disturbed home. He grew up in a stable, loving and unexceptionable, working-class family in California where all was well until he was 14. Then, as I learned from talking with his elderly father, Phillip took without permission the motorcycle of his elder brother and crashed it. He was taken unconscious to a hospital for brain surgery, specifically the removal of a frontal subdural hematoma. Following this, he underwent a rapid and drastic personality change in a manner analogous to that of Phineas Gage in the 1848 iron-bar accident (H. Damasio et al., 1994). Phil became obsessed with wanting to rape virgins. He also became heavily involved with alcohol and psychotomimetic drugs: marijuana, LSD, methamphetamine, cocaine, creating a self-induced manic-like psychosis with grandiose delusions as though he were God-like, or perhaps God himself. He raped a woman in Nevada and was sent to prison for "50 years," only to be released after 11. He had raped many girls before that, but (as so often happens in such cases) they refused to testify against him. He now abducted 11-year-old Jaycee Dugard, keeping her a sex-slave in his backyard for 18 years, with his wife (who was infertile) looking the other way. Phil had two daughters by Jaycee, who never went to school or saw other people. At 29 Jaycee was able to flee, reuniting with her mother who had long given up hope of ever seeing her daughter again. Garrido was sentenced to life in prison; Jaycee was awarded 20 million dollars by the state of California. The immensity of evil here beggars description. Over and above the anguish of the victim, who had to bear up under the indignity of her misuse and love her rape-children, there are her parents and their three decades of suffering at not knowing their daughter's fate. And yet in Europe a still worse story emerged: that of the Viennese Nazi-sympathizer Josef Fritzl (Glatt, 2009), for whom there was no mitigating circumstance like psychosis: unlike Garrido, Fritzl was a pure example of psychopathy overlain with a sadism of mind-numbing proportions. Fritzl had constructed an impregnable bunker beneath his own house, in the "upstairs" of which he lived with his wife and seven children. He already had a history of rape when he was 32, for which he served 18 months. When he was 49 he forced his eldest daughter Elizabeth down into the bunker, where he repeatedly assaulted and raped her, siring an additional seven incest-children by Elizabeth. One died shortly after birth (whom Fritzl disposed of by tossing him in the furnace). Three were allowed upstairs to be raised by his wife as "foster children." The other three saw the world only in two dimensions, like the creatures chained in Plato's cave, seeing only images on a wall in front of them (Plato's Republic §514a–520a), as projected by a fire in back of them. Elizabeth was held captive for 24 years, freed only in 2008, thanks to the illness of her daughter Kerstin, requiring "outside" attention. She and the three children now live under different names in a remote Austrian village, reliant on psychotherapy that would take more than a lifetime to be completely effective. The evil of Fritzl, besides being "new" is also unique in the world's literature. Fritzl described his early years as ones in which he grew up as an only child without a father, raised by a mother whom he alternately depicted as "the best woman in the world," and as an abusive harridan who never gave him a kiss and beat him till he lay in a pool of blood on the floor. Even if the latter scenario could be verified, it cannot suffice to account for the man's savagery and indifference to human feelings.

Mass Murder

Because of the large number of deaths resulting from each mass murder, this form of violence has the most electrifying effect on the public. There is no hesitation about calling these murders "evil," and to this unanimity of sentiment is added an element of quantifiability not easily achieved in relation to other species of violence. I have been able to create a spreadsheet, tallying the mass murders—both those meeting FBI standards (4 or more deaths in one incident) and mass murders manqué (where the killer's intention was to perpetrate a mass murder, but the toll fell short of 4)—since 1900; effectively, a 114 years of mass murder (Stone, 2014). These incidents include 227 occurring in the U.S. and 97 in other countries. Looking at the murders decade by decade, it turns out that in the years 1900 through 1969 there were 38 that I could identify in the U.S. and 12 abroad. But in the years 1970 through 2013 there were 203 in the U.S. and 45 abroad. These figures represent the more highly publicized incidents and do not, for example, include every instance of "familicide" (a man killing all his family and often himself)—a variety of mass murder not always readily accessible outside governmental organizations. But the sudden jump from no more than eight mass murders in a decade, prior to 1970 to figures of 22, 32, 75 and 51 in the U.S., during the decades from 1970 through 2009 (and in the teens in other countries, as opposed to just zero to four prior to 1970) creates a visible dividing line between Old and New Evil, vis-à-vis the phenomenon of mass murder. What accounts for this abrupt transition? This becomes clear when we look at the means employed by the killers. Before 1970, semiautomatic pistols and rifles accounted for three out of 50 mass murders in the U.S. and other countries combined. From 1970 on, a dramatic increase in the use, especially in the U.S., of semiautomatic weapons: 102 out of 258 in both domains, an increase from six to 40%. The years 2010 through the first half of 2014 are barely half a decade, but already in the U.S. 23 of the 36 mass murders so far have been carried out with semiautomatics: 64% of the total. Semiautomatic rifles in particular were developed in World War II (such as the AK-47 and the Uzi) but could not be readily purchased by people in everyday life until the late 1960s. One of the three American mass murderers who used semiautomatic weapons before 1970 was a veteran (Howard Unruh, in 1949).

An unfortunate stigma has attached to mental illness as conferring a predisposition to commit mass murder, because of several recent high-profile cases: three involved autistic men in their twenties (Seung Hui-Cho in Virginia Tech; Adam Lanza in Newtown, Connecticut; and Elliot Rodger in Santa Barbara); drug-induced psychosis was present in another (Jared Loughner in Arizona), and paranoid schizophrenia in yet another (Aaron Alexis in Washington, D.C.). James Holmes in Aurora, Colorado, exhibits the traits of schizotypal personality. Collectively, these men were responsible for the deaths of 97 persons. Two points need to be emphasized. First, approximately 160 deaths per year from mass murder in the U.S. in recent years account for only 1% of the 16,000 gun-murders in the country. Second, in my survey of mass murderers (97% of whom are men) over the past century, only about 22 to 25% could be considered "mentally ill," if by this phrase one means persons with a frank psychosis or an Asperger-type autistic condition. Many others are men with paranoid traits—who become violent when disgruntled and suddenly overcome with rage—following job-loss, rejection by a lover or divorce. But they were not "certifiably" psychotic. There have always been disgruntled men (and a few women), but the New Evil, in relation to mass murder, is this: the rendering easy the acquisition of semiautomatic weapons. We often know less than we wish, concerning the psychodynamics and precipitating factors in mass murder, since about half die by suicide or are killed by the police *in flagrante delicto*.

Regarding the more typical (and non-psychotic) mass murderer, the case of Wade Michael Page is illustrative. Page grew up in Colorado. We know little about his family other than that his parents had divorced; his father remarried, and later his stepmother divorced him. Page spent about six years in the Army but was demoted and then discharged for misconduct because of drinking and being absent without leave. Returning to Colorado as a truck-driver, he was fired for drunk driving. He became involved in white-supremacist Neo-Nazi groups, living now in Wisconsin—where his neighbors knew him as a "loner" who avoided eye contact. For a time he had a girlfriend, herself part of the Neo-Nazi group, but even she eventually rejected him, as did his boss from his most recent job. It was after these most recent failures that, in the summer of 2012, he purchased a semi-automatic gun and took out his disgruntlement on the worshipers at a Sikh temple in the southeast corner of the state. He murdered six of the worshipers before he then, as the police closed in on him, killed himself. Why the Sikhs? We don't really know. My best guess is that Page, with his hideously distorted values, probably imagined that those peaceful turban-wearing people were Muslims and therefore "had it coming to them" for 9/11. In the aftermath of 9/11 many Sikh taxi-drivers in New York City, for example, were injured by thugs who mistook them for Muslims (as if it were now "open season" on Muslims). Another guess: Many men who commit mass murder are dismal failures in their everyday lives, feel hopeless accordingly but decide to vent their rage by taking down as many other people as they can during their final suicidal act—going down in what for them is a "blaze of glory." In this way they garner their "fifteen minutes of fame" (Andy Warhol's tongue-in-cheek promise to the average person) so that their lives would not be totally forgotten. It may not be a psychodynamic in the usual sense but is certainly an explanatory motive—when a "nobody" like Page, or like Mark David Chapman (the killer of the famous John Lennon), becomes through murder—a "somebody."

Murder with Aggravated Circumstances

The mundane murders that fill spots in the back pages of our tabloids are of course evil in their own way, but they do not startle us and do not often evoke the horror that defines evil—especially the New Evil, where something different, something we have never before witnessed or heard of rivets our attention: murder, with what I call "aggravated circumstances."

One such case was the 1974 Ogden, Utah, murders at the HI-FI Shop. The ringleader in the robbery plan was a Trinidadian, Dale Pierre, whose carpenter father had emigrated with the family to Brooklyn. Dale was an incorrigible juvenile delinquent, expelled from school because of his fiery temper and numerous thefts. He had dreams of amassing great wealth and of impressing everyone with flashy cars. Dale joined the Air Force as a ground-crew worker in Ogden. He continued to steal, and when he was about to be disciplined by a sergeant whose car he had stolen, he bayoneted the sergeant to death—but for want of definite proof was not arrested. At this point, he convinced two acquaintances to join him in robbing the record shop. There were at first two employees and a young customer—joined a few hours later when two of their worried parents also showed up. Dale and an accomplice tied them all up at gunpoint and forced them to drink Drano [a sodium-hydroxide based industrial cleanser], burning their mouths and esophagus. Dale shot four, killing two, and then raped the female employee before killing her also. One man still seemed alive, so Dale, after trying to strangle the man with a wire, pushed a pen into his ear, stomping on it such that it emerged from his throat, yet the man survived. He required nine months of surgery to deal with the mouth and esophagus injuries. Never fully overcoming the trauma, he died in his early 40s. This was regarded as the most heinous crime in Utah history up to that time or since. Dale and his accomplice were ultimately executed. The third man, driving the getaway car, was given a lighter sentence. Dale Pierre was one of those fortunately rare individuals whose lives seem consecrated to the Satanic every hour of their waking life.

Another psychopath of that mold, Phil Skipper, was equally a stranger to compassion. Like Pierre, he qualifies as an "evil person," as opposed to the far more common situation: a person guilty of one or two evil acts. Skipper's father was serving a life sentence—for rape, aggravated sodomy, and murder. Phil and his wife lived a marginal existence in rural Louisiana, with no known occupation apart from robbing graves. Phil took in as a kind of stepson Johnny Baillio, whom he used to tie to a tree, burn with a cigar and then force at knifepoint to give him oral sex. Next to the trailer where Phil lived with his family was a house owned by a Black woman, Genore Guillory. Genore had a good job and was very generous, giving the Skippers money for food, diapers and other necessities. She even (unbeknownst to them) had included them in her will for a substantial sum. But when her dog killed the Skippers' pet goat, Phil's bigotry was switched on to the "max," and he told his buddies (all of whom were Ku Klux Klan enthusiasts): "Let's go kill us a nigger!" whereupon they proceeded to stab, shoot, and finally bludgeon her to death with a bat. They all then gang-raped her post mortem. Right after, Phil, surprisingly *au courant* despite his illiteracy, forced a Black man at gunpoint to masturbate into a cup so that Phil could then toss the contents over Genore's body, misleading the police into thinking the killer was a Black man. For a time he and his gang returned to their main source of revenue: stealing jewelry and gold from graves. Phil and his accomplices were caught eventually when one of the gang bragged to someone about the crime. Phil and his main "helper" were given life sentences; the one who confessed got five years. Besides his miserable upbringing and culturally sanctioned bigotry, "bad genes" may have been a factor in the crime as well, given the incarceration of Phil's father for the same trio of rape, sodomy and murder.

What makes the murders in this section singular and different from earlier examples is a kind of devilish ingenuity in their planning, relying on mechanisms hitherto unheard of: the painful murder by lye in the Utah case, the use of someone else's DNA to throw police off the scent in the Phil Skipper case. Making a corpse disappear was not unheard of in bygone times, but the methodology in recent times sometimes beggars the imagination. Such is the case with the Brazilian soccer goalee, Bruno Fernandes, in his efforts to cope with a recalcitrant mistress. He had been carrying on an affair with a model, Eliza Samudio, who became pregnant in 2009. Unwilling to pay support for a love-child, Bruno insisted she abort the pregnancy, but she refused, despite an effort by Bruno's associates to force her to take an illegal abortion drug. Bruno warned her: "You don't know what I'm capable of! I'm from the favela!" [the slums of Rio]. The baby was born and then taken by Bruno's wife, Dayane, to a different slum in Belo Horizonte. Bruno next hired a friend to "take care of" Eliza who was then tortured, strangled and dismembered. Her body parts were then fed to Bruno's 10 Rottweiler dogs, the inedible portions buried in concrete. One of Bruno's cousins later had a pang of conscience and told the authorities, whereupon Bruno was arrested, sentenced to 22 years and sent to prison. Briefly. Shortly after, another soccer team obtained permission from a judge for Bruno to play in future matches—with the proviso that he be accompanied by police escort. Bruno's motives were mainly to avoid humiliation and expense (though he was by now quite wealthy). Though an egotist with no firm moral center, it is not clear whether Fernandes would meet criteria for psychopathy. As to "absence of remorse," yes: when convicted, he lamented that "Now I won't be able to play in the 2014 World Cup."

Less in doubt is the psychopathy of Noel Doorbal (P. Davidson, 2009). A Trinidadian born to a mother of 13, alternately abusive and neglectful, he became a body-builder and "muscle" for a Miami gang that specialized in luring rich businessmen with temptations of "big deals." The businessmen would be kidnapped and then tortured into revealing their credit-card codes, bank codes and safe numbers. The men would afterwards be killed, dismembered and stuffed in oil-drums here and there around Miami. Doorbal, when arrested and convicted, ended up on Florida's Death Row, where I interviewed him for Discovery Channel TV. Con-artist to the end, Doorbal said he would okay the interview but only if we first paid him a thousand dollars to help out his daughter. We did, only to discover moments later that he had no daughter. He then declined the interview. In the Old Evil days before the late '60s, there were men in the Cosa Nostra who operated on their victims in a comparable fashion, but Doorbal and his boss, Daniel Lugo, were not Mafiosi. They developed their scam on their own.

Rape

Because so many victims are reluctant to come forward, rape is the most under-reported and insufficiently punished of the violent crimes. There has been some improvement over the past 30 years, thanks to the possibility of identifying many of the perpetrators via DNA-analysis. This has led to a kind of arms-race: the sophistication of the crime-scene specialists versus the cleverness of the offenders—as we saw with Phil Skipper and his spreading another man's DNA over his murder-and-rape victim. Cleverness aside, some of the rapists in modern times have subjected their victims to a kind of *cruelty* that, with rare exceptions, such as the Northcott case in the 1920s (Flacco, 2009) was scarcely ever recorded in the past.

As a 13-year-old in 1998, Donald Collins raped an eight-year-old boy, Robbie Middleton, and then tied him to a tree and poured gasoline over him, planning to burn him beyond recognition so as to avoid being implicated in the crime. The boy survived, horribly disfigured even after innumerable operations. Shortly before his death at 21 (of complications of his wounds) Robbie did identify his assailant, who was subsequently put in prison for life and fined, symbolically to be sure, $150 billion for the parents.

The 2005 crime of John Evander Couey in Florida against nine-year-old Jessica Lunsford—kidnap, sexual assault, and burial while alive in a garbage bag in a shallow grave—earned Couey, 47 at the time, the death penalty. He had an extensive record of sex offenses going back to when he was 20—at which time he was sentenced to 10 years for molesting a girl in her bedroom—but, as with Phil Garrido, was released soon after, free to reoffend. Couey made repeated sexual offenses upon his release—culminating in the rape-murder of Jessica.

In the last few years several of the most bizarre examples of rape-murder came out of Canada. The story of Luka Magnotta (true name: Eric Clinton Newman), born in Toronto in 1982, surpasses what we might find in the most morbid of pornographic novels. There are some relevant psychodynamics. His parents divorced when he was quite young; the maternal grandparents who then raised him also divorced. Extraordinarily vain and preoccupied with his looks from his earliest days, he changed his hair color often, and at 20 became a stripper in porn flicks, preoccupied at the time with cosmetic surgery. At 22 he engaged in credit-card fraud; his attorney allowed as how his client may have psychological issues (but these are not spelled out). He now became known for his boundless narcissism, even of the most elementary sort (like the mythological Narcissus—who became so enamored of his own image that he pined away until he was metamorphosed into the flower that bears his name): Luka was obsessed with his looks and made endless photographs of himself. At 24 he dated a transgender female; after their break-up he changed his name to Luka Magnotta. The following year, a turning point in his life, he boasted (falsely) on the Internet that he "dated"

Karla Homolka, the former wife of serial killer Paul Bernardo. He worked as a gay escort and created bizarre online postings of violence. His violent streak was actualized in 2010—by placing kittens in sealed bags, sucking the air out till they suffocated and then showing the gruesome process on YouTube. Animal-rights activists were outraged and raised money for his capture. He killed more kittens in 2012 and added new postings of necrophilia. Finally in May of that year he stabbed to death a male Chinese student, committing necrophilia and cannibalism with the corpse, which he then dismembered and sent various pieces to Canadian political organizations. Hands and feet arrived in Vancouver; the head some months later in Montreal. By now he was very much a suspect. He fled to Europe but was soon caught (as Narcissus might have been, had he been a contemporary) looking at pictures of himself on the crime-newscasts in Berlin. There are numerous Internet videos of Magnotta (before his arrest) speaking and posing in the most haughty and self-satisfied manner about his gay liaisons and sexual exploits. Our vocabulary of personality disorders is ill-equipped to characterize persons like Magnotta. His narcissism so far exceeds the egocentricity of the average "narcissist" we encounter in everyday life or in our psychiatric practice that to call these and Magnotta by the same term fails to distinguish the typical from the level *beyond* the extreme that he occupies. His trial took place in December 2014, and despite his having mounted an insanity defense, he was ultimately convicted. But anyone who has listened to his videos would grasp that, while meeting criteria for narcissistic and also for psychopathic and sadistic personalities, there is not a shred of evidence for psychosis.

What strikes us as "new" about the crimes of Magnotta is the quest for notoriety through acts of perversity never before attempted: killing kittens for YouTube, mailing body parts to politicians, guaranteed to make a story for the 11 o'clock news. But for sheer barbarity nothing stands out like the rape-murder of Sedley Alley, described by FBI profiler John Douglas (2013) as "unmitigated evil." Born in 1956, Alley had drowned his first wife in a bathtub shortly after she filed for divorce. The evidence fell short of definitive, and he was never charged. A few years later in 1985 he overpowered a 19-year-old Marine corporal Suzanne Collins in the park the evening before she was about to graduate from aviation school. After bludgeoning her into near unconsciousness, he thrust a two inch thick, nearly yard-long tree branch through her vagina and up past her abdomen and diaphragm, puncturing her lung, killing her. He had also bitten her left breast. For this macabre rape by an inanimate object Alley was given the death penalty. But legal customs had changed. Unlike the Greenlease kidnappers for whom execution was swift, inordinate wrangling delayed execution in Alley's case for 22 years – or, as Douglas pointed out – three years longer than the life of his victim.

After hearing about the Sedley Alley case, I found myself wanting to add yet another compartment to my Gradations of Evil Scale: a "23" to represent an evil more horrifying even than those in "22." I left the scale as it is, but Alley would not have been the sole occupant. There would be a secure place for Michael Rafferty, 28, and his accomplice, Terri McClintic, who in the spring of 2009 in Ontario abducted eight-year-old Tori Stafford. Michael used his 19-year-old girlfriend to lure the girl into his car. They stopped briefly so Terri could purchase garbage bags and a claw hammer. Rafferty had searched the Internet for child pornography in the months before the kidnap, making special queries relating to the violent sexual assault of prepubescent girls. Rafferty proceeded to rape the girl repeatedly and then killed her with blows of the claw hammer that lacerated her liver and crushed her skull. Her body was not found for two-and-a-half months, decomposed and hidden under a pile of rocks next to a tree. Rafferty was sentenced to life—which in Canada means possible eligibility for parole after 25 years. There was confusing testimony at the trial, each claiming the other struck the hammer blows. But this was moot as to the sentencing, since Rafferty was clearly responsible for the rape, which would have cost him 25 years anyway. McClintic herself was no stranger to violence: She had previously stabbed a man, assaulted and partially blinded her adoptive mother and killed a dog, putting it in a microwave when she was a child. As for Rafferty, Judge Thomas Heeny condemned him for snuffing the life of an innocent girl in order to gratify his "twisted and deviant desire to have sex with a child," adding, "Only a monster could commit such an act of pure evil."

Reminiscent of Phil Garrido and Cameron Hooker, a case of prolonged sequestration and rape of not one woman but three came to light in May of 2013, when the no longer adolescent captives were rescued from the shuttered Cleveland home of Ariel Castro (Hall, 2013; M. Knight & M. Buford, 2014). Two of the girls were friends of Castro's daughter. Earlier, Castro had been abusive to his own wife, beating her when she was recovering from brain surgery and shoving her down stairs. Michelle Knight, Amanda Berry and Georgina DeJesus were abducted in the 2003/2004 timeframe. During their captivity, Michelle was impregnated five times, but Castro beat and starved her so as to induce miscarriages in all five. He also impregnated Amanda, who had a daughter. He kept the captives chained to a wall for lengthy periods, allowing little time for toilet and less for showers and often threatening to kill them for any infraction of his "rules." In many ways Castro was more evil than Garrido or Cameron: Castro did not have the extenuating circumstance of being psychotic like Garrido. Also, Garrido did not subject Jaycee to the kinds of torture Castro meted out to his harem. Cameron, let it be said, though he made Colleen call him "master," subjected her only to oral sex, since he had the delicacy to regard vaginal sex with her a violation of his conjugal obligations to his wife. There were obviously no such islands of conventional morality in Castro's makeup. A month after being sentenced at trial to life plus a thousand years Castro abbreviated his own captivity by hanging himself in his cell.

Serial Sexual Homicide

When we speak of serial killers, we are usually referring to men guilty of serial sexual homicide. Doctors and nurses who poison hospital patients are sometimes called Angels of Death (such as Dr. Swango and nurse Charles Cullen in the U.S. and Dr. Shipman in England), another and less common variety of serial killers. Still rarer are mothers who suffocate one baby after the other, such as Mary Beth Tinning (newborns) or Martha Johnson (young children). Serial killers, in general, have been known since the early nineteenth century, but those committing serial sexual homicide were all but unknown until the 1860s, and even then only a few were recorded per decade. From this point on, I am going, for brevity's sake, to use the phrase "serial killer" only as referring to those committing serial sexual homicide. From the standpoint of New Evil, a graph showing the frequency of serial killers during the past century in the U.S. shows a dramatic upsurge beginning in the 1960s. The curve peaks in the 1980s and then begins to descend, although to levels still much greater than what we saw up through 1959 (Aamodt, 2014). The number of serial killers is considerably greater in the U.S. than in any other country, even when adjusted for country population. It does not appear that the level of cruelty inflicted by serial killers has worsened in recent decades, so what is new as to the New Evil, with this type of crime, is not their gruesomeness but their frequency. Dr. Herman Mudgett, for example, converted a Chicago pharmacy into a torture chamber in the 1880s where he tortured and murdered a large but unknown number of young women (Franke, 1975). Mudgett had been raised in comfortable circumstances and had not been abused. Jesse Pomeroy, in contrast, born the same year as Mudgett (1860), had been severely beaten by his father until his mother left when Jesse was about 11 (Schechter, 2000). Jesse had the characteristics of the "callous-unemotional" youths Moffitt has described. He tried, when he was 12, to castrate a boy of six; at 14 he castrated a boy of four, whose right eyeball he also punctured (perhaps in revenge for Jesse having been taunted at school because of his right-eye cataract). He tortured cats even as a child of five and when not quite 15 sexually mutilated and killed a girl he waylaid as she was on her way to a bakery. Pomeroy was arrested, dying after 56 years in a Boston prison.

In our era—the 1960s and beyond—the profile of serial killers more closely resembles that of Pomeroy than of Mudgett. As Aamodt has shown, and is in accordance with my own series of 168 full-length biographies of serial killers, the great majority come from the U.S. (76% in my series), and the great majority come from homes where there was physical or sexual or verbal abuse (singly or in different combinations) of the boys who went on to become serial killers. Less than 10 percent come from homes that were intact, and minimal or negligible as to adverse life events (meaning not even perinatal traumata, head injury or epilepsy). Those that emerged from good homes (and whose mothers did not abuse drugs during pregnancy) are of special interest, because their personality pathology (usually along the lines of psychopathy admixed with sadism) points instead to hereditary predisposition. Mental illness (as manifest by an early diagnosis of schizophrenia or bipolar disorder with psychosis) was less common among serial killers (12% in my series) than among mass murders (22% in my series of 310 mass murderers).

The serial killers of the current era that stand out, in a manner of speaking, from the crowd of other like-minded men are those who have added an extra dimension of the diabolical to their repetitive crimes. Some have created complicated torture chambers on their own property. This was the case with David Parker Ray and his infamous "Toy Box" (a trailer outfitted with implements of torture) in New Mexico and Leonard Lake and his accomplice, Charles Chitat Ng (Harrington & Burger, 1999; Lasseter, 2000). Ray and Lake, albeit heterosexual, developed a violent hatred of women. Lake came by his more understandably: His mother had abandoned him, leaving him with her parents, and never reunited with him. Ray was beaten severely, but by his alcoholic father, not his mother. Lake had fantasies of enslaving women, writing in his diary: "God meant women for cooking, cleaning house, and sex. And when they are not in use, they should be locked up." He and Ng created a combination cabin and torture chamber in a remote spot in southern California—where they kidnapped and tortured women (and a few of their husbands). As to the diabolical nature of the tortures, Lake would at times kidnap a woman and her baby, separating them (as he was separated from his mother? was that his "dynamic"?), tying up the woman, putting her limbs in a vice, and telling her: "You wanna' live: You're gonna cook for us, and clean for us, and fuck for us!" The woman would beg to see her baby—whom they of course had already killed, but telling her that they didn't think she deserved to see her kid. In a similar fashion, David Parker Ray (Glatt, 2002), would use his accomplice, Cindy Hendy, to lure young women from bars in their small town in New Mexico—first to their house, then into the adjacent trailer: the Toy Box. Each victim would be immobilized and hoisted by pulleys, making it easier for Ray to insert various torture devices into their bodies. Ray would then force the victim to hear a tape-recording he had prepared, describing in the most humiliating and frightening detail what was about to happen to her. When I interviewed Cindy Hendy for Discovery Channel, I also acquired copies of Ray's tape (in written form it is 17 pages long, single-spaced), along with his pornographic drawings of women in various torture poses (Ray was a gifted artist and a skillful mechanic). Ray insisted the women always call him "master," which I believe supplies a clue to one of his central psychodynamics. Serial killers share an inability to form enduring relationships of mutual trust and respect with their sexual partners, whether straight or gay—because they are psychosexually weak men driven to compensate for their insecurity by the grandiose mechanism of imagining themselves "masters" or even "gods." They also exhibit an array of paraphilias that also bespeak sexual weakness: why, after all, would a man who felt secure in his partner's love and loyalty need to resort to bondage, date-rape drugs, necrophilia, pedophilia or a host of other abnormal sexual practices—by way of shoring up his doubts about masculinity and attractiveness? But what is "new" about the New Evil in serial killers like Ray and Lake that was not seen in serial killers of the 1860–1960 century is the profound and prolonged *psychological* torture of their victims that preceded the physical torture, itself prolonged far beyond what was noted in their earlier predecessors, with the possible exception of Mudgett.

Ray and Lake are not alone among contemporary serial killers who brought to their thirst for torture an originality—a *virtuosity*, for want of a better term—of sadism that lets the world know: *this never happened before*. These men were what the FBI calls the "organized" type of serial killer: bright, methodical, employed and suave socially.

Among these "virtuosi" was a Canadian Air Force colonel, Russell Williams, who in his pre-crime days was privileged to ferry Queen Elizabeth back and forth when she visited Canada (Gibb, 2012). Williams was the elder of two sons of a British couple who later moved to Canada. His mother was considered a stunning beauty, but prissy and cold. Williams grew up to be socially distant and aloof, meticulous, perfectionistic, and rigid. He married an older woman, and they opted to have no children and for many years no sex. At 44 long-repressed transvestic urges passed from fantasy into action: He broke into people's houses and stole women's bras and panties, dressing himself in those items in his secret moments. The following year he graduated to rape, and finally to prolonged rape with elaborate video-filming of the torture and rape of his victims—making snuff-films of the dying women. When arrested, he confessed—with the promise (later broken) that the police not reveal the kiddie-porn in his computer. Williams led a double life for many years (transvestism does not start at 44), the eventual crimes against women suggestive of a love-hate relationship with his mother. From a psychodynamic standpoint, at least, that is a common forerunner of transvestism: a wish either to recapture (by transiently "becoming" a woman) the lost and loved mother, who may have died during the man's childhood—or a wish to "be" the fantasied "good" mother the man never had. We do not know enough about the details of Williams' life to pinpoint the motives precisely. His brother, at all events, became a physician and is considered normal. In my series, there were only eight other transvestites (i.e., about 5% of the 168). What is special and "new" about Williams is his professionally set up and prolonged filming of his torture, multiple day-long rapes, and eventual murder of his victims, presumably for his future secret enjoyment of the CDs he thus created.

Another serial killer given to extremes of sadism was Randy Kraft (McDougal, 1991). Born in 1945, he grew up in a lower middle-class

Presbyterian family in California, the fourth child and only son. The family was conventional and non-abusive. Kraft dated occasionally in high school and was at first politically conservative. At 19 he worked in a gay bar and around that time acknowledged his own homosexuality, though he did not reveal this to his family until a little later. His mother was accepting; his father, initially outraged. Very bright academically, he graduated college with a degree in economics, joining the Air Force the next year at age 23 but was discharged the next year, apparently because of the non-acceptance of his orientation in that era. He resumed work as a bartender. His first victim was another gay bartender, in 1969. This was when Kraft was not quite 25, similar to the age of the "first rape" by a serial killer: 29 in Aamodt's study; 27 in mine. From then until his arrest in 1983, Kraft pursued a career of strangling or shooting men, including many from the armed services, some gay, some straight, most tortured in excruciating ways before being killed, amounting altogether to 67 known victims, although the total may have neared a hundred. The lucky ones were killed after being "doped" with alcohol laced with tranquillizers. Besides raping his victims initially, Kraft would castrate some, and in others insert long objects into the rectum, or glass rods into the urethra then stomping on the victim's penis so as to splinter the glass inside. Many bodies were mutilated in still other ways and then beheaded. Kraft was ultimately convicted and put on Death Row in San Quentin in 1989, where he remains to this day 25 years later (executions no longer taking place in California). A destabilizing factor may have been a head injury with unconsciousness at age one, which may have contributed to his abnormal PET brain-scan years later showing frontal-lobe underactivity and temporal lobe hyperactivity. As to a psycho-dynamic factor, intense self-hatred of his homosexuality projected onto his male victims (many of whom were gay) may have underlain his sadistic behavior toward men. In my series of 168 serial killers, 24 were either exclusively homosexual (21) or bisexual (3), 14.3% or about 3 times the population average among males. As with Ray and Williams, what is "new" about the evil of Kraft is the combination of extremity and originality of the tortures to which he subjected his victims—in peacetime and by lone individuals. There is, after all, nothing new or extreme about man's capacity for torture within the context of wartime or institutions. The depraved Roman emperor Caligula violated the sphincters of his victims in ways similar to that of Kraft, but Caligula was the emperor and enjoyed what he did by way of showing who held absolute power in his domain. In fourteenth-century England, Mortimer, the lover of Queen Isabella, had the feckless King Edward II killed in the dungeon of Berkeley Castle by having a red-hot spit thrust into his rectum and bowels (it was unlawful to kill a king in a way that left marks on his body)—or so the story goes (A. Fraser, 1999). But that was authorized regicide, not murder by a citizen. Torquemada and the Spanish Inquisition were as devilishly inventive as the worst of our serial killers, as were the Conquistadors in sixteenth-century Peru, the Argentine militia under Peron, the Brazilian military against the "leftists" in 1969–74, etc. The list is very long. As for Randy Kraft, very few men survived his assaults and torture. One survivor, Douglas B. Winters, wrote me in connection with my Discovery Channel program about evil, telling me what he endured in 1977 at the hands of Randy Kraft and about the many years he has spent trying to recover from the effects. He and his wife hope to write a book about male-to-male victimization by rape, which they are still working on. He did write a comment about Nancy Rae's 2007 book on male rape, *A Matter of Time*, stating: "Society needs to understand the unique, yet common issues and conditions male/male rape survivors live with daily. Most of us live and function with untreated post-assault sexual trauma, alone ... most of us overreact or shut down many times daily."

Torture without Murder

In certain instances of torture that stops short of murder but that involves disfigurement (usually of an attractive woman), the crime seems in many ways worse than outright murder. The victim is forced to live with a radically abbreviated ability to lead an enjoyable life because she fears to show herself in public and becomes a pariah with limited chance for a normal life. Crimes of this sort are common in the Islamic world, as documented by Taslima Nasreen (2012). In her blog she writes: "Acid attack is common in Pakistan, Bangladesh, India, Afghanistan, Nepal, Cambodia and a few other countries. Men throw acid because they are angry at us for ending relationships and for refusing sexual exploitation, proposals of marriage ... for attending schools, not wearing Islamic veils, for laughing loudly." The accompanying photos are painful to look at. One such "before-and-after" picture shows Pakistani Fakhra Younus who had been attacked by her husband, a member of the Punjab Assembly, after she left him. After 39 unsuccessful reconstructive surgeries, Fakhra committed suicide. In 2011 Iranian Majid Movahedi tossed acid and blinded a woman who refused his marriage offer. There are cases closer to home. In 2007 Herbert Rodgers in Vermont, estranged from his ex-wife Carmen Tarleton, broke into her house and in front of their two children doused her with lye, giving her a chemical burn over 90% of her body (he also beat her with a baseball bat) on the assumption that she had "cheated" on him. She later made a partial recovery, thanks to being given a face-transplant. As Rodgers sat in prison for his 30-year sentence, he did express a bit of remorse, especially when it became clear to him that she hadn't cheated on him after all.

Uxoricide

There are many more cases of men killing their wives than of wives killing their husbands, which is why we have a word for the former (uxoricide) but not for the latter. In my 199 True Crime biographies of spousal murder, 139 are committed by husbands; 60 are, if I can suggest a term, *mariticides*: husbands killed by wives. Women are much less prone to torture than men are, so not surprisingly the more dramatic of the recent cases involve uxoricide. With respect to the concept of a New Evil, what we look for is a level of sophistication and originality in the murder of a wife of a sort that rarely or never was noted in the uxoricides of previous times. There is no novelty, after all, in the way Henry VIII dispatched Anne Boleyn or Catherine Howard. Anne failed to produce a (viable) son and was executed on trumped-up charges; her first cousin, Catherine Howard (19 when Henry was already 49) was executed because of her infidelity. Fast forward 400 years and we find Chester Gillette pushing his pregnant girlfriend out of a boat in one of New York's Adirondack lakes. Her drowning was likewise a murder with more malice than method. In their excellent review of murder in Chicago in the 1910–1930 period, Bowman and Altman (2003) show how the 391 women who during those years were murdered by their husbands were killed primarily on *impulse*. Their husbands were jealous or outraged when their wives made motions to divorce or paranoidally suspicious that their wives were being "unfaithful" even though they were not. This led quickly to a "divorce by bullets," guns being used in 2/3 of the murders. The most dangerous time for an abused wife was (and still is) when she attempts to leave. A typical example: 50-year-old Anna Carlson in 1927 "was killed by her husband who stabbed, choked, and finally beat her with a shovel in a drunken rage" (p. 778). Ten years later in Washington state, Hallie Illingworth (née Latham) was murdered by her husband after a violent quarrel. She disappeared, her body not found until three years later when her remains turned up in a lake, identified by her dental records. The husband had thrown her body there, pretending she had run off with another man. Though sentenced to life for this impulsive murder, he served only nine years before being paroled.

Impulsive uxoricides still make up the largest portion of wife-murders. But we are now beginning to see what are called "instrumental" murders, by men who go to great lengths to kill a wife in some elaborate, highly novelistic, too-clever-by-half way, reveling in the assumption that they *definitely* will not get caught. Even though the police (whom these husbands regard as brain-dead) know that, confronted with a murdered wife and a live husband, 19 times out of 20 it was the husband (even if he was in Zanzibar at the time and had hired a hit-man). In my biography study, with 139 cases, only 11.5% of the men killed their wives impulsively; another 8% started out with an impulsive murder, but then marshaled their ingenuity to make the murder appear accidental. Only 11% ever confessed, and 60% either "staged" the murder to appear accidental (or done by someone else) or else hired a hit-man. The uxoricides in this group were economically privileged, compared with the general population: 66% belonged either to the upper or upper-middle class; many were highly educated and clearly thought themselves sufficiently gifted to bamboozle the authorities. Dr. Chris Hill, a physician, for example, injected feces into his wife's vein, killing her with the ensuing septicemia so as to be free to be with his mistress. An uxoricide of that dreadful nature never having been done before, it qualifies, I believe, as a "New Evil." Another "perfect murder" that didn't end so perfectly was that of the anesthesiologist Carl Coppolino who, in 1965 murdered both his wife (also a physician) and the husband of his first mistress, using a curare-like drug (succinylcholine) that was part of his everyday muscle-relaxant equipment. He figured the embalming process would get rid of all the blood and hence all trace of the poison. He was eventually found guilty, though sentenced to only 2nd-degree murder, rather than 1st-degree (implying pre-meditation, which was obviously present), and he was paroled 12 years later for "good behavior."

À propos succinylcholine, a more recent "staged" uxoricide was that of William Higgs, an ex-Navy man with three divorces and two bankruptcies behind him, when in 2003 he married Katie Augustine, a state controller in Nevada (G. King, 2008). By now he was an intensive-care nurse at a local hospital. Not honoring his marriage vows (except "till death do us part"), he took up with another woman three years later and severed the fourth marriage with the aid of succinlylcholine, borrowed from the emergency-room tray. Injecting some into Katie, he then called 911, pretended to give CPR and pretending to the ambulance crew that she had had a heart attack. A nurse at his hospital overheard him telling someone that you could kill a person with succinylcholine because it left no trace. She tipped off the police, and the drug was then found in the dead wife's urine. A man with the narcissistic traits of psychopathy (but not so many of the behavioral ones), he was sentenced to 25 years.

A New Orleans real-estate man, Ed Post, began to pine, in what seemed like a mid-life-crisis, for the wife of his best friend. During a weekend meeting in another city, he drove from the meeting site to his wife's hotel. He drowned his wife, Julie, in the hotel bathtub, then drove back 200 miles at night so as to be in time for a breakfast meeting, as though he'd been in that town the whole time. And then drove back – only to "discover" his wife's body in the bathtub. It did not escape the attention of the authorities that he had taken out a $700,000 insurance policy on her life a few weeks before the "accident."

A 1998 uxoricide in upstate New York truly met criteria of a *this-never-happened-before* type of New Evil. James Cahill III had married Jill Russell, a much more successful person than he. He worked various jobs, got fired and went into debt, as an ineffectual layabout who always came in last at whatever he tried. Jill became the breadwinner, left with the task of restoring the lights, the electricity and the car-registration, which James couldn't afford to keep up. She met a much more successful man whom she planned to marry, once she divorced James. When James tapped her phone and realized there was another man, he became enraged with jealousy and smashed

Jill's skull with a baseball bat, pretending this was in "self-defense" after she "attacked him with a knife," for which he offered his clumsily self-inflicted arm cuts as "evidence." He was arrested, but his mother put up the $100 thousand bail. Meantime, Jill was slowly recovering in the hospital. James now purchased cyanide through the Internet, as though for photo-chemicals, and had it mailed to a different location where he could intercept the package so that it need not bear his home address. He then sneaked into the hospital, dressed as a woman janitor with an orange wig and a broom, and found Jill's room where he proceeded to kill her with the cyanide. He will remain in prison till he is about 80. Another narcissistic man with psychopathic traits, James exemplifies the wife-killer who has just enough education to lull him into the belief that he can outsmart the police. The reader may already be familiar with the similarly "clever" stories of Charles Stuart in Boston and Justin Barber in Florida, both of whom shot their wives to death (Charles, to escape fatherhood; Justin, to escape debt) and then shot themselves in the leg, as though some unknown (and imaginary) assailant had tried to kill the couple, managing only to kill the wife.

In my review of spousal murders in this generation, I note that the men are more apt to use cunning and trickery than the women, But there are exceptions. Kimberly Hricko, for example, had married in 1989 when she was 21. She grew tired of her husband and also began an affair nine years later with a man she hoped to marry. To accelerate the transition, she invited her husband, Steven, to a hotel for a Valentine's Day weekend where they sat and watched a TV murder mystery. Kimberly, a surgical technician, had access to that same paralytic drug, succinylcholine, which she then injected into her husband. Perhaps uncertain how foolproof this method was, she also set fire to the hotel room with an accelerant, and—to make the death appear accidental—propped the death scene with a cigar and liquor, although Steven neither smoked nor drank. Nor, as it turned out, was there any soot in his lungs, meaning that he was dead before the fire started. She also hoped to profit from the $400,000 insurance policy she had taken out for him, in her favor, shortly before the fateful weekend. Kimberly at her trial was sentenced to life in prison for the premeditated murder, and another 30 years for the arson.

Commentary

My contention that there has been an increase in the nature of violent crimes within the past 50 years, compared with the pre-1960 or 1965 period, is based on my survey of several thousand criminals from 1900 to the present. I have more extensive biographical data from the more recent years than the pre-1960 period, but in general, and even combing through newspaper archives in the first half of the 1900s, I have found few crimes in the earlier period that rise to the level of "evil," in the sense of containing elements of the depraved, sickening and bizarre qualities that identify a crime (or a criminal) as "evil." This seems so, even though the number of violent crimes has for the most part decreased. The murder-rate in the U.S., for example, had been about 10 per 100,000 per year in 1980; now down to about 5.6 (still higher than the 1.0 or less in Europe or Japan).

Cultural trends and sociological explanations, admittedly, are often suspect, for want of sufficient data amenable to proper statistical analysis. One is left with impressions—which are still of value, if only in that they can spur interest in further research that may bring greater clarity to the issues, and an enhanced ability either to confirm or reject one's previous hunches.

Lasch in his *Culture of Narcissism* (1979) spoke of the declining importance of the family in our society over the past century; he felt that a hitherto more "inner-directed" personality type was giving way to a peer-oriented, other-directed type and alongside these changes, a lessening of impulse controls (p. 238), i.e., of what neurophysiologists are currently calling "diminished frontal-lobe inhibitory control." Lasch also stressed the heightening of "anxious concern with the impression we make on others" (p. 243) as an important ingredient in narcissistic personality, as opposed to a healthy self-reliance. Along similar lines, others have spoken of a shift from an "idealistic" to a "sensate" culture, as underlying the increase in narcissism. Those are other expressions for devotion to what's best for one's community versus preoccupation to just what "I" want.

The evil behaviors of the persons highlighted in this chapter take these qualities to the extreme: narcissistic preoccupation with the self passing over into indifference to the feelings of others and to callousness. To be sure, in some cases there are genetic predispositions to "zero empathy" (specifically: absence of the *compassionate* form of empathy) that precede exposure to family and society and facilitate the commission of the heartless crimes we label as evil.

Relations between the sexes play an important role in this apparent transition from the "old evil" of past generations to the "New Evil" we now confront. In the area of serial sexual homicide this is a key variable. Case in point: the typewriter was invented in about 1867 by Christopher Sholes in Milwaukee. It was not long before women of meager means, here and abroad, who had few ways of making money apart from prostitution could now earn a respectable living as typists. No longer could men (of equally meager means) buy sex for two shillings (or the equivalent). Some experienced outrage and turned to serial rape and murder, the first such being recorded in the 1870s. For decades serial murders continued, but at a slow pace: a few instances per decade, mostly in the U.S., England and Western Europe. In the 1960s several societal events altered that pattern. The widespread availability of The Pill (and other easier means of contraception), the feminist revolution of the late 1960s and in the U.S. the 1973 *Roe v Wade* decision making backroom abortions with coat-hangers no longer necessary.

The divorce rate soared in the U.S. (and in other developed countries) during the '60s. All these changes meant that many men, working-class men in particular, could no longer mistreat their wives and still count on their remaining at home. The precipitous rise in serial killing began in the '60s, peaked in the 1980s and has only recently begun to decline (to levels still far above those of the pre-1960 period). Many men, for similar reasons (break-up of the traditional family), grew up lost, deprived of a steadily available mother; some developed the kind of hatred of women, while remaining heterosexual, that we saw in Leonard Lake. Women had greater opportunities to break free from unpleasant men, such as when Dorothy Stratten, the Playboy "centerfold" discovered by Paul Snider, a psychopathic pimp in Vancouver, was inveigled into marrying him. But when Dorothy was then invited to Hugh Hefner's mansion in Chicago, her beauty, and unusually sweet personality attracted the Hollywood director Peter Bogdanovich. She made plans to leave Paul and marry Peter. That was the "breaking free," but when Paul discovered this, he became violently jealous and shot her to death (and them himself). Many of the uxoricides in recent times, including the particularly evil ones, can be understood as the violent protest of fragile men unable to tolerate women's greater freedom.

Parallel to greater freedoms for women and greater control over their bodies and their fate (still lamentably short of the ideal), there are fewer adoptees who come from educated and well-to-do biological parents. Too often, promiscuous teenagers get pregnant by men of dubious reputation, offering their babies, often genetically handicapped and adversely affected by maternal drug abuse, to the public. It is politically incorrect to speak openly about such matters, but they are true nonetheless. So it is not surprising that the percentage of adoptees among serial killers (such as David "Son of Sam" Berkowitz, Ian Brady, Gerald Stano, Larry Eyler, Charles Albright ...) is six to eight times the national average. Likewise higher is the percentage of adoptees among men committing other forms of violent crimes, such as Josh Komisarjevsky, mentioned in the text. Adoption aside, the rate of births to unmarried mothers without a high-school degree was 61% in 2013, compared with 9% for unmarried mothers with college degrees (*The Economist* 412, July 2014, pp. 21–25). The propensity to crime among boys raised without a father, especially in economically poor circumstances, is much greater than is the case with boys from well-off, "father-present" families (Lykken, 1995).

The motivation in most serial killers is *vengeance*, against women, in the heterosexual killers. Homosexual killers appear to be consumed with an often unacknowledged hatred (absorbed often enough from their fathers and from peers) against themselves and their own sexual preference. As societal attitudes have begun to normalize in recent years, perhaps there will no longer be an over-representation of "gays" among serial killers as there has been heretofore. Similarly the recent decline in prevalence of serial killers can be accounted for in part by a greater acceptance of women's rights vis-à-vis freedom, work and control over their sexual and reproductive fate: better than 30 years ago, though still a long ways to go.

The aforementioned factors do not explain the recently increased tendency, if my observations are correct, not only toward the heinousness of certain violent crimes, but also to a curious kind of luxuriating in such crimes as exemplified in the creation of torture chambers where warped individuals (men, almost invariably, and of a diagnostically psychopathic bent) indulge in protracted and exotic tortures never before imagined, let alone acted out. I think in this regard of the Sifrit couple: an ex-Navy SEAL Benjamin, and his wife Erika (Phelps, 2009). At one point they kidnapped a couple in Maryland, forced them to strip, and killed them, whereupon Ben had sex with the woman's decapitated head, and was sexually aroused with the dismemberment. He then took photos of the scene as "trophies." This is not only "thrill seeking"—seen so commonly in psychopathic persons (as an antidote to boredom)—but the seeking of a perverse thrill no one had thought of before. I must suppose that for Ben much of the thrill lay in its uniqueness, becoming in effect, a narcissistic "triumph." You will not find such examples in Lasch's *Culture of Narcissism*. In persons like Ben, there is no longer a barrier between "what I feel like doing" and "what I will go ahead and do." This is a new narcissism: one that feeds on social disconnectedness and anomie, the entitlement of a perverse god to whom ALL is permitted: a further extension, one could say, of the feeling of inauthenticity and emptiness of which Lasch wrote concerning the typical narcissist of his time (p. 239). In serial killing, thrill seeking as a primary motive was much less common than vengeance, and was noted mostly in the men who had not been mistreated in their early life. An example is Larry Bittaker, on Death Row in San Quentin for the past 33 years (Markman & Bosco, 1989). In my correspondence with Bittaker, he avoids the details of the murders (shoving an ice pick through the ear of the adolescent girls he and his accomplice, Roy Norris, had raped) but acknowledges the non-abusiveness of his parents; the main motives emerged as thrill-seeking and the need to dominate women.

Another factor that may help account for the viciousness in certain contemporary crimes of violence is an inconsistency in the judicial system. The percentage of the population incarcerated in the U.S. is much higher than in other developed countries, excessively so. Many are kept in prison for minor felonies like possession of small amounts of marijuana. Others, having committed violent crimes, especially rape, are released prematurely for "good behavior." Premature release was a feature in 56 (33%) of the serial killers in my study, many of whom had been convicted of rape originally: men such as Rodney Alcala, Arthur Shawcross, Jack Unterweger. Others had previously committed violent crimes of a different sort: Ted Bundy, Clifford Olson, Gary Taylor, Derrick Todd Lee. What these men had in common was psychopathy (as a full diagnosis, not just a few traits). Their example should teach us something about the length of prison sentences. The age-old tradition of equating crime-X with time-Y (where one is free after he has "paid his debt to society") needs modification. Antisocial men and women with negligible psychopathy "scores" often deserve brief sentences and are capable of rehabilitation. That is what did not happen with Stanley "Tookie" Williams, former head of the Los Angeles "Crips" gang. Tookie spent many years in San Quentin's Death Row for killing four people during his early 20s. During his prison years, he matured, outgrew his "gang" mentality and wrote several books urging young boys not to get caught up in the gang life as he did. He became a spiritual leader, nominated five times for the Nobel Peace Prize, before he was unwisely and unnecessarily executed in 2005 (Williams, 2004). If justice triumphed, the psychopathic serial killer Rodney Alcala would have taken Tookie's place; the once-but-no-longer antisocial Tookie should have been released long before to pursue further his goals for the welfare of the community. With the psychopath, in contrast, the notion of *paying one's debt to society* in some specified number of incarcerated years is not meaningful. The risk of recidivism, especially in those with violent tendencies, is too great. Gary Taylor, for example, shot women in their backside with a B-B gun as an adolescent; raped and almost murdered a woman when he was 20; ended up in a forensic hospital, where he was considered "sociopathic and alcoholic," but released so long as he promised to take medicine for his drinking and to check in periodically with the hospital (Imbrie, 1993). Instead, he stopped "checking in" and quickly built a soundproofed torture chamber in his house where he set about raping, torturing and mutilating prostitutes, burying them in his backyard. Had the hospital personnel taken their diagnosis seriously rather than lightly (and not released him), 20 lives would have been spared.

Inconsistencies and certain weaknesses in the law also play a role in some types of "New Evil" cases. Bullying, in several of the cases mentioned above, led to suicide of the victims. Judges have given light sentences or no sentences at all to the aggressors. As a result, the message does not get broadcast to the public in general that bullying that leads to suicide is not very different from murder. There are principles in law, supposedly still valid, sometimes referred to under the titles: *Fragile Skull* and *But-For*. If someone armed only with a gun made of licorice sticks up an elderly person who then drops dead with a heart attack over the sudden fright unaware that the gun was just candy, the victim could be said to have a "fragile skull" (the point being that a stronger, younger person wouldn't have died); however. BUT FOR being accosted with that pretend weapon, the death would not have occurred. Ergo: murder. The crime was the direct cause of the person's death. But currently the law seems to have become too lenient, and the bullying goes on. When the Rutgers student Tyler Clementi jumped off the George Washington bridge in 2010 after his roommate secretly filmed him having sex with another man and put the film on the Internet, BUT FOR that secret filming then made to go "viral," Clementi, perhaps a bit more fragile than some other gay roommate, would not have committed suicide. Dharun Davi, the roommate, was therefore responsible for the death, though he did not have murder as his primary intention. It was a kind of murder, but the judge did not charge him with a crime. In my view this form of New Evil could be substantially reduced if it were well understood that such acts would lead to severe consequences for the perpetrator.

As for mass murder, the psychodynamics and motives are the same as they have always been: disgruntlement over the loss of a job or lover; a paranoid cast to the personality; limited adaptiveness; a thirst for vengeance. The new element in this old evil is the ease (in the U.S.), during the past 50 years, in the acquisition of semiautomatic weapons. This accounts, it would appear, for the greater frequency of mass murders and the greater victim-toll. Apart from drastically reducing availability of such weapons, it is not easy to see how this trend can be reversed.

Among the crimes most readily experienced as evil are rape (included repetitive rape without murder), rape with torture and serial sexual homicide. From a psychodynamic standpoint they can be said to represent a distinction without a difference, since the underlying psychodynamics are quite similar even though for the victim life versus death is a crucial distinction. To my way of thinking, all rape involves torture, since in the "mildest" of cases, the victim must cope with pain, degradation and humiliation. But "rape with torture," literally implies the addition of intentional infliction of intense physical pain and often mutilation. In his excellent monograph on rape, Groth (1979) mentions that some rape victims wished they had been murdered rather than raped. The statistics on rape are of uncertain validity, since many women prefer not to divulge what had happened to them, and the courts too often downgrade a rape to some lesser offense. Still, the picture is disturbing. Since 1960, for example, the murder rate in the U.S. has fluctuated from 5.1 per 100,000 in 1960, up to 10.2 in 1980, and gradually back down to 4.8 in 2010. The incidence of rape in 1960 was recorded as 9.6 per 100,000 in 1960; shot up to 36.8 in 1980, 41.2 in 1990, before dropping to a still high figure of 18 in 2010 (http://www.disaster.com/crime/uscrime.htm). Groth dispels the illusion that rape is a crime driven by sexual desire. Instead, "rape is serving primarily nonsexual needs. It is the sexual expression of power and anger" (p. 2). He adds that "Rape is always a symptom of some psychological dysfunction, either transient or repetitive. It is usually a desperate act that results from an emotionally weak and insecure individual's inability to handle the stresses and demands of his life" (p. 5). In his taxonomy of rape, Groth points to three main motivations: *anger, power* and *sadism,* examples of which he offers in his chapter on the psychodynamics of rape. These motives may of course be conflated in individual cases. One man might be prompted to rape out of anger at an abandoning or cruel mother. Another might turn to rape as an antidote to feelings of masculine weakness and social ineffectiveness. Men of the latter sort often show the "master-slave" dynamic, insisting upon being called "master" by the woman he treats as a slave. This dynamic often shades over into the sadistic variety. Serial killer Mike DeBardeleben, who when young had been tortured by both parents, turned to torture himself, even penning a manifesto about sadism. In it he wrote: "*The central impulse is to have complete mastery over another person ... to become her god ... and the most radical aim is to make her suffer ... The pleasure in the complete domination over another person is the very essence of the sadistic drive*" (Hazelwood and Michaux, 2001, p. 88). Some repetitive rapists stop short of murder, deriving their satisfaction mainly from the psychological suffering of their victims, as in the case of Fred Coe, a psychopathic man from a wealthy family, whose 25 rapes in the Spokane area in the early 1980s seemed to have been fueled in part by a need to overcome a sense of failure in the occupational world (Olsen, 1983). His indifference to conventional morality may have been helped along by similar moral lacunae in his mother who, when Coe was sentenced at trial, tried to hire a hit man to kill the judge. Crime statistics do not subdivide rape and serial killing according to an anger/power/sadism schema, so we cannot tell whether the "New Evil" (the sadistic cases) in this domain is all that new. As Sarah McMahon and Karen Baker remind us (2011), acknowledgement of sexual violence as a major social problem came relatively late in the U.S., spurred by the civil rights and feminist movements of 1960–1970. So we don't know how much the apparent increase in rape since 1960 stems from a true increase in verifiable cases, and how much is a reflection of heightened awareness and readiness on the part of women (and men) to come forward and lodge complaints. Judging from earlier (and necessarily incomplete) records, it does appear that rape and serial killing of the *sadistic* kind, where the torture component is maximized and carried out at times with a kind of malicious inventiveness, is taking place more often in our time than in times past (before 1960).

Coda

To account for some of the psychological motives—the psychodynamics—that serve as the springboard to atrocities in peacetime, we should pay attention to cultural changes that, for a time, favor certain types of violent crimes, while suppressing others. We have already noted how the kidnaps in the pre-1960 era were primarily about money. The ransoms demanded in the Ross and Lindbergh cases were made during times of economic depression in the U.S. Beginning in the 1960s a number of societal changes were taking place. The women's movement and better and more widespread means of birth control led to greater sexual freedom. For some (mostly men) freedom edged over into license. Psychiatry had a hand in this also. Freud and the pioneers, though never condoning excess, did help the culture overcome Victorian inhibition and move toward greater freedom in sexual expression. Alongside this there was a move away from the strict morality of the earlier era toward an emphasis on "I": the needs of the Self as opposed to the Group. We now began to see kidnap primarily for sexual reasons. This took on a number of forms: repetitive rapes but without murder (Fred Coe); solitary rape with murder of a particularly vicious sort (John Evander Couey, Richard Davis), kidnap to effect prolonged sexual slavery (Ariel Castro, Josef Fritzl) and kidnap as a first step in serial sexual homicide (David Parker Ray).

The 1960s also saw declining religious affiliation in the U.S. and Europe, a marked increase in divorce rate and in boys raised without fathers (as well as an increase in the proportion of children born outside wedlock). The use of mind-altering substances also changed dramatically after the 60s. Counterculture guru Timothy Leary preached "Turn on, Tune In, Drop out!" encouraging the use of LSD and other drugs, which for many replaced the reliance on alcohol. Many men in the last 50 years, contemplating a violent crime, have primed the pump toward actually committing the crime through the prior use of cocaine, methamphetamine, and a host of other drugs rarely available before 1960.

The '60s was a bad decade in any case: the unpopular Vietnam war, Charles Manson, the assassinations of President D Kennedy, Robert Kennedy and Martin Luther King, Jr., whose message "Learn, Don't Burn" appears to have died with him. In America many young people lost faith in the country and turned instead to a self-centered philosophy of self-fulfillment and doing whatever you want. Several mass murderers have prefaced their attacks with the words "I'm going to be famous!"—the epitome (more the nadir, actually) of the new narcissism, which has become an important ingredient of the New Evil. Elliot Rodger, the mass murderer of the Santa Barbara students, wrote in his manifesto, for example: "I am more than human, I am Elliot Rodger ... magnificent, glorious, supreme, divine!"—but for those murderous acts, he would have spent his days in obscurity, as would Jared Loughner, Adam Lanza, James Holmes and Seung Hui Cho, whose names are now known to everyone. In the new narcissism one saw entitlement carried to extremes hitherto unknown. We saw this with many of the recent spousal murders, behind which was the motto, so it appeared: "if I can think it, I can do it, and I can get away with it." The staging of a murder so as to look like an accident is now a feature of many wife-murders, something almost unknown before the 1970s. Also the boundless narcissism of Luka Magnotta, who fled Canada only to be arrested while watching the video of his crime at an Internet café in Europe. Or the plot in 2012 by a New York policeman, Gilbeto Valle, to kill, cook, and eat women, beginning with his own wife. He shared his plan with others via the Internet, was arrested and spent a year in prison before being released for "insufficient evidence" (the plot was never carried out). Because one can use false names and give vent to the most depraved fantasies, thanks to its anonymity, the Internet itself seems to have facilitated the expression—and at times to the implementation—of twisted dreams hitherto unknown outside the pages of salacious crime novels. Among the crimes of extreme self-centeredness, however, none compare with the murder of pregnant women for "fetus-snatching"—the newest and arguably the most repugnant form of the New Evil, unknown before 1987.

It is customary for the older generation to decry the bad habits of the younger generation, as though mankind is surely headed for a terrible fall. The great and ascetic preacher, Saint John Chrystostom in the fourth century, spoke pessimistically about the young boys of his day who let their hair grow so long and what this portended for the future. Yet here we are 1800 years later, still thriving as a species, despite our flaws. There does appear, at least in the West, a coarsening of the culture: a less strict morality, a weakening of religion, more divorce and broken families, less cohesiveness with one's community, more self-centeredness and insistence on instant gratification, greater disillusion with government and with these societal changes, a greater despair and distrust. As a side effect of such changes, morbid sexual crimes now overshadow the "traditional" economic crimes (such as robbery and kidnap for ransom), and we are witnessing a greater tendency to crimes of callousness and violence, of varieties rarely or in some cases never before witnessed. To understand the New Evil, it is essential to understand not only the psychodynamics of the individuals who commit the violent crimes of our day, but also the societal dynamics that affect the culture surrounding and giving shape to the men and women responsible for this violence. This chapter represents an attempt to bring some clarity to these important issues.

References

Aamodt, M. (2014). *Annual Report: Statistics on Serial Killers*. Radford, VA: Radford University and Springfield College.

Baron-Cohen, S. (2003). *The Essential Difference: Male and Female brains and the Truth about Autism*. New York, NY: Basic Books/Perseus Book Group.

Baron-Cohen, S. (2011). *The Science of Evil: On Empathy and the Origins of Cruelty*. New York, NY: Basic Books/Perseus Book Group.

Bayle, P. (1696). *Dictionnaire Historique et Critique*. Amsterdam, the Netherlands: chez Reinier Leers.

Bowman, C. G. and Altman, B. (2003). Wife murder in Chicago: 1910–1930. *Journal of Criminal Law and Criminology, 92*, 738–790.

Capote, T. (1965). *In Cold Blood*. New York, NY: New American Library.

Clarkson, W. (1995). *Whatever Mother Says: A True Story of Mother, Madness, and Murder*. New York, NY: St Martin's Press.

Craig, I. W. and Halton, K. E. (2009). Genetics of human aggressive behavior. *Human Genetics, 126*, 101–113.

Damasio, H., Grabowski, T., Frank, R., Galaburda, A. M. and Damasio, A. (1994). The return of Phineas Gage: Clues about the brain and skull of a famous MA patient. *Science, 264*, 1102–1106.

Davidson, P. (2009). *Homicide Miami*. New York, NY: Penguin Books.

Dean, J. (2008). *House of Evil.* New York, NY: St Martin's Press.
Douglas, J. (2013). *Law and disorder.* New York, NY: Kensington Publishers.
Fass, P. S. (1997). *Kidnapped: Child Abduction in America.* Cambridge, MA: Harvard University Press.
Flacco, A. (2009). *The Road out of Hell.* New York, NY: Sterling Books.
Franke, D. (1975). *The Torture Doctor: The Only True Account of the Greatest Criminal the Police have Ever Handled.* New York, NY: Hawthorne Books.
Fraser, A. (1999). *The Lives of the Kings and Queens of England.* Berkeley, CA: University of California Press.
Frick, P. (1998). Callous-unemotional traits and conduct problems: Applying the two-factor model of psychopathy to children. In D. J. Cooke, A. E. Forth & R. D. Hare (Eds.), *Psychopathy: Theory, Research and Implications for Society.* Dordrecht, the Netherlands: Kluwer, 161–187.
Gibb, D. (2012). *Camouflaged killer: The Shocking Life of Colonel Russell Williams.* New York, NY: Berkley Books.
Glatt, J. (2002). *Cries in the Desert.* New York, NY: St. Martins' Press.
Glatt, J. (2009). *Secrets in the Cellar.* New York, NY: St Martin's Press.
Glatt, J. (2010). *Lost and Found.* New York, NY: St Martin's Press.
Groth, A. N. (1979). *Men who rape: The Psychology of the Offender.* New York, NY: Basic Books.
Guinn, J. (2013). *The Life and Times of Charles Manson.* New York, NY: Simon & Schuster.
Hall, A. (2013). *Captive: One house, Three Women, and Ten Years.* New York, NY: Penguin Books.
Hamilton, E. and Cairns, H. (Eds.). (1961). *Plato: The Collected Dialogues Including the Letters.* Bollingen Series, LXXI, 575–844. Princeton, NJ: Princeton University Press.
Hare, R. D. (1991). *The Hare Psychopathy Checklist Revised.* Toronto, Ontario: Multihealth Systems.
Harrington, J. and Burger, R. (1999). *Justice Denied.* New York, NY: Plenum Books.
Hazelwood, R. and Michaud, S. G. (2001). *Dark Dreams: Sexual Violence, Homicide, and the Criminal Mind.* New York, NY: St Martin's Press.
Heidenry, J. (2009). *Zero at the Bone.* New York, NY: St Martin's Press.
Hughes, D. T. (1992). *Lullaby and Good Night.* New York, NY: Picket Books.
Imbrie, A. E. (1993). *Spoken in Darkness.* New York, NY: Plume Books.
Kellerman, A. L. and Mercy, J. A. (1992). Men, women, and murder. Gender specific differences in rates of fatal violence and victimization. *Journal of Trauma, 33*, 105.
King, G. C. (2008). *An Almost Perfect Murder.* New York, NY: Pinnacle Books.
Knight, M. and Buford, M. (2014). *Finding Me: A Decade of Darkness, a Life Reclaimed.* New York, NY: Weisman Books.
Lasch, C. (1979). *The Culture of Narcissism.* New York, NY: W. W. Norton.
Lasseter, D. (2000). *Die for Me.* New York, NY: Pinnacle Books.
Lasseter, D. (2006). *If I Can't Have You, No One Can: A Deadly Stalker's Twisted Passion.* New York, NY: Pinnacle Books.
Leibniz, G. (1710). *Essais de Theodicée sur la Bonté de Dieu, la Liberté de l'homme et l'Origine du Mal* (1990) Theodicy. Chicago, IL: Open Court Classics. tr. EM Huggard (English translation).

Lykken, D. T. (1995). *The Antisocial Personalities*. Hillsdale, NJ: L. Erlbaum Associates.

McMahon, S. and Baker, K. (2011). Changing perceptions of sexual violence over time. *National Online Resource Center/Violence Against Women*, 1–22.

Markman, R. and Bosco, D. (1989). *Alone with the Devil*. New York, NY: Bantam Books.

McClellan, W. (1993). *Evidence of Murder: The Perfect Marriage and the Almost perfect Murder*. New York, NY: Penguin/Onyx.

McDougal, D. (1991). *Angel of Darkness: The True Story of Randy Kraft and the Most Heinous Murder Spree of the Century*. New York, NY: Warner Books.

McGuire, C. and Norton, C. (1988). *Perfect Victim*. New York, NY: William Morrow.

Moffitt, T. E. (1993). Adolescence-limited and life-course persistent antisocial behavior. *Psychological Review, 100*, 674–701.

Nasreen, T. (2012). "No Country for Women." http://freethoughtblogs.com/taslima/2012/07/14/our-men-throw-acid.

Olsen, J. (1983). *Son: A Psychopath and his Victims*. New York, NY: Dell Books.

Phelps, M. W. (2009). *Cruel Death*. New York, NY: Pinnacle Books.

Rae, N. (2007). *A matter of Time*. Indianapolis, IN: AuthorHouse.

Rosencrance, L. (2006). *An Act of Murder*. New York, NY: Pinnacle Books.

Rothgeb, C. and Cupp, S. (2005). *No One Can Hurt Him Anymore*. New York, NY: Pinnacle Books.

Sauerwein, K. (2008). *Invisible Chains*. Guilford, CT: The Lyons Press.

Schechter, H. (2000). *Fiend: The Shocking True Story of America's Youngest Serial Killer*. New York, NY: Pocket Books.

Stone, M. H. (1993). *Abnormalities of Personality: Within and Beyond the Realm of Treatment*. New York, NY: W. W. Norton.

Stone, M. H. (2009). *The anatomy of Evil*. Amherst, NY: Prometheus Books.

Stone, M. H. (2014). Mass murder, mental illness, and men. *Violence and Gender, 2*(1), 51–86. doi:10.1089/vio.2015.0006.

Stone, M. H., Krischer, M. and Steinmeyer, E. (2005). Infanticide in forensic mothers. 1. An evolutionary perspective. *Journal of Practical Psychiatry, 11*(1), 35–45.

Stout, M. (2005). *The Sociopath Next Door: The Ruthless Versus the Rest of Us*. New York, NY: Crown Publishing.

Williams, S. T. (2004). *Blue Rage, Black Redemption*. New York, NY: Simon & Schuster.

Part III

Clinical Applications

Chapter 7

Trauma and Evil

Questions of Ethics and Aesthetics for a Profession in Crisis

Oren Gozlan

Since World War II, the phenomenon of trauma has become central to our understanding of the cultural, political and psychological challenges that define what it means to live in the postmodern era. Bohleber reminds us that "psychoanalysis began as a theory of trauma" (2010, p. 101) by linking the roots of hysteria to memory, and more precisely to the failure to remember, which leads to repetition and to the conflation of self and other, past and present, here and there. Since trauma is at the origin of the psychoanalytic project, perhaps it should not surprise us that the question of origin has haunted the psychoanalytic understanding of trauma since its very beginning. Can trauma be traced to a single childhood event? What is the role of fantasy in experiencing an event as traumatic? Are events such as war or the witnessing of acts of evil sufficient to trigger a traumatic response or do they need to converge with a primary experience of trauma to elicit symptoms? And what about the experience of insidious, repetitive trauma that is not "outside the range of human experience" (DSM III-R)? Can we predict who will be vulnerable to trauma, or is the wish to predict a repetition itself of the mechanisms of trauma to which we are all subject? The question of origin, however, turns into a crisis of belief when the witness—for instance, a mental health professional—becomes contaminated and affected by the horror she is witnessing. How does the expert account for her own vicarious trauma, and what kind of questions does this crisis of witnessing open for the field?

In this paper, I turn to the case of Dr. John Bradford, a Toronto based forensic psychiatrist who, in the process of watching a video filmed by the perpetrator himself, experiences a breakdown. The case will be used to consider questions of affect, trauma and ethics in the process of witnessing acts of evil and how these matters affect the expert's challenging task of distinguishing sanity from insanity and trauma from ordinary distress.

This paper does not intend to offer an explanation for acts of evil or of the psychiatrist's breakdown but instead, to explore several affective challenges that are tied to a profession charged with the responsibility of witnessing evil and ascertaining sanity, to the extent that these questions exert pressure on the psychiatrist's mind. The issue, in other words, concerns the traumatic effect of the profession's handling of diagnosis and trauma on the psychiatrist. Bradford, I claim, is a psychiatrist who does not know himself. This surprising statement will be examined shortly. The larger question this essay asks is whether there is a relationship between witnessing evil and the need to obliterate the self.

After watching hours of tape taken by convicted killer ex-Colonel Russell Williams, Dr. Bradford experiences a breakdown while driving home. Williams, a colonel in the Canadian Army, was charged in the slayings of Jessica Lloyd, 27, and Cpl. Marie-France Comeau, 38, as well as with forcible confinement and sexual assaults on two other women. The tapes Bradford watched were filmed by Williams himself. The videos recorded his rape and murders, as if he could rape and murder forever. Bradford is a forensic psychiatrist who has analyzed the videotapes of many notorious criminals in both the U.K. and Canada, but something unexpected happened to Bradford. His exposure to Williams' tapes unhinged his mind and led to a breakdown that at first, Bradford denied. He began drinking, became suicidal, and was unable to work through his distress. He experienced panic attacks and decided that he could not continue to examine videos documenting heinous crimes or assessing criminals. Given that Bradford was not new to the practice, one may wonder what happened to him in the process of examining Williams' self-taped evidence. Bradford's breakdown will be used as an entry point for the discussion of the effects of evil on the witness. I suggest that a psychic breakdown may be a necessary ethical positioning in the act of witnessing evil.

Theory of Trauma in the Face of Evil

Bradford tells us that his impression of Williams, with whom he had spent days in an intense interview process, was that he was "an ordinary man." In Dr. Bradford's opinion, Mr. Williams "wasn't a psychopathic individual who suddenly at 45 years of age started to kill women. (...) Something happened in his life, which has never been in the public domain, I'm not at liberty to talk about it, and that made a change." (CBC-Canada, 2014) Bradford also reflects on his own breakdown after watching Russell Williams' tapes: "It's like a switch went off in my head and I just broke down." "I get tears occasionally, but this was sobbing, out of control." (CBC-Canada, 2014) Bradford's narration of his own breakdown parallels the manner in which he theorizes Williams' shift from an "ordinary man" to a murderer and a rapist—a sudden, total transformation. In Bradford's view, both Williams and he became unrecognizable.

In tracing his own undoing, Bradford recalls being particularly disturbed not only by witnessing Williams rape and murder his victims, but by hearing the voices of the women, listening to the interactions and knowing how the scenes would end. What unhinged him was the sheer helplessness he felt when watching Williams engage in unjustified acts of evil, hearing the victims' cries, and knowing the end of the plot. But being forced, almost sadistically, to watch these scenes orchestrated by the perpetrator who had used technology to elaborate his fantasy, also played a role in rendering the psychiatrist helpless. Bradford's act of witnessing the victim's profound suffering as well as his own breakdown may allow us to understand the structures that sustain hatred and aggression and the way our own vulnerability must be considered in raising the question of how we respond to the other's suffering. What happens in and through the traumatic reception of hatred and violence? In and through the witnessing of the desire to destroy? Did Bradford identify with Williams' victims, and did this identification turn the psychiatrist into the helpless girl about to be killed? In attending to the phenomena of identification, we may begin to unravel the dilemmas of the transference, fragmentation and loss, "attachment and dissociation" (Britzman, 2000, p. 31) in the process of witnessing evil.

Bradford does not recall experiencing any distress while watching countless videos depicting rape and murder. In fact, even while watching Williams' tapes, he does not succumb to anxiety. In attempting to trace Williams' own turn from sanity to insanity, the missing link between fantasy and reality, Bradford's self goes missing. He feels detached and determines that he can and should be able to examine these disturbing acts as one observes subjects at a lab. Believing himself to be a "tough guy," the experienced psychiatrist did not expect that his expertise would fail to protect him from becoming affected by what he studied. Bradford's own surprise at finding himself affected raises important questions regarding the way in which dissociation plays out in the very way in which trauma is approached in psychiatry. What are the implications of the assumption that the psychiatric profession can and should dissociate itself from the object of its studies?

Bradford's case provides a frame within which to consider a constellation of dilemmas related to the ways in which we are affected by horrific acts. What does it means to witness others who have been subjected to evil and what questions does this act of witnessing raise for the profession? The case provides us with a context in which to ask how a diagnosis may change the diagnostician and what would it mean to provide a diagnosis dislodged from affect? At bottom the issue is ethical, and it addresses the implications of the profession's (dis)attachment from its object of study for the recognition of human suffering. I propose in this paper that Bradford's crisis parallels a larger crisis in the field of psychiatry that can be understood as a problem of transference that relates to the profession's position of certainty that grounds diagnosis as a defense against affect.

Crisis of Ideality

Through Bradford's case we can begin to problematize the epistemological tenets that ground psychiatric knowledge: its search for the origin of trauma, its denial of repetition as an essential aspect of the trauma experience and its desire to position the clinician outside of the experience. Bradford makes the arbitrary statement that he does not believe in the diagnosis of Post-Traumatic Stress Disorder and raises qualms about the primacy of childhood trauma in etiological theories. Bradford's statement introduces another dimension of the inherent challenges of the profession, those pertaining to the job itself. We could say that the profession's demand of objectivity translates into the psychological numbing of the clinician as a defense mechanism against becoming response-able. The affective tensions are such that when the defenses shatter, the clinician does not understand what the shattering itself means. What Bradford could not anticipate is that he would encounter a case that would animate his own breakdown—a primal dread from which his professional frame failed to protect him. Bradford could not be contained by the professional apparatus, but what is interesting about his response is that he does not understand his own susceptibility. I suggest that Bradford's dismay at his own breakdown and his disbelief in the diagnostic category of PTSD remind us that our profession is in crisis. As I will attempt to demonstrate in this essay, psychiatry's investment in deciphering truths through the search for empirically verifiable evidence and its intolerance of the inevitable ambiguity and density of human narrative inevitably break down when it comes to trauma.

Bradford's approach to the case is grounded on a perspective that that links trauma to a "real," external event. He links Williams' breakdown to a secret "event" that cannot be disclosed and his own breakdown with his watching of Williams' tapes. In both cases, something akin to an explosion, to a sudden psychic disorganization is said to have produced a seemingly complete change in identity. This notion of a sudden turn precipitated by a singular event may tell us something about the relationship between theory and the history of one's own education. Is his narrative affected by theories of trauma prevalent in his profession? Bradford's narrative leads us to question the stability of identity and the possibility of self-transformation. With the term "destructive plasticity" (2012, p. 2), Catherine Malabou describes the phenomena of being radically and suddenly changed by an event or experience with the power to split the individual though a "sudden interruption" that gives rise to an "absolute other" that gradually takes over the subject's identity. This sudden shift in identity is characterized by the impossibility of return to or reconciliation with the former self. Malabou describes this shift as a becoming "unrecognizable to ourselves" in the process of encountering our absolute Other. But this otherness is not a transformable core, it is rather a cleft that remains inaccessible and unchanged in the face of any psychological intervention. The origin of such "interruption," she argues, cannot be traced back to childhood trauma or repression and, therefore, it cannot be worked through analytical transference. Destruction, she suggests, is also formative: It shatters the self with no possibility of return.

Malabou's argument poses a challenge to psychoanalysis because it proposes that in some cases, trauma is not repressed or "interiorized" (p. 81) and therefore the desubjectification that follows is not caused by repression or unconscious negation. It is a response to the destruction of the psychic apparatus rather than a matter of the subject's capacity to tolerate enigma or conflict. Malabou's approach seems to echo the biological approaches that wipe away affect by leaning on neurobiological explanations of the effects of trauma on a body that does not signify. The impact on the body is said to be "beyond affect" in that trauma is understood as destroying the very psychical structure that gives rise to affect or meaning.

Can we approach Bradford's breakdown in the way Malabou proposes, as a traumatic response that cannot be traced back to childhood and the return of the repressed? I would like to consider the relation between Bradford's own desubjectification and the larger crisis in the professional field to which he belongs. The crisis can be related to the tendency within the mental health profession to think about assessment and treatment as mechanized formulaic techniques to be applied to a "passive patient" (Leader, 2011, p. 4), as techniques that have no affective influence on the subjectivity of the clinician. This resistance to acknowledge the effects on the clinician of observing and assessing trauma speaks to the field's inability to address, psychologically and ethically, the defenses against affect that generate dissociated responses on the part of the professional. What is most problematic about this dissociated response is that they repeat and reenact the trauma s/he's attempting to understand.

Allergy to Affect

In his book *Unhinged: The Trouble with Psychiatry*, the Bostonian psychiatrist Daniel Carlat argues that psychiatry gave up on "understanding the mind" (p. 5) and has turned instead into a foreclosed system of thought convinced of its ability to develop cures by tracing symptoms to causes. Psychiatry, as Carlat observes, is in crisis because it does not question the premises of its own discourse and cannot understand the effects such discourse has on the knowledge it produces, thus leading to alienation and ideality. As a discipline rooted in medicine, psychiatry reflects those it seeks to cure, including psychiatrists themselves, who are subject to helplessness, idealization and glorified emotional distance. Idealization (i.e., of observable "facts," empirical knowledge, the authority of the DSM) is a way to fend off identification, avoid painful conflicts and doubt, ward off loss, in short, a defensive maneuver that itself becomes traumatic by foreclosing meaning and the ability to become attentive to suffering, one's and other's.

Carlat observes that through the "rote approach to treatment" (Carlat, 2010, p. 15) that characterizes psychiatry, the field has become "unhinged" from its "original mission—to discover the causes of mental illness and to treat those causes (p. 15). For Carlat, the crisis lies in the tendency of the discipline to move away from listening to the patient's suffering and toward medication. There is an allure in the idea that biological causes for suffering can be found and treated and there is also a fantasy of legitimacy that accompanies scientific knowledge. Does psychiatry's love affair with science impact its capacity to confront difficult, painful knowledge? Perhaps psychiatry, psychology and psychoanalysis become unhinged precisely when the search for original causes and the aim of cure replaces the capacity to tolerate the unknown and to help the patient give meaning to her suffering. What is at stake is not a shift away from the "original aim" of the profession but rather an understanding that becoming unhinged is a necessary step in developing the discipline's ability to confront destruction, sustain desire and propose an ethics of care that can tolerate conflict and ambivalence.

Bradford's case can help us consider psychic breakdown as a function of dissociation, passivity and identification with helplessness. His surprise at his own unhinging also raises a question about a possible relation between the denial of psychic reality and self-destruction. In examining Williams' disturbing videos, Bradford confronts helplessness in the face of meaningless suffering and reacts with emotional numbness. Bradford's surprise at his own breakdown perhaps suggests an identification with the very meaninglessness he was witnessing. To the extent that psychiatry's move toward "effective action" is also a move away from words and their inevitable ambiguity, it is also a move away from passion and curiosity (Phillips, 1998). Consistent with Carlat's observation about the automatization of psychiatry and its abandonment of its original aim of "understanding of the mind," Bradford's surprise at his own breakdown can be interpreted as a denial of psychical reality as promoted and sustained by the discipline.

In his book *The Beast in the Nursery* (1998), Phillips reminds us that silence is a sign of blocked curiosity and simultaneously a precondition of thinking that is vehemently disowned: "children are always encouraged to lose the knowledge that they do not know how to speak (properly)" (p. 45). For Phillips, language is a "mixed blessing" because although it allows us to address the other as well as contain difficult emotions, it also veils the inarticulate self. Language helps us sublimate, but when idealized as stable and exhaustive, it can also be used defensibly to disavow inchoateness. Language, in other words, can be used to deaden curiosity because education also takes the form of adaptation that hinders our capacity to tolerate the breakdown of meaning: a loss of idealized identifications, of fantasized self-sufficiency.

The Kleinian concept of Paranoid Schizoid ideation can help us understand some of psychiatry's proclivity to turn away from ambivalence and loss through idealization, indifference and the denial of susceptibility. Forgetting one's helplessness, hatred of the human condition and disavowal of vulnerability are, for Klein, typical forms of defense against separation. The hatred of emotional life contributes to compliance with authority insofar as it creates a hermetic structure where knowledge becomes split off from what destabilizes it. What is disavowed is the meaning-making capacity of narrated experience, the working through of one's history and, hence, of one's dependency, desire and fear. The shrinking of self-curiosity can be observed in psychiatry and psychology's attempt to make individuals adapt to what is considered as ideal functioning in an ill-functioning society. The psychiatric DSM classification of human suffering into different "disorders" and the focus in psychology on "evidence-based" knowledge denies the "affective relation between knowledge and character" (Britzman, 2014, p. 11) and falls into what Kristeva calls the, incredible "need to believe" (2007, p. 722). This need to believe is a form of refusal of loss through the enactment of adolescent's wish for certainty that activates the search for an idealized love object. For the adolescent, the polymorphous sexuality of childhood, characterized by un-sublimated curiosity and the capacity to be surprised, is tempered by the belief in the possibility of absolute satisfaction (Kristeva, 2007) via an object of desire. Adolescence marks the point where increased pressures to conform and be intelligible crushes more imaginative ways of presenting ourselves, turning desire into dogmatic conviction. Returning to Freud's sexuality papers, Phillips (1998) describes Freud's child researcher as "an artist because he wants to be a failed scientist" (p. 35). There is a conflict between ideality and sexuality, love and hate, conviction and surprise that affects our thinking and learning. This conflict can be articulated as an aesthetic dilemma, situated between the desire for stability and intelligibility, on the one side, and curiosity and the capacity to tolerate not-knowing, on the other. But a resolution of this conflict through conformity, adaptation and a belief in objective, absolute truth moves us away from our own inchoateness and toward a mythical lull of safety. "The work of education," Britzman writes, "will have to disillusion the phantasy" (2014, p. 12) of completion brought on by splitting.

But the tendency in psychiatry and psychology to rely on the medical model's quasi-scientific claim of prediction and control idealizes the historization of facts and description of symptoms over the subjective recreation of affective ties to one's history. The individual under study becomes an object, and his subjectivity is stripped away by the rejection of the meaning that the individual gives to her experience. What becomes invisible in this mechanical procedure of observation and fact finding is the susceptible self of the clinician and, hence, her capacity to act ethically. Bradford's unaffected, numb witnessing suggests what he cannot articulate: an identification with the killer's meaninglessness and the victims' helplessness. But his numb gaze also suggests Bradford's deadened curiosity as reflected in his inability to ask himself what impact the story he is listening to has on him and what his disaffected witnessing might mean. There is something sinister in Bradford's story that may reveal a structural dimension of the psychiatric practice in relation to how diagnoses are made. For a diagnosis may function as a defense against feelings of uselessness when used to replace curiosity with an answer that trivializes suffering. If a diagnosis contains a kernel of a triumphant, manic defense against the vulnerability of not knowing, it becomes a pretext for the playing out of the very thing it tries to contain. In that configuration, trauma is an identifiable event that undoes us, and the treatment that can restore us back into "normality" is based on the therapist's ability to recognize what is missing, to name pathology and disentangle it from normalcy. However, Bradford's story may also illustrate how curiosity is re-opened when something cracks a smooth story.

Bradford's enigmatic comment about his relationship with diagnosis and trauma—his surprise at his own fragmentation and his disbelief in the existence of Post-Traumatic Stress Disorder—provoked a strong reaction from psychologists who understood it as an implicit admission that he does not believe his patients. It is hard to make sense of Bradford's disbelief in the psychiatric diagnosis, and we can only speculate about what it is exactly that he does not believe in. Is his a disbelief in the adequacy of the diagnostic category to account for the horrors he is witnessing and finds impossible to make meaning of? Or perhaps it is a disbelief in how he himself could be affected with Post-Traumatic Stress Disorder? I believe that Bradford's stance articulates a pervasive believe shared in his profession, which assumes that the clinician's role is to remain an objective observer, unaffected by his patients. But what has Bradford observed in failing to maintain an objective gaze? And how has his becoming-affected turned into disbelief?

Sadism at Its Best

Bradford's astonishment over his own affective reaction to horror raises questions regarding the relationship between the "psychiatrist as the strong personality" (Parker, 2011, p. 35) and the fragility of a self that fails to protect itself against being affected by her practice. It may speak of a pervasive stance within the "psy" profession that promotes the virtue of remaining unaffected, objective and omnipotent while approaching knowledge as dislodged from psychic pain. What do we really know about the human psyche, including our own? There is a resistance to consider psychic breakdown in a serious way and to consider what can be learned about the profession in and through the breakdown itself.

Bradford's disbelief at his own crisis points at a dissociative dynamic inherent in the diagnostic process that, uncannily, replicates the very thing it is attempting to explain. Bradford's difficulties in understanding suffering and his disbelief in the PTSD diagnosis, on the one hand, and his identification with Williams' sudden change, on the other, point to an invisible conflict within a profession torn between using language as means of understanding and using diagnosis to defend itself against being affected by words. To the extent that the diagnostic process attempts to contain the anxiety of that which cannot be fully known, it inevitably fails. For the clinician who is burdened with the task of witnessing a victim's suffering, a diagnosis helps very little in understanding both the horror itself and the effects of witnessing such horror on the clinician himself.

Bradford's composure and seemingly unaffected stance before his breakdown can be read as a triumphant defense against the great difficulties in working through the horror and evil he had witnessed. But his reaction may also be symptomatic of the immense challenge that is to listen to accounts of suffering and of his failed attempt at artificially containing the anxiety of not understanding. Undoubtedly, the profession fails to account for the limits of its own understanding, which leaves it vulnerable to breakdown. This breakdown in the profession is indicative of its incapacity to accept the human condition: its inescapable vulnerability, dependency and traumatic confusion between self and other, victim and victimizer, abuser and viewer.

Bradford's stance raises questions about those discourses within the discipline that are structured around a fantasy of a non-existent subject (patient) in relation to an all-satisfying other (therapist) (Parker, 2011). In this fantasy, the clinician—like an idealized lost object—can repair the loss, once it is identified and objectified via diagnosis of symptoms. But is there an alternative to diagnosis?

The question of diagnosis opens us to the dilemma of communication and the primal agony of not being able to communicate what one thinks. Learning to listen to the other's suffering brings us to the aesthetic wavering between being recognized and confronting one's own destruction. It animates the fear of the social anxieties through a body that reverberates, collapses and loses its fragile intelligibility. Witnessing the other's suffering also means bearing witness to one's impact on the other and this emotional predicament of suspension between beauty and horror, self and other, pushes for stability through diagnosis and idealization of knowledge. There is a wish to move closer to the "truth" of the scene to comprehend or apprehend it at the same time that it triggers a recoil from feelings of abjection and painful identifications with victim and victimizer. Bradford's distrust of the PTSD diagnosis raises questions regarding the challenge of exploring emotional experience and responding to events that have no obvious justification or causation. His stance expresses the conflict of simultaneously wanting to understand and resist experiences of profound terror, evil and loss. Is the clinician's attempt to trace horror back to a root cause a way to contain his own traumatic contamination? Is the focus on facts rather than on narrative and meaning a way to distance oneself from the transferential impact of witnessing evil or horror?

Certainly, Bradford's surprise at his own breakdown may be one way of avoiding painful helplessness. Getting closer to the details of the crime or to testimonies of what has happened can be used as a defense mechanism to ward off the anxiety emanating from the unconscious relevance of the painful material to the clinician's own life. However, his admission of disbelief at his own breakdown and his distrust of the PTSD category may betray psychiatry's investment in knowledge as transparent and non-slippery, where deeply ingrained assumptions are employed as criteria to evaluate and situate patients, not as lived positions but as ideologies (Parker, 2011, p. 42). Ian Parker notes that the psychiatric apparatus problematically attempts to "render pathology visible" (p. 30) through the gaze of the expert on the passive patient. As such, the psychiatric frame serves as a shield against the aporetic relation between body and psyche through creating a totalizing system that places the diagnostic signifier and its promise of mastery (Parker, 2011) as "other" to the psychiatrist.

The most obvious implication of psychiatry's defensive tendencies in approaching horror is that the victim is excluded. In avoiding the painful identification with the trauma of the other, the clinician manages to circumvent the meaning-making process necessary to understanding suffering as well as the structures that uphold senseless acts of evil. If trauma, as Britzman (2000) describes it, is an "incapacity to respond adequately to a terrible shattering event, the incapacity to think an afterward, and to make meaning from the ruins of experience, aftermath of this event" (p. 33), it follows that that which cannot be thought or owned as an experience will be repeated in the attempt to "make from loss a learning" (p. 33). But the work of learning to live with one's loss involves coming to terms with the ambivalence that accompanies it into consciousness. Like the patient's resistance to work through ambivalent feelings regarding a loss, the clinician also refuses the loss of her idealized residence in knowledge by maintaining the belief in her ability to act as an objective observer. When the clinician encounters the patient's inhibited mourning and incapacity to experience, the clinician's attempt to retrace the trauma to an original event actually repeats the patient's resistance to lose its hold on the idealized lost object. In taking an objective stance, the patient is turned into an object of history while the history of her disowned affect is missed.

The Fall of the Expert

The search for an objective origin of trauma expresses the aftereffect of trauma itself precisely through the resistance to making memory from what cannot be remembered, only experienced and symbolized. Once Bradford observed something he could not understand, he could no longer hold on to his position of expert. Experiencing Williams as an "ordinary man" and then confronting his acts of rape, torture and murder led Bradford to feel fooled. When the "subject supposed to know" can no longer count on his expertise he is shattered by the limits of his knowledge. For Bradford, something happened in the grip of transference where murky identifications rendered him helpless, numb and overwhelmed with meaninglessness. Watching Williams' tapes was not only disturbing for their violent content; it was precisely the meaninglessness of his acts of violence that couldn't be processed by the viewer.

There is a link, I suggest, between the meaninglessness of evil and the detatchment it fosters. The identification with meaninglessness, the moment at which the symptom comes to replace the inchoateness of experience, materializes as an appeal for an answer, to which the diagnosis caters. I would like to argue that his identification with meaninglessness turned Bradford into an unaffected observer, thus allowing him to witness countless act of evil without becoming unhinged while numbing him to the registration of trauma he disavowed in his patients. In this sense, Bradford's case illustrates the way in which diagnosis may be used as an armor, transforming the position of expert into a tool with which to repel the chaotic otherness of trauma.

Ethics of Care

Bradford's narrative falls apart when he can no longer avoid his own vicarious traumatization whose symptoms, as described in the PTSD diagnosis, he had denied. At this point we have to raise more questions about his negation. His breakdown began much earlier than the explicit symptoms of alcohol drinking, uncontrollable crying outbursts and anxiety episodes: It was already evident in his incapacity to experience pain, in his ability to remain unaffected and replace thinking with instrumental reason.

In his 1974 article, Winnicott theorizes the "fear of breaking down" as the defensive stance against coming to terms with "the unthinkable" (p. 1). The fear of breakdown is a fear of something that had already happened, an "original agony" experienced as a state of non-differentiation, a failure of embodiment or "indwelling" (Winnicott, p. 2). The fear of breakdown refers to an anticipatory anxiety over a state of uncertainty that is unbearable to the self. Is witnessing the other's pain an experience of fear of what has already happened? Does it refer to the fear of becoming unhinged by traces of encounters that have not been yet registered?

For Winnicott, a breakdown constitutes a reenactment of the failure of an environmental provision. The breakdown follows the anxiety of what is coming. It is therefore an in-between state in what has happened but has not yet been experienced, what has not happened yet and what is about to happen. As such, breakdown signifies the weight of the aesthetic conflict and gives rise to aesthetic dilemmas. The aesthetic conflict, as defined by Meltzer and Williams (2008), refers to the encounter of the baby with the infinite enigma of the maternal body: a conflict of beauty, knowledge and truth, a conflict articulated by Meltzer as a conversion of passion for and hatred of knowledge, an attempt to apprehend and repel the object that mesmerizes and frightens us (Gozlan, 2014). The "beauty" for the clinician is the truth of diagnosis and the objective knowledge that is idealized. But there is also the truth of uncertainty, of what cannot be known, remembered or experienced. Bearing this tension in the face of the other's suffering often leads to a splitting that removes the cries of the other from the witness' experience, as if they were "coming from nowhere" (Felman and Laub, 1992, p. 169). Yet, it is precisely the inability to experience that makes the experience hover "everywhere," uncontained. The observer becomes confused with what he observes: He is both inside and outside the crime scene.

In encountering the other we are faced with a paradox that Meltzer articulates through his notion of the aesthetic conflict. It refers to the tension between attempting to relate to the other while experiencing the impossibility of "apprehending" the Other. We are always in uncertain terms in relation to the other, and this gives an aesthetic quality to every human encounter. The aesthetic dilemma that Bradford's case raises for us is twofold: How does one create meaning and sustain affect in the face of horror? How does one move closer to events that have no reason (Britzman, 2000) without losing one's mind? And, if facing an event that exceeds our capacity to process or discharge our affect also threatens the boundaries of our ego and hinders our capacity for thinking, how are we to consider questions of ethics in relation to witnessing?

The aesthetic dilemma of being simultaneously fascinated and repelled by unrepresentable evil leads to a breakdown. But a breakdown is also a point of transformation—a breakthrough. Through his breakdown, Bradford becomes other to himself and is able to see the other. For Bradford, the question of ethics begins with a falling apart that cracks open his previously self-contained narrative. It is the breakdown that allows him to witness the way in which the very meaninglessness of the scene affects him, precisely because it decenters him and forces him to encounter his own subjectivity.

Psychoanalysis reminds us that all narrative is a repetition that smoothes over the cracks of our necessarily fragmented story. The story that psychiatry tells itself is one of idealization and mastery that attempts to mask the messy encounter between the patient's and the therapist's unconscious and therapist through a one-dimensional, exhaustive story. Our incapacity to hear the story within the story, the story that exceeds our knowledge, prevents us from making meaning out of the meaninglessness of trauma. To go beyond the familiar story that provides us with an illusory reassurance of our coherence and knowledge we must be disrupted by affect so that we can decipher our own identification. In other words, an ethical encounter must risk an engagement with difference, with what is other, and in Lacanian terms, with what is Real. In facing evil we face an irreducible otherness, but in facing this troubling excess, we encounter ourselves. Psychiatry and psychology's emphasis on adaptation and mechanization is an attempt to assimilate the other into the self, one that can be contained, understood and helped. Psychoanalysis, on the other hand, brings us to question the limits of our knowledge by inviting us to confront, in the transference, that which resists coherence. Encountering our empty face, the "demonic" face in which I do not recognize myself, opens the possibility of relating to someone who has lost his humanity (Ruti, 2012, p. 194). We may argue that our ethics are closely bound with our capacity to mourn the loss of knowledge, the desire for intelligibility and self-coincidence. They compel us to relate to the psyche as an enigma and correspondingly to take critical distance from science's promise in the objective separation between the clinician's self and its other.

Bradford's breakdown reminds us of how the armor of objectivity and professionalism cannot guard us against the inhumane otherness of the Real that tears the fabric of our intelligibility and sense of safety. What is hard to bear is the unconscious intensity of that which cannot be signified or predicted. Encountering the Other involves bearing witness to that which is estranging and inarticulable for both the self and the other. In Bradford's case, this means that the enigma of otherness is shared by both the clinician and the other (patient, perpetrator). Neither is in a privileged position to articulate or make sense of his desire. The malignant, dangerous jouissance of the other poses a challenge to the observer's capacity to bear conflict and hence to feel or relate to the enigma of the other's thanatic jouissance.

Facing unintelligible horror means to encounter radical otherness, where the unreadable face of the other and our own bafflement become confused. Being confronted over and over again with images of intolerable pain and excitation makes it impossible to locate the origin of repetition compulsion. Is it Williams' sadistic compulsion that excites and frightens Bradford or is it his own? The confusion between self and other, external and internal reality, limits our capacity to tolerate ambiguity. Perhaps it is the irresistible and compelling nature of the scene that draws Bradford to watch it again and again, as if under the spell of a diabolical possession that both fascinates and frightens him. His incapacity to process, work through or discharge the excitation threatens the boundaries of the ego and its psychical capacity to articulate or bear a conflict that needs to be expelled from the self (Verhaeghe, 2004). The boundaries of the ego are therefore at risk of loss, making despair and trauma subject to repetition through projection and identification with violence and arousal.

If we consider Bradford's experience as part of a larger crisis within the profession, we may say that his vicarious traumatization was an effect of both the act of witnessing repeated scenes of horror and the failure of his profession to provide him with a signifying frame that could contain him. The instrumental discourse of psychiatry—and of empiricist psychology that follows in its footsteps—attempts to hide a structural void, where elaborate attempts at classification, objectification and normalization transform what should be a practice of care into a perverse search for mastery. The preference for explanation rather than interpretation as well as the promise of objectivity, predictability and emotional distance translates into totalitarian thinking and omnipotence in the clinician's practice.

What is denied in medical and psychological approaches is the Real of history (Lacan, 1977), which stands both in lack and in excess of one's intelligible narrative. Between the denial of history and the search for unequivocal origin—a positive event to which the experience of trauma can be traced—there is no position the psychiatrist can occupy from which to productively mourn his own helplessness. Bradford's breakdown provides a grounds for a larger critique of psychology and psychiatry's attempt to replace meaning-making with the fantasy of objectivity, prediction and control. Bradford's breakdown also signifies the radical failure of representation that is inherent to trauma, a failure foreclosed by a profession unable to assume the capacity of being affected as a means of being awakened to psychic life. In short, psychic breakdowns give rise to aesthetic dilemmas that productively interrupt idealization and compel us to face anew the singularity of the other.

The defense against trauma is itself traumatic—obscuring the witness' own psychic needs and his capacity to form a transferential relation to the suffering of the other. Bradford's incapacity to apprehend his own identification and repulsion, his uncontained affect and numbness, prevented him from mourning his own limitations. The psychiatric stance, like that of the witness, involves a crisis and a struggle to hold on to sanity in the face of the ineffable. To attend to the other's devastation requires a confrontation with one's crisis and its reverberations with one's own history.

Witnessing, as Laub reminds us, involves being witnessed. As the listener moves away and toward the horror he or she is also witnessed by his or her own observation. The interviewer becomes a participant in the re-experiencing of the trauma and what one witnesses in the narration of horror is a fragment of memory that cannot contain the reality it attempts to apprehend. In the process of distorting what is too painful to bear, memory is turned into a wall that bars the victim from speaking or relating. It is only through the struggle to make meaning from the enigmatic turmoil of identification and projection that one avoids becoming a deadened object or a victim to the deadening objectification of knowledge. And so, the other's silence and our muted affective response to the other's narrative may become complicit the very act of forgetting.

Ideology forecloses the capacity for "empathetic unsettlement" (LaCapra, 2001, p. 41) that defines the ethics of witnessing. The idealization of science and the certainty of diagnosis circumvent the question of how we come to know the Other. The wish to remain an objective and unaffected subject-supposed-to-know forecloses the therapist's own capacity to mourn. The deafness of the clinician that Carlat (2010) and Parker (2007) lament, and which is reflected in the common belief that the clinician must not take herself as the object of research or examination (Parker, p. 27), denies its own denial. We may speculate in this regard that watching Williams' videos faces the psychiatrist with his own blind spot—the point at which he misses the encounter with his own trauma. Now he becomes a witness to his own disrupted self. The act of witnessing incomprehensible suffering makes the witness disappear precisely because what is witnessed cannot be registered or contained. This unacknowledged disintegration translates into Bradford's failure to believe his patients' own traumatic unhinging.

Psychoanalysis reminds us, however, that the practitioner must not only be aware of his or her reaction to the traumatic material he is witnessing but also to the impact the patient's own experience has on the practitioner's thoughts and actions. Britzman's (2000) response to the question of what it means to become an ethical subject in relation to the other resides in the clinician's ability to hold herself within questions, particularly when facing significant suffering where ethics seem to be suspended. What Britzman suggests is that the ethical imagination must be mourned (2000, p. 38) and that part of the process of mourning involves the practitioner's own capacity to be affected by painful testimonies and accept the inevitability of helplessness in the face of trauma that has already taken place. The listener is situated between the trauma that has been and the precarious attempts to prevent its repetition. The difficult challenge in witnessing trauma consists of sustaining the impossibility of an exhaustive signification while containing the urge to understand and rescue. The capacity to listen to the singularity of pain, to be touched by what has not been experienced by the victim herself, means that the witness must become aware of her own ambivalence.

What Bradford's case suggests is that through the inevitable anxiety of a breakdown one can regain the capacity to think. The foreclosure of psychic conflict and pain through the medicalization of treatment and the illusion of knowledge produces a surplus anxiety about one's fallibility and precarious susceptibility in the face of profound trauma. What is forgotten is the tenuousness and instability of the practitioner's own education, which ends up being defensively protected rather than reflected upon (Britzman, 2000, p. 37). The encounter with unintelligible suffering demands that the analyst follows the obscure and dark path of her own breakdown rather than fall into numbness and a phantasy of rescue where both reactions bracket out the subjectivity of the patient as well as that of the therapist. This very enigma, of uncontained affect and numbness, of registration without experiencing the intimacy of the encounter with suffering, is not felt by Bradford until his breakdown. Detached and silent, the psychiatrist witnesses Williams' repetition of meaningless attacks, as if the scene will never end, until he snaps. Bradford feels helpless not only in his incapacity to act, but in his inability to feel, think or register what he had witnessed.

If uncontained emotions and numbness are transitory identifications (Britzman, 2000, p. 35) that help us repel the otherness within ourselves, how do we uphold an ethical position in relation to that which cannot be represented or contained? How can the unrepresentable be represented, or in the words of Felman, how can the witness bear witness "to the witness' inability to cross the bridge towards the Other's life or death?" (1992, p. 200).

Bradford's numbness and emotional collapse illustrates this paradox that Britzman articulates through the distinction between "the time of trauma from the trauma of time" (2000, p. 35). The collapse of the professional armor in the face of horror represents the transferential projections that must be worked through in order to engage ethically with the other, to move past trauma, or move trauma to the past. Paradoxically, a return to thinking occurs in the belatedness of breakdown, in the afterwardsness of affect (Laplanche, 1999). The impossibility to trace affect to a univocal origin forces us to encounter a trace of our own loss and pain that precedes the encounter with the horror and suffering we are witnessing. However, if the desire for idealized knowledge and omnipotent mastery is to be interrupted, the urge to close down on knowledge through idealization must be worked through so that the therapist's self does not go missing.

Witnessing and diagnosing radical violence produces in the clinician a loss of reason, of words and of the belief in the profession's authority. The helper needs help, and this is a difficult position to assume for the expert. But what kind of help are we referring to? The clinician is crushed under a blow of meaninglessness, for there is no time in evil—no before or after, no since or until, only an atemporal present. Meaninglessness is devastating for the psychical apparatus that searches for meaning and symbolization.

A breakdown provides a way out of the entrapment in the atemporality of transference, an attempt to escape the mad oscillation between the victim's helplessness and the perpetrator's detached madness. It is from this place of breakdown and interruption that we may begin to open ourselves to the unknown, the un-intelligible and the unexplained, to wake up to our own disclaimed history by placing ourselves back in time and turn our loss into memory.

References

American Psychiatric Association (1987). *Diagnostic and Statistical Manual of Mental Disorders*, Third Edition-Revised. Washington DC.

Bohleber, W. (2010). *Destructiveness, Intersubjectivity and Trauma: The Identity Crisis of Modern Psychoanalysis*. London, UK: Karnac.

Britzman, P. D. (2000). If the story cannot end: Deferred action, ambivalence, and difficult knowledge. In R. J. Simon, S. Rosenberg, & C. Eppert. (Eds.), *Between Hope and Despair: Pedagogy and the Remembrance of Historical Trauma,* 22–57. Lanham, MD: Rowman & Littlefield Publishers.

Britzman, P. D. (2014). Thoughts on the fragility of peace. *Life Long Learning in Europe*. Issue 2, http://www.lline.fi/en/article/research/422014/thoughts-on-the-fragility-of-peace.
Carlat, D. (2010). *Unhinged: The Trouble with Psychiatry—A Doctor's Revelations about a Profession in Crisis*. New York, NY: Free Press.
Carson, A. (2012). *Antigonick*. (A. Carson. Trans.). Toronto, Canada: McClelland & Stewart Ltd.
CBC Canada. (2014) Dr. John Bradford won't work Magnotta case because of PTSD.Retrieved from www.cbc.ca/news/canada/dr-john-bradford-won-t-work magnotta-case-because-of-ptsd-1.2571463.
Felman, S., & Laub, D. (1992). *Testimony: Crisis of Witnessing in Literature, Psychoanalysis and History*. New York, NY: Routledge.
Freud, S. (1974). Beyond the pleasure principle. In J. Strachey (Ed. and Trans.). *The Standard Edition of the Complete Psychological Works of Sigmund Freud, 18*, 1–64. London, UK: Hogarth Press. (Original work published 1920).
Gozlan, O. (2015). *Transsexuality and the Art of Transitioning*. New York, NY: Routledge.
Kristeva, J. (2007). Adolescence: A syndrome of ideality. (*M. Marder & P.* Vieira, Trans.). *Psychoanalytic Review, 94*(5), 716–725.
Lacan, Jacques. (1977). *Écrits: A Selection*. (Alan Sheridan, Trans.). London, UK: Tavistock.
LaCapra, D. (2001). *Writing History, Writing Trauma*. Baltimore, MD: Johns Hopkins University Press.
Laplanche, J. (1999). *Essays on Otherness*. New York, NY: Routledge.
Leader, D. (2011). *What is Madness?* London, UK: Penguin Group.
Malabou, C. (2012). *Ontology of an Accident. An essay on destructive plasticity*. (Carolyn Shread, Trans.). Cambridge, UK: Polity Press.
Meltzer, D., & Williams, M. H. (2008). *The Apprehension of Beauty: The Role of Aesthetic Conflict in Development, Art, and Violence*. London, UK: Karnac Books.
Parker, I. (2007). *Revolution in Psychology: Alienation to Emancipation*. Ann Arbor, MI: Pluto Press.
Parker, I. (2011). *Lacanian Psychoanalysis: Revolution in Subjectivity*. New York, NY: Routledge.
Phillips, A. (1998). *The Beast in the Nursery*. New York, NY: Pantheon Books.
Ruti, M. (2012). *The Singularity of being: Lacan and the Immortal Within*. New York, NY: Fordham University Press.
Verhaeghe, P. (2004). *On Being Normal and Other Disorders: A Manual for Clinical psychodiagnostics*. New York, NY: Other Press.
Winnicott, D. (1974). Fear of breakdown. *International Review of Psycho-analysis, 1*, 103–107.

Chapter 8

Witnessing Evil

Coline Covington

Introduction

Kovno 1941

Report of a photographer:

At the beginning of the Russian campaign on the morning of 22 June 1941 I was transferred with my unit to Gumbinnen. We remained there until the following Tuesday, 24 June 1941. On that Tuesday I was ordered to transfer from Gumbinnen to Kovno with an advance party. I arrived there with the head of an army until on Wednesday morning (25 June 1941). My assignment was to find quarters for the group following us. My job was made substantially easier because we had already pinpointed a number of block houses for our unit on an aerial photograph of Kovno that had been taken beforehand.

There were no more significant clashes in the city. Close to my quarters I noticed a crowd of people in the forecourt of a petrol station which was surrounded by a wall on three sides. The way to the road was completely blocked by a wall of people. I was confronted by the following scene: in the left corner of the yard there was a group of men aged between thirty and fifty. There must have been forty to fifty of them. They were herded together and kept under guard by some civilians. The civilians were armed with rifles and wore armbands, as can be seen in the picture I took. A young man – he must have been a Lithuanian - … with rolled-up sleeves was armed with an iron crowbar. He dragged out one man at a time from the group and struck him with the crowbar with one or more blows on the back of his head. Within three-quarters of an hour he had beaten to death the entire group of forty-five to fifty people in this way. I took a series of photographs of the victims … .

After the entire group had been beaten to death, the young man put the crowbar to one side, fetched an accordion and went and stood on the mountain of corpses and played the Lithuanian national anthem. I recognized the tune and was informed by bystanders that this was the national anthem. The behaviour of the civilians present (women and

> children) was unbelievable. After each man had been killed they began to clap and when the national anthem started up they joined in singing and clapping. In the front row there were women with small children in their arms who stayed there right until the end of the whole proceedings. I found out from some people who knew German what was happening here. They explained to me that the parents of the young man who had killed the other people had been taken from their beds two days earlier and immediately shot, because they were suspected of being nationalists, and this was the young man's revenge. Not far away there was a large number of dead people who according to the civilians had been killed by the withdrawing Commissars and Communists.
>
> (Klee, pp. 31–32)

Report of a lance-corporal in 562nd Bakers' Company:

> On our way through the city of Kovno. ... I saw a crowd of people gathered in a square somewhere in the centre of the town. I stopped my vehicle to find out what was going on. I had to climb on to my vehicle to be able to see as my view was blocked by a wall as well as the large number of people standing round. From where I was standing I saw Lithuanian civilians beating a number of civilians with different types of weapons until they showed no more sign of life. ... (I was told) that the people being beaten to death were all Jews who had been apprehended by Lithuanians in the city and had been brought to this square. The killings were carried out by the recently released Lithuanian convicts. Why these Jews were being beaten to death I did not find out. At that time I had not formulated my own thoughts about the persecution of the Jews because I had not yet heard anything about it. The bystanders were almost exclusively German soldiers, who were observing the cruel incident out of curiosity.
>
> (Klee, pp. 32–33)

These two accounts of the Kovno massacre of Jews in June 1941 are echoed in different ways and in different circumstances by numerous other accounts of public cruelty and mass killings witnessed across Europe during World War II. They are also, of course, not confined to Europe or WWII; they are hauntingly familiar around the world in the genocides of Khmer Rouge in Cambodia, Rwanda, Kosovo and Sri Lanka and continue today notably in the Middle East fundamentalist killings claimed by ISIS.

Witnessing evil takes different forms and occurs in different contexts. It is not a phenomenon conducive to a single theory but is highly contingent on how it happens, where it happens, when it happens and to whom it happens. Context and relationship are foremost in trying to piece together what mental processes may be at work.

An important aspect of relationship is the actual physical distance between the bystander and the scene of cruelty. We no longer have to be on the spot to see atrocities occurring, sometimes in real time. Being in the position of witness is something we are increasingly exposed to in our day to day lives through television news coverage alone. Although questionable morally, our degree of distance tends to be associated with our degree of responsibility; the farther away, the less responsible we perceive ourselves to be. In some respects distance lets the voyeur off the hook of intervening. He is not actually there to do anything. It also allows for wider audience viewing, as we have seen recently with the Jihadi filmed beheadings accessible to the world via the Internet. Klee, referring to Kovno and other similar reports, describes this phenomenon as "execution tourism" (Klee).

For the purposes of this chapter, I am leaving aside the psychology of the distant voyeur and will focus specifically on bystander relationships where some form of intervention is possible, despite what may be apparent conditions of coercion or fear. These are the bystander relationships that raise the question, "How could they stand there and watch without doing anything?" They are situations in which the actions witnessed "overstep proper limits" or "exceed due measure." This is the etymology of evil. Primo Levi describes the impossibility of evil and refers to the German adage, "What may not be cannot be" (Levi, 1987). They are actions that break and overturn the moral order of life. We typically think of extreme actions such as cruelty or mass killing within this category. They are actions that take place, significantly, in public. But there are also actions that take place in private, e.g., within the confines of family life, that upset the moral order. These too have their witnesses.

One of the difficulties in understanding the mental processes that occur in witnessing evil is that the material is most often second hand and what we can extrapolate from it is inevitably speculative. There is now an extensive body of literature that documents witness accounts of atrocities of various kinds in different parts of the world. But these accounts do not attempt to describe or explain the psychodynamics that take place within the individual or the group who are witnesses. While there are recognized psychological processes attributed to witnessing atrocity, such as dissociation, denial, repressed sadism and so on, these too tend to be speculative in their application. However, the psychoanalyst is in the privileged position of being able to hear first-hand accounts from patients who have experiences of witnessing atrocities, sometimes as a result of war or political conflict, but also within their own families. These accounts are not speculative; on the contrary, they are palpably real and help us to map out the dynamics of witnessing evil at a micro, individual level.

I am going to illustrate the complexity of bystander relationships by focusing first on a clinical example of a woman patient who witnessed the regular abuse and beatings of her young daughter by her husband. From this example of witnessing continuous cruelty within the private confines of the family, I will speculate on the dynamics that may have been at work in witnessing the sudden atrocities in Kovno and on witnessing atrocities over an extended period of time in the community surrounding Mauthausen concentration camp in Austria, as representative of many such events that occur elsewhere. The clinical account provides a direct exposition of the dynamics of witnessing evil that I hope will shed light on the dynamics of witnessing in other contexts. I want to stress that this example is one amongst several possible dynamics that are operative in witnessing atrocities. Nevertheless, extrapolating from a specific, detailed account may help us to think about the question, "How could they watch without doing anything?" on a deeper level.

Private Witnessing

A young woman in her mid-30s was referred to me for treatment through her divorce lawyer. Cary had been married for six years and had a daughter, aged five, who had appeared in school one morning with a badly bruised cheek. This was not the first time Agnes had appeared in school with bruises, but on this occasion the teacher was suspicious and, taking Agnes aside, asked her what had happened. Agnes burst into tears and said that she had fallen against a radiator and complained that she still had a headache. The teacher asked how this had happened and Agnes then admitted that her father had hit her. The teacher contacted a social worker and Cary was told that if there was any further sign of abuse, Agnes would be removed from the home. This threat triggered a violent conflict between Cary and her husband, ultimately leading to divorce proceedings.

Cary soon told me that she had also been regularly beaten by her father when she was a small child and was concerned about her daughter but at the same time was confused about what discipline was appropriate and what was not. Her mother had insisted that her father had beaten her because he loved her and did not want her to grow up as a spoiled child. But she also remembered that there were times when he beat her excessively and only stopped when he seemed spent. On these occasions, she remembered having to wear long sleeves to school to hide the bruises on her arms, much like her daughter, and how ashamed she had felt. Cary described her father as very strict. He controlled everything within the family and her mother deferred to him completely. Her mother was very loving to Cary and her younger brother, often sneaking them treats after they had been punished by their father. Whenever Cary misbehaved, her mother never raised her voice but looked at her with a pained expression on her face. There was a distinct split in Cary's mind between her punitive, sadistic father and her passive, loving mother.

Cary had worked as her husband's secretary and immediately developed a powerful crush on him. Mark was very exacting in his work and emotionally controlled, hardly ever praising her and often pointing out how she could improve. However, he would also spontaneously buy her flowers or small presents, and she took these as signs of his affection and care for her. After a brief courtship they married, and Cary quickly became pregnant. Her husband was a conscientious provider but was emotionally cold and withdrawn. When they were together with friends, he would either suddenly display affection toward her or just as suddenly be openly critical and demeaning. After Agnes' birth, Mark criticized every aspect of Cary's mothering. Cary's confidence and self-esteem, already at a low ebb, became increasingly undermined as her dependency on Mark grew.

Although Mark was never physically abusive toward Cary, he began hitting Agnes as soon as she could walk, explaining that she had to learn the difference between right and wrong and was too young to reason with. Cary admitted that this upset her but believed her husband knew best and that she could only comfort Agnes when she was hurt and upset. As Agnes grew up, the beatings became more violent. There were times, Cary said, when Agnes screamed so much that Mark put duct tape over her mouth so the neighbors wouldn't be disturbed. Cary insisted on being present when Mark beat Agnes as she felt that this way she could ensure he would not go too far. When Cary told me this, as an attempt to reassure me, I realized the extent to which she had dissociated from her own sadistic feelings and how complicit she was with her husband's behavior.

After nearly a year of analysis, Cary recounted a terrifying dream she had had over the weekend. She told me:

> I was with a group of adults and various small animals. Someone had caught an animal—it was a mixture between a kitten and a ferret—and had wrapped it up and laid it on its back. The adults were encouraging the other animals to go near it and suddenly the other animals began to bite it and eat it alive in front of me. The adults were standing around, encouraging the animals, and were clearly excited by what was going on. I was paralysed with horror and I knew there was nothing I could do to stop it. I could see the ferret's eyes looking off into the distance as it was being killed. I feel sick even describing it to you. I woke up and immediately thought that you would comfort me if I told you the dream, just as my mother used to when my father beat me.

In hearing Cary's dream, I felt both repelled and fascinated by the idea of watching the small animal being eaten alive. I was also aware of thinking, "This is just a dream." I understood my reaction as counter-transference and wondered whether Cary was inviting me to kill off my feelings, and hers, by understanding her experience as a nightmare and nothing more. I would then have re-enacted the role of her impassive mother who could not see the need to intervene. I remarked that although Cary wanted me to comfort her, perhaps she also wanted me to see, as she did in her dream, the full horror of this cruel killing and that it wasn't just a nightmare that would vanish in the cold light of day.

Cary replied,

> It's strange that you say that because this is exactly what my mother never did. She never acknowledged that what was happening was wrong or cruel. She always said, "It's over now. Don't think about it," as if it was a kind of nightmare. In fact, by comforting me, she made me feel proud that I had survived so well, as if I was a brave girl and could endure anything. I suppose, ironically, it was like being one of Pavlov's dogs—I was beaten and then rewarded for it!

I said, "Not only rewarded, but made to feel that the violence was justified and that your father knew what was best. His punishments could not be questioned because they were meant to be in your own interest. You weren't meant to think about it, only to obey."

Cary became silent and then began to sob, saying, "I hate my mother! I hate her for watching—and for comforting me, for pretending to love me. She was like the adults in my dream who got excited when they saw the little animal being killed. She's despicable. ... And I was the ferret being brave and no longer feeling. I hated myself for being so little and weak and helpless."

I asked, "Is this what you hate in your daughter? And what you don't want me to see?"

> I don't want you to see that I've been like my mother—that I watched Mark beating Agnes because it excited me. I think Agnes became all that I hated in myself, all that I wanted to destroy and I could remain her loving mother if I wasn't the one who was hurting her. I used to have fantasies when Mark was beating her, that he would really hurt her, break her arm, or smash her face in, or crush her. I was terrified by these images but I couldn't stop them in my mind. ... I'm now remembering a time when my mother and my brother were both watching as my father beat me—and I suddenly caught them sniggering together.

Cary's admission of her own sadism along with her recognition of her mother's sadism marked an important step in beginning to understand how she had been taken over by the perverse norms of her family that she too had lived out with her husband and daughter. She could also see how the repeated trauma of her own childhood had not simply anaesthetized her to the trauma she was complicit in inflicting on her daughter, but it had necessitated a suspension of belief inside of her as a way of sustaining family life. Cary tried to reassure herself by telling herself, "one day this will be over, everything will be all right."

Cary's description of her hatred of herself—and of her daughter—as weak and helpless can be understood as a form of identification with the aggressor. She aligned herself with her abusive father as an attempt to regain some sense of control over her life and to adopt the system of power he represented within the family so that she could survive psychically. However, as she later acknowledged, she also wanted to kill off her feelings of vulnerability, pain and terror, as in the excited killing of the small animal in her dream. Cary's fantasies of wanting her husband to physically harm, if not kill, their daughter provided an enactment of wanting not only to kill off this sensate part of herself but also to destroy the mental perception of being abused. She wanted to eradicate the disjunction in her mind between her actual experience of abuse and the normative moral code within her family that converted hatred and abuse into expressions of love. The trauma of her childhood had to be repeated as a way of cancelling out irreconcilable belief systems within herself.

In admitting her sadistic fantasies toward her daughter and herself, Cary articulated the dilemma she faced if she had intervened. She explained,

> If I had told my husband to stop or if I had physically tried to stop him from beating Agnes, everything would have fallen apart. I would certainly have been afraid that Mark would turn on me—and if this happened then I would be back again as a child being beaten by my father but with the new horror that my mother had done nothing to stop him because of her hatred towards me. And I would also have had to face my own hatred and step out of what felt like a shield of innocence.

Collective Witnessing

Just as Cary had her own history of family abuse and trauma that unconsciously shaped her role as a bystander, those who witnessed the killings in Kovno were similarly caught up in a subtext of relations that kept them inert in the face of horror. The killings witnessed by the photographer and the lance-corporal in Kovno took place in the context of war, reprisals and powerful national ideologies that swept populations along in a moral fervor built on highly stratified classification systems to identify the enemy. Witnessing various forms of cruelty and abuse is almost unavoidable for those living in war zones. In this respect a kind of norm or expectation of cruelty is established that becomes part of life, just as Cary came to expect to be beaten by her father as part of the daily fabric of her family life.

The accounts in Kovno illustrate not only the random nature of witnessing atrocities, e.g., the lance-corporal happens to come upon the killings in the square without prior warning, but they also highlight the different relationships held by various bystanders to the perpetrators, to other groups of bystanders, and to the victims. In Kovno at least three groups are identified as local Lithuanians, including Lithuanian convicts, Germans and Jews. The Russians have left behind their own trail of murders and witnesses. These relationships need to be differentiated and elucidated in order to begin to understand the psychodynamics of witnessing cruelty.

The photographer who stumbled across the public beatings in Kovno explains in his report that the young man who was beating the Jews to death one by one was doing so in revenge for the murder of his parents, killed by the retreating Russian Commissars and Communists on suspicion of being nationalists. This explanation provides a specific narrative meaning to the event and can be seen as an attempt to restore some sense of moral order. The killings can be understood as not simply random and arbitrary, but as a restoration of justice and, perhaps most importantly, as an assertion on the part of the Lithuanians that they were back in control after being invaded and overpowered by the Russians.

Although the Russians had retreated, they remained present in the wounded minds of the Lithuanians. Since June 1940, the Lithuanian territories had been occupied and subsequently annexed by Russia. Lithuanian nationalists were arrested, and the Jewish population was singled out for attack, their communal organizations dissolved and much of their property confiscated. A week before German invasion, the Russians had ordered mass deportations across the Baltics, including hundreds of Jews. At the same time, the Lithuanian Activist Front, founded by nationalist emigres in Berlin, fanned the flames of anti-Semitism that had been ignited under Russian occupation. The German conquest of Lithuania was perceived initially as a liberation that would restore Lithuanian independence. Compliance with German anti-Semitism became for many the price to pay for independence. To support their own anti-Semitic policies, Germans also blamed the Jewish community for Russian annexation. For the Lithuanians, the Jews became the logical scapegoats; they became the black sheep that had caused the invasion and sublimation of the Lithuanians. The Jews became the enemy within the group who had complied with and encouraged Russian takeover.

Against this backdrop, the Kovno killings take on a particular meaning. The single-handed slaughter of nearly 50 Jews reinstated the strength of the Lithuanian turned victor, as dramatically marked by the Lithuanian killer as he stood on the corpses of the Jews he had murdered and played the national anthem. The fact that the bystanders joined in, celebrating their nationality, indicates the degree of trauma experienced within the group that was both expelled and repeated in this act of violence. Cary's mother and brother also watched as her father beat her, keeping solidarity in the family. Justice is meted out and the violence of the past displaced onto others in the present.

While the enemy is symbolically expunged in the form of an "other" and the group strengthened against further external threat, there is also a ritual extermination of the weakness and vulnerability that was so cruelly exposed by the Russian invasion. The group vanquishes its weakness by enacting what was done to them onto others. This identification with the aggressor ensures a sense of safety while the collective trauma is transferred onto the "other."

What is also significant, as we learn from the lance-corporal's report, is that "the killings were carried out by the recently released Lithuanian convicts." Many of these convicts would have been imprisoned under Russian orders and at least in this respect, like the young man described in the photographer's report, would have experienced particular animosity about what had happened to them. Because of this, the former convicts represented the larger group's subjugation and captivity and were also the ones to lead the community toward freedom and power.

The fact that it was the ex-convicts who conducted the killings also perhaps enabled the group to rid themselves of moral responsibility as they watched one murder after another. Turner observes that just as we turn our enemies into the "other" so that we can direct our aggression toward them without concern or guilt, we are equally liable to categorize the evildoer as "other" (Turner, 2009). In this way we project our own potential for cruelty onto an "other" and dissociate ourselves from such actions. This was essentially how Cary viewed her husband; he was not only the ultimate authority with total power but on a less conscious level, he was the one with dirty hands while she maintained her "shield of innocence."

The reports written about Kovno express the horror not just of the public cruelty taking place but of the passive witnesses who allowed it to happen, clapping after each beating and singing the national anthem when it was all over. Women, holding small children, were positioned in the front for the best views and stayed until the end. Although this may be reminiscent of the crowds that public executions have attracted throughout history, the incongruence in Kovno is that the Jews had not committed crimes but had become the target for reprisals nevertheless. At least amongst the local population, this was hardly "execution" voyeurism but rather a distortion or subversion of reality in order to reverse the effects of collective trauma.

It is possible to understand the group of witnesses as being swept along in a kind of mass hysteria that counteracts feelings of fear and helplessness. Fear triggers the physiological response of releasing adrenalin and, like a pack of animals on the chase, those engaged in violence and those witnessing it enter into a drama that is overwhelmingly exciting and awful. This was how Cary had described the humans in her dream as they excitedly egged on the animals to kill the small animal. It was also how she described her father's excitement as he beat her until he was "spent." The chase had started a momentum that could only end in annihilation.

Witnessing extreme violence perpetrated on the "other" may also assume the function of a kind of ritualized cleansing that cancels out the taint of evil. It is a witch hunt that is intended to restore purity within the group, especially when the group leadership is under threat. In other circumstances with different collective histories, e.g., amongst concentration camp prisoners, the failure of the group to intervene may be due to overwhelming fear of being killed themselves, reinforced by their identification with the victim. But in the Kovno incident, the victims were already seen as "other" and outside, if not an active threat to the Lithuanian community; identification could then be neutralized by this form of distancing and group cohesion strengthened.

The bystanders of the atrocities in Kovno were not passive—people clapped and sang, mothers were pushed to the fore so that their children could see, and presumably remember, the events that were meant to signal freedom for Lithuania. Rather than identifying with the victims, the group could instead identify with the killer who served as a conduit for their own sadism, omnipotence and fantasies of revenge. The group could keep their hands clean and maintain the paranoid splitting necessary to keep what is bad outside and "other" as a defense against past trauma and present reality.

Although the Germans at first promised independence, a promise that was subsequently withdrawn, they held ultimate power over the conquered Lithuanian territories. They were the new masters. The applause for the killings magically transformed what we can see as an evil act, i.e., an act that destroys moral order, into an act that restores moral order. It is subsumed under the common good. Allegiance to the new rule, accompanied by its own set of beliefs, becomes supra-ordinate to everything else as a way of surviving and managing overwhelming fear and what is essentially unthinkable.

Belief Systems, Ideology and Trauma

When we view others witnessing atrocities, we are often unaware of the context in which the atrocities are committed and in which the witnesses exist. The prisoner of war who witnesses a fellow prisoner being beaten to death may to our eyes have no choice but to watch helplessly, for intervention would mean certain death. However, the civilian passing by as others from a different race are beaten to death is in a very different position and may, at least in principle, have a range of choices on which to act. Although the difference in these examples is that one population is imprisoned and the other is not, what we may overlook in both is the importance of the role of popular and political ideology in shaping not only the norms of what is acceptable behavior and what is not but also the values we confer on ourselves and others.

It is important not to underestimate the power of ideology in shaping our behavior toward each other and in influencing our conception of morality. Within a family, parental values and beliefs determine not only behavior but the ideals to which children aspire and that are associated with acceptance and love. This is also true within the larger group, especially when survival may depend on adherence to the group's values. In his 1926 paper,

"Inhibitions, symptoms, and anxiety," Freud stresses the danger of being excluded from "the horde" (Freud, p. 139). To be set apart or excluded is the most feared condition in any society because it severs the person from his existence and sense of self. When faced with an ideology that is based on excluding—and exterminating—those who are categorized as "other," the fear of breaking ranks becomes even more extreme.

Witnessing evil, i.e., an act that breaches our moral order, is traumatic because it destroys not only the set of beliefs that form our ability to go on being in the world, but it also threatens our relationship with our internal objects, or those relationships that have created our set of beliefs about the world. The evil act is a rent in our belief system that stops us from being able to continue to function in the way we have before. The parameters that constitute what makes us feel safe have suddenly and unrecognizably altered. Our internal objects become crippled, sometimes to the point of irrevocable damage, and can no longer be safely relied upon to guide us. Some degree of alliance, if not identification, results as a means of adapting and surviving within a new reality that brings with it a different belief system.

We can understand some of the complex reasons the Kovno group not only witnessed the killings of the Jews but applauded them. Because of a confluence of war time trauma and changing political masters, the killings of people who had only recently been members of the wider community could be justified under a new belief system that accorded with the ruling ideology. Anti-Semitism had been promulgated by the Russians and then the Germans. In accord with recent policies of ethnic cleansing, the Kovno population could well have regarded these killings as not only what was required by German authority but moreover what was "right." Milgram's 1963 study of obedience first graphically demonstrated that people will inflict pain on others when ordered to do so by a higher authority not simply because they are following orders but because they believe the authority knows "best" and will protect their interests and the interests of the group. There is no reason to believe that witnesses to cruelty inflicted on others will behave any differently (Milgram, 1974).

The local Kovno population did not comprise all of the witnesses to the killing of the Jews. We learn from the reports of the German photographer and lance-corporal that the bystanders (i.e., those not amongst the Kovno residents) were "almost exclusively German soldiers" and watched out of "curiosity." These bystanders were witnessing violent acts that, at least on first glance, made no sense to them and were beyond the pale. The lance-corporal states clearly, "At that time I had not formulated my own thoughts about the persecution of the Jews because I had not heard anything about it." The ideology of ethnic cleansing had not been promoted amongst many of the German troops at this point and would not have provided a rationale for this public atrocity. However, the fact that none of the local population viewing this event was showing disapproval or trying to stop it may have signaled to the Germans that there was a subtext that they could not know and therefore could not interfere with.

While the German soldiers were not actively participating in the violence, they were not attempting to stop it either. In their curiosity, were they trying to accommodate something that might otherwise be unimaginable that was now part of their reality—a foreign ideology that was only just coming into awareness? Or is watching in this context, like "execution tourism," a means by which the unimaginable is made into a drama being enacted by others that can be distanced and separated from the viewer?

The failure to intervene in this situation can only be partially explained away as morbid curiosity. Distancing is one way of vicariously expressing sadistic fantasies that can be projected onto the "other" and denied within the observer. Yet this explanation does not take into account that witnessing an atrocity is a traumatic experience in itself. There is a sudden disjuncture between the observer's set of beliefs of the world and how it operates and a world in which such expectations and rules of behavior no longer apply. The paralysis that ensues reflects a shattering of one's belief system and the struggle to reconcile what seems to be a contradictory or opposing reality. In the midst of this confusion, the bystander is confronted with a parallel reality that threatens the core of his personal and social identity. In this respect, the fear of intervening may not be as much the fear of physical harm as a fear of being overtaken by an alien (or perverse), more powerful belief system. Non-intervention is then not due to denial, or curiosity, but to an attempt to maintain a distance from the event in order to sustain one's own belief system and to find a way of continuing to exist in the face of annihilation of one's reality.

There is also the fear, and difficulty, of engaging in violence. Sociologist Randall Collins argues: "Violence is hard, not easy. Virtually no cultural discourse admits this; neither perpetrators nor pro-violence groups, nor victims, nor altruistic or righteous observers-from-a-distance. Everyone thinks violence is easy to perform, whether one brags about it, fears it, or hopes to eliminate it. But the micro-situational realities of talking about violence fall into ritual patterns of bluster and bluff, and these rituals provide an ideology that covers up the real nature of violence—that it is hard to perform, that most people are not good at it, including the ones who are doing the bragging and swaggering" (Collins, 2008 pp. 23–24). Intervening means being prepared to act outside one's experience and to be violent in order to stop violence; it means stepping over the line of "what may be" into a world of "what cannot be." In defending one's belief system the person who intervenes risks becoming a perpetrator as the distinction between ritualized posturing and actual violence collapses. Anyone who acts has inevitably dirtied his hands; anyone who does not act is also implicated, morally. No one remains innocent or unscarred.

Trauma is a shock against which the psyche cannot defend itself; it threatens to destroy the hermeneutic narrative that enables us to live in the world and establish moral order. The failure to intervene can perhaps be understood as a means of protecting the psyche, not just from being tainted by what is perceived as bad or outside one's moral code but, fundamentally, as an attempt to preserve one's own internal objects and set of beliefs and the division between "what may and may not be."

Distancing and Cooperation

> In the Concentration Camp Mauthausen at the work site in Vienna Ditch inmates are being shot repeatedly; those badly struck live for yet some time, and so remain lying next to the dead for hours and even half a day long.
>
> My property lies upon an elevation next to Vienna Ditch, and one is often an unwilling witness to such outrages.
>
> I am anyway sickly and such a sight makes such a demand on my nerves that in the long run I cannot bear this.
>
> I request that it be arranged that inhuman deeds be discontinued, or else be done where one does not see it.
>
> (quoted in Horwitz, p. 35)

This letter of complaint, written in 1941 by Eleanore Gusenbauer, a local farmer, describes the plight of residents living near the Austrian concentration camp of Mauthausen who could not avoid witnessing atrocities on a daily basis. Recognizing that it was unlikely that the atrocities could be stopped altogether, the residents could at least be shielded from them; they could be conducted out of sight.

When the sight of atrocities could not be avoided, what many residents resorted to was "prudent disregard" (Horwitz, 1910, p. 35). Expressing criticism or shock at the ill-treatment of prisoners could result in arrest and imprisonment. Even minor complaints or gestures of sympathy, for example from civilians working alongside prisoners in the rock quarries of the Vienna Ditch, could lead to loss of employment. This was also the case in other areas of local employment, including office work where civilians would be cognizant of the cruelties to which prisoners were habitually subjected.

Turning a blind eye out of fear of the consequences of not doing so made witnesses complicit in the rule of terror imposed by the camp and effectively extended the camp perimeter to the boundaries of the town's jurisdiction. Residents became a subservient class within the regime, under close surveillance and subject to the tyranny of the camp. Mistrust, profiteering and increasing isolation from the world outside pervaded the area.

The psychological effect on civilians was most vividly apparent amongst those working in Castle Hartheim, 18.6 miles west of Mauthausen, where inmates were transferred to their deaths in the newly constructed gas chambers. Many of the civilians working in the Castle claimed that they were forced to cooperate with what was going on for fear of losing their jobs. Personal will was sacrificed to the expediency of survival. There was no choice.

Horwitz describes this state of mind:

> Persons who worked in Hartheim maintained years afterward that they wanted to leave but were unable to do so. In explaining their inability to extract themselves from their predicament, they explained that all such efforts were "pointless" or "without result." They wanted to leave, they said, but all attempts they characterized as hopeless. The phrases themselves, common to bureaucratic procedure and authority, once assimilated, absorbed, and given expression in common speech, reinforced passivity. These expressions comprised a framework and guide to mental categories of moral paralysis. Protected thereby from thoughts of individual responsibility, the employees appeared for work day after day.
> (Horwitz, p. 80)

The workers attributed their passivity, or what Horwitz refers to as moral paralysis, to resignation and helplessness. Whatever alternatives might have been available to them were either "pointless" or would worsen their position. Their cooperation in the regime of the Castle, perhaps like the German soldiers in Kovno, enabled them to tolerate the trauma of something that was too powerful for them to alter and to preserve the continuity of an internal world that in their perception could be viewed as temporarily disabled. The distinction between belief systems could be maintained through prolonged dissociation; the horrors were executed by others, not themselves. Here again, physical avoidance was used to relieve workers of responsibility. What they did not see or touch, they were not responsible for. At the same time, they could perform their bureaucratic tasks conscientiously as this was congruent with their own aspirations of what it means to be a good worker. In this way, a moral code could be sustained, not in the belief that what they were being asked to do was "right" but in the belief that it was inevitable dirty work that had to be done. As Cary tried to convince herself, the workers wanted to believe the nightmare would end and life would resume as normal.

I have elaborated some of the psychic strategies and defenses adopted by the local population in the community of Mauthausen and nearby Castle Hartheim who were exposed to atrocities over a prolonged period of time. In both locales the totalitarian regimes established by the camps, very similar to the iron fist with which Cary's father ruled his family, were terrifying and extensive, inculcating complete obedience in the service of a higher authority. And yet, life for these communities carried on, albeit in restricted forms. The population could use the technique of distancing themselves from what was essentially inhuman and unthinkable, but they were still aware of what was happening to the prisoners at their doorsteps. Denial and dissociation were hardly viable strategies. Psychic survival in this situation is perhaps most dependent on the capacity to suspend belief. By this I mean the capacity to hold one's internal belief system in suspension while adapting to tyrannical conditions (e.g., being a "good" office worker) so that some semblance of a recognizable moral order can be maintained.

Conclusion

The bystander who fails to intervene may be entranced by seeing the sadistic fantasies in his own mind being powerfully played out in reality. Paradoxically, putting a stop to the atrocity is also an act of recognition that it is happening in reality, not in fantasy. As Cary stated, such an act forces the bystander to take hold of and act on his own hatred; the "shield of innocence" is broken. As long as the bystander watches without acting, he can remain relatively untainted. The cruel drama unfolding in front of him can be explained in terms of something "other," some temporary aberration. The bystander can still walk back into his known world, or at least this is the delusion.

In much of the literature on witnessing evil, the bystander is regarded from a moralistic perspective; the act of witnessing is inextricably bound to moral obligation. As Vetlesen sums it up, "not acting is still acting" (Vetlesen, p. 237). Cohen divides the position of the bystander into two categories as those who passively support and those who passively oppose the atrocity (Cohen, 2001, p. 147). But human responses are not so neatly divided; they are nuanced and contextualized just as our conception of what is moral tends to be. These views of the bystander lack the ambiguity and complexity that, at least in the case of Cary, are clearly evident in the mind of the bystander.

The passivity of the bystander is not simply due to repressed sadism and unconscious complicity, nor is it due only to fear and dissociation. It can be regarded as a response to a trauma that suddenly turns the relations that have been experienced as reliable and known on their head. Even in cultures in which extreme violence is habitual, as in Cary's experience of her childhood and marriage, extreme cruelty and violence remain outside thought and therefore outside emotional containment. The bystander is in a twilight zone, neither actively engaged in the event nor entirely passive, simultaneously identifying with both abuser and victim, albeit, in the case of identifying with the abuser, this may be unconscious. Because of this dual identification, taking action is equivalent to entering the world of abuser and victim with the attendant risk of becoming one or the other. Entering into the fray removes the presence of an observing other, of a witness who can see that reality has been ruptured.

While I have tried to elucidate some of the psychological defenses and dynamics that take place in the minds of those who witness evil, the role of the bystander as observer is important in itself in terms of preserving a potential space, between realities, in which what is abhorrent can be held in stark relief against the background of everyday life. The bystander is at worst complicit and at best witness to "an impossible reality" (Levi, 1987). Until we are put to the test, the question as to what any of us would do in such circumstances remains open.

References

Cohen, S. (2001). *States of Denial: Knowing about Atrocities and Suffering*. Cambridge, UK: Polity.

Collins, R. (2008). *Violence: A Micro-sociological Theory*. Princeton, NJ: Princeton University Press.

Freud, S. (1926). Inhibitions, symptoms, and anxiety. *The Standard Edition of the Complete Psychological Works of Sigmund Freud, 20*, 75–176.

Horwitz, G. J. (1990). *In the Shadow of Death: Living Outside the Gates of Mauthausen*. Oxford, UK: The Free Press.

Klee, E., Dressen, W., & Riess, V. eds. (1988). *"The Good Old Days": The Holocaust as Seen by Its Perpetrators and Bystanders*. Old Saybrook, CT: Konecky & Konecky.

Levi, P. Beyond judgment. *New York Review of Books*, 17 Dec. 1987, 14.

Milgram, S. (1974). *Obedience to Authority: An Experimental View*. New York, NY: Harper & Row.

Molina, A. M. (2001). *Sepharad*. London, UK: Harvest.

Turner, K. (2009). *Cruelty: Human Evil and the Human brain*. Oxford, UK: Oxford University Press.

Vetlesen, A. J. (2005). *Evil and Human Agency: Understanding Collective Evildoing*. Cambridge, UK: Cambridge University Press.

Notes on Contributors

John Beebe, M.D. is past President of the C. G. Jung Institute of San Francisco; Distinguished Life Fellow of the American Psychiatric Association; and first American co-editor of *The Journal of Analytical Psychology*. He is the author of *Integrity in Depth*, co-author of *Psychiatric Treatment: Crisis, Clinic and Consultation*, editor of *Terror, Violence, and the Impulse to Destroy*, and co-editor of *The Question of Psychological Types: The Correspondence of C. G. Jung and Hans Schmid-Guisan*.

Coline Covington, Ph.D., B.P.C. is the former Chair of the British Psychoanalytic Council and is a Training Analyst and Supervisor of the Society of Analytical Psychology and the British Psychotherapy Foundation. She is a member of the International Dialogue Initiative (IDI), a group formed by Prof. Vamik Volkan, Lord Alderdice and Dr. Robi Friedman to apply psychoanalytic concepts in understanding political conflict. Dr. Covington's publications include *Terrorism and War: Unconscious Dynamics of Political Violence* (Karnac, 2002), *Shrinking the News: Headline Stories on the Couch* (Karnac, 2013), and *Sabina Spielrein: Forgotten Pioneer of Psychoanalysis*, 2nd edition (Routledge, 2014). She is a regular columnist for *The Week* online.

Oren Gozlan, Psy.D., ABPP is a clinical psychologist and a psychoanalyst in private practice and a professor and director of Clinical Training at the Adler Graduate Professional School in Toronto. He is a Diplomate in Psychoanalysis with the American Board of Professional Psychology where he serves as Treasurer. He is the Chair of the Gender and Sexuality Committee of the International Forum for Psychoanalytic Education. Dr. Gozlan has published articles on gender, transsexuality and psychic difference in various psychoanalytic journals. He is the author of *Transsexuality and the Art of Transitioning: a Lacanian Approach* (Routledge, 2015) was published in 2015.

Sean J. McGrath, Ph.D. is a professor of philosophy at Memorial University of Newfoundland where he researches and teaches in the areas of metaphysics, classical German philosophy (Kant to Heidegger), phenomenology and hermeneutics and psychoanalysis. After graduate work at the University of Toronto in both theology and philosophy, he graduated in 2002 with a dissertation in philosophy supervised by Graeme Nicholson, later published as *The Early Heidegger and Medieval Philosophy: Phenomenology for the Godforsaken* (Catholic University of America Press, 2006, reprinted 2013). In 2008 he published a second book, *Heidegger: A (Very) Critical Introduction* (Eerdmans), which was commissioned by the Centre for Theology and Philosophy at the University of Nottingham. That same year he was awarded a Humboldt Fellowship for two years of research in Germany on the topic of the historical and systematic connections between psychoanalysis and German Idealism. The fruit of that research was published in 2012 as *The Dark Ground of Spirit: Schelling and the Unconscious* (Routledge). He is the co-editor of *A Companion to Heidegger's Phenomenology of Religious Life* (Rodopi, 2010) and the editor of *Analecta Hermeneutica*, an annual journal on philosophical hermeneutics and related fields. He serves as the co-chair of the North American Schelling Society (which he founded with Jason Wirth in 2011) and as a member of the executive committee of the Canadian Society for Continental Philosophy.

Jon Mills, Psy.D., Ph.D., ABPP is a philosopher, psychoanalyst and psychologist. He is professor of psychology & psychoanalysis at the Adler Graduate Professional School in Toronto and is the author of many works in philosophy, psychoanalysis and psychology including 13 other books. In 2006, 2011 and 2013 he was recognized with a Gradiva Award from the National Association for the Advancement of Psychoanalysis in New York City for his scholarship, received a Significant Contribution to Canadian Psychology Award in 2008, a Goethe Award for best book in 2013 and the Otto Weininger Memorial Award for lifetime achievement in 2015 by the Section on Psychoanalytic and Psychodynamic Psychology of the Canadian Psychological Association. He runs a mental health corporation in Ontario, Canada.

Ronald C. Naso, Ph.D., ABPP is a psychoanalyst and clinical psychologist in independent practice in Stamford, CT. He is currently a Director and Secretary of the American Board and Academy of Psychoanalysis (ABAPsa) as well as a member of the ABAPsa workgroup responsible for the development of educational and training standards adopted by the Commission for the Recognition of Specialties and Proficiencies in Professional Psychology. The author of numerous papers on psychoanalytic topics and associate editor of *Contemporary Psychoanalytic Studies*, contributing editor of *Division/Review* and the *Journal of Psychology and Clinical Psychiatry*, his book entitled, *Hypocrisy Unmasked: Dissociation, Shame, and the Ethics of Inauthenticity* was published by Aronson in 2010.

Robert Prince, Ph.D., ABPP is past Co-chair of the Interpersonal Track of the NYU Postdoctoral Program in Psychotherapy & Psychoanalysis, past President of Psychologist-Psychoanalyst Clinicians and past Section Representative to the Board of Directors of the Division of Psychoanalysis of the APA. He is the author of *The Legacy of the Holocaust*, the editor of *The Death of Psychoanalysis* and *Trauma and Culture*. He has also written more than 30 articles and chapters.

Michael Stone, M.D. is a professor of clinical psychiatry at the Columbia College of Physicians and Surgeons in New York City. His psychoanalytic training was also at Columbia. Currently he is on the staff at the Columbia Psychoanalytic Institute and also at the Mid-Hudson Forensic Psychiatric Hospital, where he teaches forensic psychiatry. He is the author of eleven books, of which the most recent is *The Anatomy of Evil,* published by Prometheus Press. Others include a long-term follow-up study: *The Fate of Borderline Patients* and *Abnormalities of Personality: Within and Beyond the Realm of Treatment*, and a companion piece: *Personality-Disordered Patients: Treatable and Untreatable. The Anatomy of Evil* was the outgrowth of Dr. Stone's 25 year research on murder and other violent crimes and of his work as host of the Discovery Channel's former series: *Most Evil.* To prepare for the TV series, Dr. Stone interviewed serial killers and other notorious murderers in prisons throughout the U.S. He has been featured in the *New York Times, The London Times, Psychology Today,* and *The Christian Science Monitor*, as well as on CNN, ABC News, CBS News, Fox News, and on radio shows including the Phil Hendrie Show, the Diane Rehm NPR Show and many others.

Index